THE FUNDAMENTALS OF WOODTURNING

MIKE DARLOW

THE LYONS PRESS

First published 1998

Layout by Stephen Joseph of Alexandria Graphics Pty. Ltd.

Cover Design by Sol Design Pty Ltd.
Cover Photograph by Nick Gleitzman

Printed by H & Y Printing Ltd., Hong Kong.

10 9 8 7 6 5 4 3 2 1

Library of Congress Cataloging–in–Publication Data

Darlow, Mike.
        The fundamentals of woodturning / Mike Darlow.
            p.   cm.
        Includes index.
        ISBN 1–55821–719–3
        1. Turning.   2. Woodwork.   I. Title.
TT202 . D36   1998
    684' .083--dc21   97–49054
                                                          CIP

CONTENTS

ACKNOWLEDGEMENTS

I have been fortunate to receive help from many individuals and organisations.

A special thank you to those who reveal all in chapter 1: Frank Bollins, Peter Lowe, Gail Redman, Walter Rissmeyer, and David Springett.

I hope that this book's coverage of turning equipment will help to foster greater cooperation and understanding between manufacturers, retailers and turners. Individuals and companies have helped with advice, transparencies, and equipment. I thank them. I have listed them below under countries:

Australia Don Akrigg, Harry Arnall, Sue Goody of Carba-Tec Pty. Ltd., Steve Durden of Durden Woodworking Machinery, John Ewart of The Woodturning Centre, Myles Herbert of Garrick Herbert Pty. Ltd., P&N, P.A. Products Pty. Ltd., Philip Marcelis of Promac Pty. Ltd., Gary Pye, John Sommerville of J.W. Ross & Sons Pty. Ltd., Vicmarc Machinery Pty. Ltd., and Woodfast Machinery Co.,

Canada Leonard Lee of Veritas Tools Inc.

England Anthony Isles of Ashley Isles (Edge Tools) Ltd., Bierton Craft Turnery, Bob Chapman Woodturning Accessories, Chesterman Marketing Ltd, Craft Supplies Limited, Melvyn Firmager, Mark Baker of Robert Sorby, and Dennis Abdy of Henry Taylor Tools Limited.

New Zealand Woodcut Tools International Ltd., Link Technology.

Sweden Kurt Johannson.

USA Richard Lukes of Beech Street Toolworks, Alan Steytler of Conover Lathe, Delta International Machinery Corp., David Ellsworth, Jerry Glaser of HiTEC Tools, Lyle Jamieson, Hugh McKay, and Denis Stewart

I have tons of wood, but on two occasions I needed special pieces. Thank you Don Akrigg and Bert Smith. I also thank Adrian Barendregt, Jack Crawford, Mike Irving, and John Powell for allowing me to photograph equipment.

I am grateful to the following people for providing information, videos, photographs, and slides: Mike Abbott, Joy Bowen of National Museums & Galleries of Wales, Philip Holden of The Society of Ornamental Turners, John Jordan, Ray Key of The Association of Woodturners of Great Britain, Albert LeCoff of the Wood Turning Center, Mary Redig of the American Association of Woodturners, Chris Stott, and Don Tietjens of the National Association of Woodturners New Zealand.

It is no good producing a book if you cannot sell it. Hugh Foster, Philip Gore, John Kelsey, Craig Osment, and Ken Raffe have given me invaluable advice and assistance in this key area.

Steve Joseph of Alexandria Graphics did the layouts. His brief from me was to fit a huge volume of information into 200 pages. He has done so with great skill, patience, and enthusiasm.

Jane Newport has researched for me in America. I hope I may be able to repay in some way when her own book is published.

I thank Nick Gleitzman for photographing the front cover, and Dale Hageman and Mike Cassidy for helping with it (Dale is "the student").

An author might work at home, but that doesn't mean he can be more accessible to his family than those who work more conventionally. I thank my sons Joshua and Samuel for their understanding and their help with the photography. I especially thank Alice for her editing, legal advice, and guidance, and for putting up with me.

INTRODUCTION

Purpose

My first book *The Practice of Woodturning* was published in 1985. In 1993 I released a companion seven-hour teaching video of the same same title. I then revised the book to incorporate the developments in turning and changes in my thinking which had occurred since 1985, and it was re-released in 1996. Both book and video are the leaders in their respective fields. But *The Practice of Woodturning* has 360 pages. I saw the possibility of a shorter book which could also take advantage of the reducing cost of color printing. But with over a hundred woodturning books available and many of them pitched at beginners, why should I add another? There are two reasons: I believe that I can give you sounder advice, and present it better.

If you are considering starting turning, have just bought or been given a lathe, or are unsure of your present techniques, then this book is for you. It has three aims:

1. To help you become familiar and comfortable in a new world, the world of woodturning.
2. To give you a sound, basic knowledge of turning and especially of turning techniques.
3. To enable you to teach yourself, if necessary in isolation, to turn surely and confidently so that you will be able to tackle most turning projects successfully.

To achieve these three aims, this book covers in considerable detail only those topics which are immediately relevant. You should also seek information elsewhere, from other turners, from other books, from magazine articles and videos. As you glean you may become concerned that advice even from highly-regarded sources is often contradictory. These contradictions in part result from the still-popular view that particular methods suit particular turners. I reject this view; first because its proponents have failed to establish the criteria which govern suitability; and second because turning techniques are about how to present the most suitable cutting edge to the wood in the best way. Surely the latter is independent of your physique, nationality or personality. Instead I believe that for each turning situation there is one (or sometimes more than one) best method, and that these best methods are the same for all. And you want to learn the best methods, not the idiosyncratic methods which "work" for a particular teacher who has never tested them against others' or subjected them to any logical examination.

I believe that the methods described in this book are the best. They result from twenty years of searching, from:

1. Discussions with other turners.

2. In-lathe trials.
3. Attempting to research and understand what happens at the tool tip during turning, and then applying that understanding to improve turning techniques and equipment designs.

Over those twenty years I modified my turning techniques as my knowledge grew. It is an ongoing process. I welcome feedback, because like turning students I have no wish to use inferior methods—nor do I wish to teach them.

In the late 20th century original designs, new techniques, and new equipment are especially valued. They are vital to woodturning's progress. But they don't lessen the relevance of traditionally-based techniques because:

1. Most of the turning techniques you will ever need are described in this book. They are with few exceptions improved versions of the techniques traditionally used.
2. Technology continues to advance and our under standing of the turning process is far greater now; therefore our tools and equipment are better and our methods sounder. This retention and improvement of traditional techniques is a testament to their basic soundness, not a case for their rejection.
3. All turnings, even the most avant-garde, are built from convex, concave, and straight profiles. These profiles are still most efficiently produced on a hand lathe by improved-traditional techniques except where tool access is especially restricted or a special effect is intended.
4. Modern turning designs are characterised by the absence of fillets and "S" curves, and a reliance on simple geometric (sometimes called Euclidean) forms such as spheres, cylinders, and straight tapers. The exercises in this book are in traditional and other styles to provide you with a full repetoire of techniques so that you can turn almost any design. I am not seeking to promote or discredit any particular style.
5. Some contemporary turning is being promoted as art. Its creators often use non-traditional turning methods and non-turning techniques such as carving, laminating, in-lathe chainsawing, charring, etc. This could be viewed as evidence that traditional methods are becoming less relevant. I view it as an expansion of the boundaries of turning.
6. The use of the same best techniques in the same turning situations by all does not diminish creativity. The contrary is true. The faster and the more certainly you can turn the designs you create, the more your horizons are widened. Competence in turning techniques is a means to an end not an end in itself.

Those who avoid or fudge gaining this competence never fulfil their potential.

It is nobody's place to dictate to you what or how you should turn, or how committed you should be to turning. Fortunately you can become competent in the basic techniques in less than a week. So resist short-cutting to the apparent glamour of the so-called advanced techniques. It usually results in:

1. Frustration rather then fulfillment because you will be unlikely to develop the skill and confidence to turn the shapes you want.
2. You basing your turning on a continuing and fruitless search for short-term fixes through wonder tools and gimmick techniques.
3. You reducing your armoury of techniques and therefore limiting the designs which you feel confident to undertake.

You may even needlessly abandon turning.

When after some days or weeks you have achieved the basic competence intended by this book, you will then be well-equipped to start to input more emotion and life into your turning. Turning is not patternmaking, the production of rigidly-defined geometric shapes. You will not often be intending to achieve a true sphere or cylinder. With most turnings you should be intending that those who later experience your turnings will have particular intellectual and emotional reactions. To promote those reactions you have to input your intellect and emotion at both the design and turning stages. No matter how detailed your design input, people's reactions to the completed turning will be influenced by your intellectual and emotional involvement as you turn. When you are confident of your technique, you will be freed to input those involvements and enjoy your skill. Your fulfillment will thus be greater.

Being competent in the basic techniques will also free you to:

1. Refine your basic skills further.
2. Learn, practice and develop more specialized techniques.
3. Increase your knowledge of equipment and our major working material, wood.
4. Shift your focus to and increase your expertise in design.

But first there is work to do.

Working Through the Exercises

The later chapters 6 to 10 cover the basic turning techniques. My approach is to enable you to teach yourself by working through a sequence of graded exercises, each fresh exercise building on the skills already attained.

Individual aptitudes vary, but you will have little difficulty in achieving turning competence if you adopt a committed approach. That means learning to walk before attempting to run, and committing four or five full days to the exercises in this book and to the making of decorative firewood.

You should work through the exercises in order. Do not start the next exercise until you have achieved repeatable competence in the current one. A catch or dig-in is just as likely with a bold early cut as with a fine, careful, finishing cut, so try not to become defensive in your attitude. Practice is important, but you must concentrate on practicing the right techniques correctly: firstly to ingrain them into your muscle memories; and secondly to become free and relaxed at the lathe.

Wood Selection for the Exercises

This book does not have a chapter on wood. The properties of woods as a working material for turners are briefly described in chapters 5 and 9. They are detailed in The Practice of Woodturning and in an extensive specialist literature.

For all the exercises you can use any species. Choose an inexpensive wood which is not too hard, relatively knot-free and straight-grained, reasonably dry, and free of cracks. Wood with hidden cracks will sound dead if you tap it on the lathe. If it is not convenient to use the sizes indicated, change, but try to keep the proportions similar.

You can practice on wood which is not well seasoned. With very wet wood you will need to wear full wet-weather gear and deal with the staining and rust-promoting sap flung out. As you progress through the exercises you may wish to finish and keep the results, but unless the wood is fully-seasoned there is a probability of distortion and cracking.

For the spindle and cupchuck-turning exercises buy sawn square-section wood—only if you intend to use the legs in exercise 6.5 do you need square-planed sections. If you are a wood harvester, you can use sound rived instead of sawn sections.

For faceplate, bowl and hollow turning you may be able to buy suitable squares or planks. Disks are available from a few specialist suppliers. But even when suitable wood sections are commercially available, they are expensive, and restricted in their range of species. Most serious bowl- and hollow-turners therefore harvest their own, often from wood which would otherwise be tipped or burned. I outline this at the start of chapter 9.

Level of Detail

Expertise in action looks simple. Its secret is simple. It is to have all the component details correct. The sweet-feeling, perfect cut which leaves a superb surface is no different. It results from using the right tool sharpened in the best way, from taking the ideal grip and stance, from holding the wood in the most appropriate way in a suitable lathe running at the optimum speed with a well-shaped toolrest correctly positioned, and from presenting the tool correctly and maintaining an ideal tool presentation as you traverse the tool at the optimum speed along the profile. To get these details right you have to know about them. This book tells you about them. Having this detailed knowledge will also enable you to analyse and correct any errors you make.

A high level of detail can be difficult to digest. I have therefore presented the techniques through a series of graded exercises described in a picture book illustration/caption/legend format. I have also tried to write clearly and concisely.

In presenting the detail I have to describe three-dimensional shapes and movements. For precision and brevity I have to use some technical terms. Those for concrete objects such as "headstock" and "chuck" seem to be readily accepted, but some turners find conceptual terms such as "rake angle" and "clearance" difficult. There is evidence that many people develop an aversion to books during their school years because of poor teaching or pressure from other students. If you are one, I hope that you will persevere with this book because I am certain that you will conclude that your extra efforts have been worthwhile.

Design

This book contains a brief introduction to design in chapter 5, but does not have a design chapter. Not because design is unimportant or should be ignored until you can turn competently, but because this book concentrates on the first hurdle, achieving competence in the sharpening and basic manipulations of turning tools. Design is discussed in some of the exercises, and in a way which is far more relevant than the usual "apply this formula" or "get the geometry righ"'. But rather than provide a skimpy and thereby unsatisfactory design chapter, I suggest that you consult *The Practice of Woodturning* and other design sources.

Units of Measurement

Our world is unnecessarily complicated by having two basic unit systems. The metric or SI system is far more convenient for turning, but I alone am unlikely to persuade many North Americans to abandon feet, inches, and fractions of an inch for millimeters. I therefore provide imperial and metric units. Having the metric units second and in brackets merely reflects the probability of lower sales for this book in metric-using countries.

When the metric value is not an exact or close conversion, there is no need for it to be.

Photography

Almost all the photographs have been taken by me, or set up by me with a family member releasing the shutter(s). I have used three techniques not often previously used in woodturning texts to provide more and clearer information:

1. Most of the shots are lit by flash. I used unusually-short flash durations which show greater detail by freezing the action. Because there is less blurring, there is little impression of movement.
2. Close-up photography has been used to clarify what is happening at the tool tip.
3. To show tool manipulations more clearly I have sometimes fired two cameras simultaneously, one camera looking in plan, the other from the side.

Photographing yourself turning has its problems. I have preferred to show the turner's view of a cut which prevented my head and body being in the ideal position. When taking several shots during a cut I had to wait between each for the flash unit(s) to recharge. The wood's off-the-tool surface is therefore sometimes not as good as it should be.

Conclusion

Despite the wonderful new media, the book remains a convenient, cheap and effective source of pleasure and information. This book is purposely packed with information because the more turning knowledge you can take in, the better will be your turning. This density of specific knowledge rather than airy-fairy platitudes may initially turn-off those who came to dislike books at school. But a particular advantage of books is that you can read them at your own pace and in your own way.

I suggest that most readers should first skim through this book a couple of times to get an overall familiarity. Only then start on the detail, taking it in manageable bites. You may have to read and think about some parts several times to gain a clear understanding—there is nothing uncommon in this. This is not a book which you read once, then ignore. You will continue to find it valuable long into your turning future.

Have a great time turning,

Mike Darlow

KEYS

Pointing and dimensioning arrows

Movement arrows

Force arrows

Cut arrows

Center lines and axes

Hidden detail

	Elevation	Section
Wood in general		
Wood, end grain		
Wood, parallel (long or side) grain		
Wood, radial grain		
Tool steel		
Cast iron, mild steel, or brass		
Parting, parting off, and V-cuts.		
Other cuts.		

Chapter One

IS WOODTURNING FOR ME?

As you are reading this, you may already be attracted to woodturning, but it may not suit everyone. Why should you want to start? It could be because you:

1. Yearn to make real things, things which are tactile and permanent.
2. Have a desire to work in wood, a natural, infinitely-variable and attractive material which is still relatively inexpensive and plentiful. If you are a committed environmentalist you can source plantation-grown wood or waste wood from, for example, trees blown over in storms or felled before construction work.
3. Want to learn, practice, and even master another skill.
4. Have limited time but want to make things. One advantage of turning is that you can produce works in minutes or hours, rather than in days or weeks, and without the need for physical strength or endurance.
5. Get turned on by tools and machinery or the idea of making and developing your own.
6. Are looking for a pastime which you can do alone or can become a source of future friendships.
7. Want to earn income. Cards on the table. You are most unlikely to get rich through turning. Having to fight off customers at craft fairs is an unlikely experience. But there are opportunities for both part-time and full-time income.
8. Would find the skill a valuable complement to another practice you are already involved in. The possession of skills in related areas increases the potential in all.
9. Are approaching retirement, and want a new, active interest.
10. Want to give to others: gifts to relatives, toys for needy children, gadgets for the disabled.
11. Are gently forced into it by well-meaning but determined spouses or relatives.
12. Like organizing or other non-production activities in addition to turning. It is obvious that some enjoy involvement in running woodturning organizations, teaching, etc. in addition to working on a lathe.

If any of the twelve situations above apply to you, then you should consider woodturning. But what is woodturning? If you start, which direction should you take? If you turn already, should you change your direction and commitment? Every turner's involvement in turning is unique and personal, and varies through time. By looking at turners and their work, past and present, this chapter seeks to give you an insight into what turning could be to you.

1.1 A BRIEF HISTORY

Woodturning was invented about 3000 years ago in the Middle East. Among the earliest records are those at Persepolis, the capital of Iran around 600 BC. Its spectacular remains are rich in limestone reliefs which record the triumphs of its rulers Xerxes and Artaxerxes who are pictured on turned thrones (figure 1.1). This use of turning was probably due to it being a new innovation, as now a prerequisite for high-fashion status.

By this time some of the practical benefits of turning would have been appreciated: the ease of producing truly circular cross-sections, the ease of ornamenting spindles and possibly other circular forms with mouldings, and the production of accurate diameter spigots for housing in drilled holes.

Turning changed little during the next two millenia. The wood continued to be held between two spike-like centers, one of which could be slid along the lathe bed and be clamped to accommodate different workpiece lengths. The wood was rotated by a reciprocating cord wrapped around it or a driving mandrel (figure 1.2).

Figure 1.1 A relief at Persepolis of Xerxes on his turned throne.

Figure 1.2 A pole lathe operated by Englishman Mike Abbott. The cord goes up to the tip of a springy sapling (the *pole*) which is out of shot. Pushing down on the treadle causes the cord to rotate the workpiece forwards against the tool's cutting edge. Releasing the pressure on the treadle allows the the pole to straighten. This pulls the cord upwards which causes the workpiece to rotate away from the cutting edge. Because of this reversing rotation the cutting is not continuous.

Figure 1.3 A lignum vitae wassail bowl in the J.B. Hawkins collection. Turned in England in about 1660. The handle at the top is used to syphon wassail into the upper reservoir. Each dipper cup can be filled from the reservoir through its own tap.

In his marvellous book *Treen and other Wooden Bygones* Edward H. Pinto states that wassailing is "associated with festive community drinking." It is believed that village virgins carried wassail bowls brimming with wassail (a punch of variable recipe) in procession. What happened afterwards is uncertain.

During the 15th century came the fundamental breakthrough, the introduction of the two-bearing headstock. Instead of a fixed spike, there is a spindle which is able to be rotated within bearings near each end. This design continues to be the basis of all modern lathes (see chapter 3). It permitted three new forms of turning: *cupchuck turning* in which the workpiece has its grain direction parallel to the lathe axis but is held only at the headstock end (see figure 1.3 and chapter 7); and *faceplate* and *bowl turning* in which the disk-like workpiece is held by only one face (chapters 8 and 9).

Until recently most turning would have been profes-

sional, although even professionals sometimes let their hair down (figure 1.4). But with the increase this century in wealth and leisure and the banishment of prejudice against trade activities as hobbies, the crafts were ripe for a revival. Since 1970 the growth in hobby turning has been spectacular. In parallel the decline in professional turning caused largely by the substitution of metals, plastics and modern designs, has ceased. Professional turners have also embraced new roles, in particular servicing the growing number of hobby turners, and turning for the craft and gallery markets.

Figure 1.4   A seventeenth-century turned armchair in ash. From Ty'n-y-cymer, Porth, Glamorgan, Wales. In the collection of the Museum of Welsh Life, Cardiff.

1.2   PERSONAL PORTRAITS

The rest of this chapter attempts to show what woodturning could be to you by looking at five turners; at their lives, their turning, and their hopes for the future.

Frank Bollins

Born 1918, Birmingham, England.
Sheet metal worker and labour union official 1934 to 1983.
Hobby woodturner since 1968.
Lives at Peakhurst, Sydney, Australia.

Frank is good with his hands, is a born organizer, and has a strong social conscience. In retrospect, his progress from sheet-metal-working apprentice via the presidency of a labour union to President of The Syndey Woodturners Guild is not surprising.

He began his apprenticeship in 1934. In 1940 he was elected as a union shop steward, subsequently rising through the union movement to become New South Wales President of the Amalgamated Metal Workers' Union from

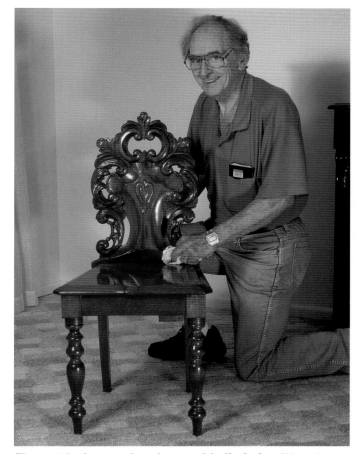

Figure 1.5   A turned and carved hall chair. Although turning is his forte, Frank's competence in a range of woodworking skills allows greater scope.

1974 until his retirement in 1983.

He was introduced to woodturning during the late 1960s when a union organiser. "In metal spinning, the annealed disks are sometimes spun over turned, hard wood formers. I was asked to encourage apprentice metal spinners to enrol in the woodturning course at Sydney Technical College. Through this they would be better able to produce these wooden formers. Few of the target apprentices were attracted, but on my inspection visit to the Tech' I was, and enrolled in one of the evening practical courses. It involved one evening each week for three years. It gave me a thorough grounding in tradition technique and detailing. I later did a carving course to complement my turning skills."

"Most of my turning has been traditional in style, probably because my turning and carving teachers favoured those styles. My wife too preferred the 18th-century English style and helped with the design of some of my more ambitious pieces. I think too that many of we older turners were late in seeing the merits in modern turning design."

"The future? With only a few years of active turning left, I am anxious to explore contemporary design and the new techniques. I want to experiment with what would have once been regarded as reject wood. And I want to get to grips with hollow turning."

Frank Bollins and The Sydney Woodturners Guild

No profile of Frank should ignore his involvement with the Sydney Woodturners Guild. Its formation resulted from the desire of those hobby turners who were attending the Tech' for an association which would bring them together and help them further their turning.

Soundings were made; a meeting called; and in 1983 the Sydney Woodturners Guild was formed with the Tech' as its main home.

Although primarily for hobbyists, the Guild enjoys the support of local professionals. Its objectives are similar to those of most woodturners' associations around the world and are:

1. To promote woodturning in New South Wales.
2. To bring together those interested in woodturning.
3. To exchange woodturning ideas and knowledge amongst members through discussions, seminars, demonstrations, recurring education, competitions, etc.
4. To encourage more interest in woodturning through displays at exhibitions, shows, fairs, etc.
5. To inform members on the availability and suitability of timbers, equipment, etc.
6. To seek to progressively influence woodturning design and techniques.

However the Guild does not believe that it should provide cheap tuition for beginners – it sees its role rather to further members' turning. But the Guild has promoted beginners' classes, especially at the local level, because it recognises the importance of starting properly through sound tuition.

Frank was involved from the start, and in 1985 was elected Vice President. He has held an elected office ever since, including that of President from 1986 to 1992.

The Tech' is centrally located, but Sydney is a widespread city of 4 million. Following the growth of informal meetings between members who lived close to one another, it was decided to encourage the formation of local groups to help the Guild better achieve its objectives. There are now ten regional groups which meet formally once every two months. The local group meetings alternate with full Guild meetings at the Tech' which are usually attended by about a hundred of its still-growing membership of over 400. Frank says, "At Guild meetings we try not to dally too long on administrative business. We usually then have a visiting speaker, often with a demonstration. Members are encouraged to describe the features of their recent work. Meetings close at about 9.30 pm after supper."

As lathes aren't easily portable, a common problem for turners' associations is to find places to meet. The Southern Group to which Frank belongs was fortunate to be offered a vacant hall on a long-term lease (figure 1.6). It now houses seven lathes and other equipment, a kitchen, and a meeting room. It is used almost every day by Group members, and visits by other groups and individual turners are encouraged.

Frank has stated, "My experiences in industry and in the Guild confirm my belief in the benefits of democratic structures for cooperative activities." I hope we would all agree.

Figure 1.6 The headquarters of the Southern Group of the Sydney Woodturners Guild. Previously used by the scouts, the building is leased from the local Sutherland Shire Council.

Peter Lowe

Born 1958, Bunbury, Western Australia.
Computer software engineer until 1994.
Professional gallery turner since 1994.
Works from home in Perth, Western Australia.

In the two decades after leaving school Peter built a successful computer software business with two older partners. In parallel he studied at night which left little time for leisure. But by 1989 he had the free time to salve the itch which had been gnawing since high school. It wasn't the result of inspirational teaching, it was the frustration of not having had enough time at school to give woodturning a proper go.

In 1994 Peter's partners decided to retire. It was a crucial time. Woodturning won and Peter became a full-time turner.

"Apart from having more time to spend with my family, the greatest pleasure comes from the friendliness of the other turners in Western Australia. All of us are working from home workshops which makes contacts so much more personal. I was concerned that by working on my own I would end up as some kind of dusty hermit, but if anything the opposite is true. There's always somebody dropping in for a chat to swap ideas and techniques or to propose some new idea for an exhibition."

One of Peter's hobby horses is the promotion of woodturning as an art form. He frequently organizes group exhibitions which promote the message that turning is not just chair legs and stair balusters.

Peter's focus is the top end of the gallery market, perhaps the most difficult area in which to earn a living. His advice to anyone considering this specialty is "Make sure your wife has a good income."

Figure 1.8 Essential Element Fire III, Peter Lowe, sheoak, 17 in (420 mm) high.

Figure 1.7 Peter Lowe has put computing behind him.

Peter most enjoys designing. A lot of time is spent with pencil and paper before he approaches the lathe. The inspirations for his vessel designs come from many sources, especially pottery. "I think I've always been a frustrated potter. I love the shapes that potters make and their luxury of being able to mold the plastic clay as well as carve it. However I don't think I could work in any material other than wood. I love its variations and surprises and the challenges which result. I won't force a design onto a piece of wood which is trying to tell me something different. Quite often an outstanding success results from exploiting a feature in the wood."

The technical challenges of taking a design through to the finished turning are almost as rewarding to Peter as those from designing. He wishes though he had more metal-working skills so that he could make his own tools.

Peter has only been turning professionally for three years, but is already becoming highly regarded in his chosen specialty of combining carving and turning. His

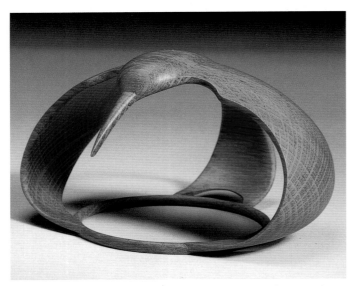

Figure 1.9 Spinebill, Peter Lowe, sheoak, 6 in (150 mm) diameter.

enthusiasm for his craft and the enjoyment he finds with other turners ensure that he'll be creating for years to come.

Gail Redman

Lives and works in San Francisco, USA.

What has brought a graduate in botany and anthropology to be one of the world's very few female production turners? Whether you call it passion or obsession, or whether it's both, you have to gain one or both if you wish to excel.

After graduation, Gail taught eight-year-olds near her native San Francisco. In part to relieve the stress of teaching she enrolled in an evening adult education class, and was introduced to woodturning. She continued turning as a hobby, exclusively bowls and platters, while teaching and travelling. The turning bug was burrowing deeper.

In 1974 she heard of the strength of professional turning in New Zealand. On her next trip via an intensive carving course in Java, she headed for Auckland. She was initially disappointed: "I wanted to be a bowl turner like Bob Stocksdale, but it was all spindle turning!" Building and furniture components, and interior design items were mass- and batch-produced for local consumption and export. Gail bowed to the inevitable, and got a start with Matloe Woodturning. Dave Wilcox ran the woodturning shop there, and Gail joined the four male apprentices. Dave had trained in England and demanded that Gail adopt his methods. Gail still believes "that the overhand grip provides more control." Gail learnt that production turning, mainly of spindles, was the only financially-viable form at that time—this was early in the conception of craft

and studio turning. She also learned the joy of true tool mastery, and started to appreciate that aesthetic challenge and complexity is not exclusive to bowls and vessels.

Production woodturning was even more exclusively a male preserve then. Sure, she got lots of ribbing, but her commitment ensured a genuine acceptance, one that was harder to find later in her native America.

In 1976 she headed home and soon found a job with the architectural turners. Haas Wood & Ivory Company. After eight months there was a downturn in Haas's business, and Gail decided to set up her own shop.

Like all who start a new business with little capital, Gail did everything, somehow. She installed, turned, maintained, cleaned up, at the same time being bookkeeper, accountant, purchasing officer, marketing manager, and PR consultant. Over 20 years on, Gail is a well-established and successful architectural and jobbing turner in San Francisco. She usually employs one other experienced turner. She's also collected a husband and turned out two children. The passion is still there, but now it has to be spread a little wider.

What about the rewards of production turning? "One is being out and about, seeing your work in situ, doing its job;

Figure 1.10 Gail Redman.

Figure 1.11 A newel post and balusters by Gail Redman. Balustrade components are the most-sought items from architectural turners.

well-pleased customers who keep coming back or recommend you; above all the satisfaction of the obsession. And there are hassles: besides a sore neck and back, the main one is the pressure from customers who need it 'yesterday'."

Turning has been a male preserve until recently. There is now a welcome and increasing number of women, especially in gallery turning. But in production turning Gail is perhaps unique.

Walter Rissmeyer

Born 1931, New York City.
Mortgage banker 1955 to 1995.
Hobby turner since 1939.
Lives at Lakewood, New Jersey, USA.

Walter's big, bluff, and cheery. He doesn't fit the desiccated banker stereotype. Think Father Christmas though, and you're close to the mark.

Walter started turning at eight after seeing a turner in action at a county fair in New York in 1939. "I was fascinated watching square blocks spin into round chair legs. I pictured all the marvellous things I could make." He immediately started to build his first lathe from a Singer sewing machine and scavenged bits.

Walter first tried a "proper" lathe at high school. He still has the cherry bowl he turned there. Within a year of leaving school he had saved and bought a Shop Smith which served as his lathe for the next twenty years. He made furniture and turned woodware—today's focus on art turning was still below the horizon.

Figure 1.12 Walter Rissmeyer in 1830's costume. The driving cord of Allaire Village's pole lathe is wrapped around the cylindrical mandrel which was used in turning the nest of three maple bowls. Photograph by Norman Moskowitz.

Figure 1.13 Walter's workshop doesn't have much wasted space. Photograph by Norman Moskowitz.

During the three decades after WWII proper woodturning instruction was almost unknown. "There were few tools, books, or magazines. Unless you were apprenticed you taught yourself by trial and error."

Walter's day job was mortgage banking. Those readers who have just started to tremble are unlikely to appreciate the stress of such work. Walter found relief in his own turning and joy through helping others to learn and appreciate the craft. Friendships with other woodworkers blossomed as they shared knowledge and equipment.

Walter is unashamedly a turner of useful items, of: bowls, mallets, gavels, letter openers, rolling pins, knitting needles, Christmas tree ornaments, candlesticks, pepper mills, goblets, napkin rings, and especially pens: the list stretches on and on. (This pleasure we turners get from converting a mere lump of wood into something of use and beauty is difficult to pin down, yet is surely one of the driving forces of human progress). Unless making a pair or a set Walter does not attempt to turn each type of item identically—one of his pleasures is to make each a little different and therefore unique.

Now retired, Walter retains his interest in mortgage banking and is a sought-after lecturer. Walter has always turned every day, but is not a batchelor! But he now has more time to devote to turning and to enjoy the increasing flood of books, videos, magazines, and exhibitions. He is an active member of many woodworkers' and woodturners' associations—we met at the First World Turning Conference in Delaware in 1993.

For Walter as for the other of this chapter's subjects, turning has offered a way to repay. He demonstrates and teaches at retirement homes, to community groups, to woodworkers' clubs, and on television. He teaches an eight-week adult-education course each fall. And if you go to New Jersey's historic Allaire Village at the weekends, it's likely you'll be able to talk to Walter in his 1830's costume as he pedals its 19th-century lathes. Don't get too close though or he'll make you swop places.

David Springett

Born 1948, Birmingham, England.
Teacher of woodwork in secondary schools in Gloucestershire, England from 1970 to 1977.
Professional bobbin turner since 1977.
Author of: Woodturning Wizardry *and* Adventures in Woodturning.
Author and publisher of: Success to the Lace Pillow *and* Turning Lace Bobbins.
Lives at Rugby, Warwickshire, England.

David turned wood at school. Like most schoolboys he was told to scrape it. He recalls, "It was a case of thrusting a blunt steel tool into a whirling chunk of wood to see which would give way first. I couldn't see how to get a smooth surface without hours of choking sanding." But despite this needless repression of his latent love of woodturning, he became a school woodwork teacher.

Anxious to do better for his students, David read the few

Figure 1.14 David Springett.

then-available turning books. Gordon Stokes struck a chord with his explanation that the bevel of the tool should rub the wood, then slowly be brought down until cutting started. " For the first time I could cut wood cleanly. I loved it. After a few weeks I could cleanly finish pieces just off-the-tool."

David passed his new skills on to his students. They too revelled in them. David continued to build his skills in his free time. Bowls became his passion. Being able to finish pieces by one process, using one machine, was an extra attraction.

John Sainsbury, since the author of several woodturning books, was employed by Record Tools to visit schools to promote and advise on turning. He held a teachers' workshop at David's school. As David was host he had to use the miniature lathe which John had brought so that there would be one per teacher. David was not immediately tempted to scale down.

In 1977 David's wife Christine started bobbin lacemaking as a hobby. Hand lacemaking using bobbins had been a major industry in Europe from the sixteenth century until the 1880s when it disappeared almost overnight with the advent of lacemaking machines. The 1970's crafts revival brought with it a renewed interest in lace, starting in its earlier stronghold of England's East Midlands, wherein lies Rugby. David volunteered to make the growing numbers of

Figure 1.16 David's turning interests are much wider than just bobbins. These turnings seem to have been turned on an ornamental lathe in which the tool is held in the machine. *Woodturning Wizardry* shows you how to turn them by hand.

bobbins that Christine needed as her interest grew. David recalled, practiced, and perfected the techniques of miniature turning which he had been shown earlier by John Sainsbury. Then other students in Christine's lacemaking class wanted David's bobbins too, and the seed of a business germinated.

David continues to turn bobbins, to write and publish on bobbins and intricate turning techniques. Christine's interest too has blossomed, and she now runs The British College of Lace which holds classes and is a source for everything a lacemaker needs.

After twenty years of professional turning within the same specialty, David still loves it. "I love every moment in the workshop. What could be better, radio on, cosy, creating pieces which people treasure. I turn hundreds of bobbins each week in small varied batches. It's not in the least tedious. It also develops, almost without you noticing it, extraordinary skills. When making less demanding cuts I let my mind wander—can I improve my techniques? How was this done? Turning wood to the highest standard, this is what I want to do with the rest of my life."

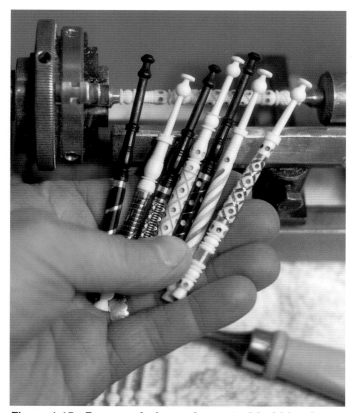

Figure 1.15 Bone and ebony decorated bobbins by David Springett.

Chapter Two

HOW TO START

You have decided to give woodturning a try. How do you start? You can:

1. Join your local woodturning club and national association.
2. Have woodturning lessons.
3. Seek out further sources of woodturning knowledge and information through books, magazines, videos, catalogues, and events.
4. Discuss woodturning with other turners, both amateur and professional.
5. Study woodturners in action.
6. Study woodturning exhibitions and displays.
7. Buy the equipment and teach yourself using this book plus other input.
8. Become an apprentice, work with a turner, become a tertiary student in a course with woodturning content.

These options are discussed below. Follow as many as you can. This book will help you whichever you choose, and especially if you choose or have to teach yourself.

Woodturning Clubs

The formation of woodturners' clubs in the English-speaking world started in Australia and New Zealand from the mid-1970s. The local clubs in New Zealand decided to form a national association in 1986 to better coordinate events and represent the interests of turners on a national level. In Australia there has never been a strong movement to form a national association—no one is sure who would man it, what it would do, and how it would be paid for. To compensate there are exchanges of newsletters, visits of one club to another, and personal contacts. In Britain and America, national associations were formed first, in the late 1980s. They then promoted and assisted the formation of affiliated regional and local groups.

The recent growth in woodturning may have started in English-speaking countries, but its growth is international with national associations and local clubs being formed in an increasing number of countries. There is a strong possibility therefore that there is a club near you. If so the best way to start turning is to join it.

Through being in a club you will be able to experience what woodturning is to others, assess whether it might be

Figure 2.1 Nothing attracts like a demonstration. Members of the Southern Highlands Woodturners Guild watch member John Powell show what he learnt on a course the week before. The Southern Highlands is a rural area a two-hour drive south-west of Sydney, Australia.

Figure 2.2 Members of the Southern Highlands Woodturners Guild. The handsome edifice behind belongs to Don Akrigg (*second from left*). He generously allows the Guild to hold its monthly meetings there. The Guild is seeking to attract younger and female members.

for you, get help and advice, strike up friendships. To find your local club (if there is one) approach your national woodturners' or woodworkers' association when one exists. Some addresses are in included in appendix 1. They can also be tracked down through your national or state Crafts Council, your national woodworking or woodturning magazines, local or specialist woodturning suppliers, industrial arts teachers and professional woodturners, or your local paper. You could ask in your local newsagent who regularly buys the relevant magazines.

If there is no local club, the above search should at least turn up locals who share your interest and you can start your own club.

Tuition

No book or video can equal first-class face-to-face tuition. Your national woodworking and woodturning magazines will carry tuition advertisements. Ask around to discover who others recommend. There is a shortage of good teachers, and unfortunately some of the better ones concentrate on teaching specialist techniques. Familiarity with this book should enable you to monitor and get the best out of any teaching. Where advice conflicts, ask your teacher to explain.

Some teachers offer individual tuition, some group. The tuition in a class of six or less is not necessarily inferior to that you would get in individual lessons. The more relaxed atmosphere when you are in a group can be an advantage. Check with the teacher whether you need to take any wood

or equipment.

If you start turning by doing a course, delay buying equipment until you feel more informed and confident of choosing wisely. If the course is a series of, say, weekly lessons, this means that you will not be able to practice at home between lessons until you are set up. This is a unfortunate, but less so than buying the wrong equipment.

Teaching Yourself

Readers remote from clubs, tuition, or from other turners, can teach themselves. Many have in the past when there was less, often far less, information readily available than there is now. The illustrations and text in this book are designed so that you can learn the basics from it alone if necessary. You will need application and care—their lack and poor tuition are the main reasons that some do not progress as they should.

Books

No matter how good you believe this book is, you should seek out as many others as you can. Few bookshops will carry many, but most specialist suppliers do, and will mail-order them to you. Some libraries have good collections.

The more sources you consult, the more conflicting advice you will find. Much of the advice must be inferior or poorly presented. Regrettably you have to decide which.

Magazines

There are now many magazines and journals which have significant woodturning content. It is particularly worthwhile to subscribe to one with local relevance. Magazines on architecture, building, the decorative arts, design, interior design, crafts, and antiques often contain articles of interest.

Videos

Video is an excellent medium for conveying woodturning knowledge. The quality of both content and presentation varies enormously, so ask around. Recommended is the companion video to my first book. Both are titled *The Practice of Woodturning*.

If buying an overseas video, check that it compatible. North America and Japan use the NTSC system; Europe, Australia, New Zealand, and South Africa use PAL.

Catalogues

The catalogues of many specialist suppliers make fascinating and informative reading. Some run to over 100 pages and are in color.

Wood Turning Center

The initiative of its director Albert LeCoff, this resource center at 42 West Coulter Street, Philadelphia, PA 19144, USA, is a must-visit if you are in the area, and is open by appointment. It has an extensive collection of turnings, slides, books, magazines, catalogues, etc. It publishes books and its quarterly publication *Turning Points* is sent free to members. The Center is an important promoter of woodturning exhibitions and conferences. Its telephone number is (215) 844 2188.

Events

National and local associations, suppliers, and other bodies increasingly hold woodturning events or hold events which incorporate some woodturning content. The scale varies from international symposiums running for some days to a local association's couple of hours promotion at a shopping center. If you are new to turning, attendance at any would be worthwhile.

Contacts with Other Turners

Through the associations and events described above you should be able to establish contacts with other turners. However much you wish to share knowledge, if you are a beginner you will be a net receiver. You will inevitably be imposing on the goodwill of others. You should telephone in advance and appreciate that if another turner agrees to see you they are putting themselves out for you. And in the case of the professional, foregoing income to see you. So don't overstay your welcome or be disappointed if some refuse to divulge their "secret" methods or give you prolonged, free tuition.

Where to See Woodturnings

Woodturnings are in craft shops, galleries, touring exhibitions, private collections, and decorative arts and technology collections in museums. Woodturning is a popular feature in heritage villages and craft fairs. Some turners have retail showrooms—a good opportunity to start your own collection. But in countries where wood has been and is used extensively in building, furniture, and domestic ware, woodturnings are everywhere. Use your eyes, the knowledge is there for the taking.

Becoming a Professional

Professional turners are a rare breed. In Australia they are perhaps 1 in 200,000 of the population. There are few because society doesn't need many. Nor does it believe that they are essential. If your ambition is to become wealthy, don't become a professional woodturner.

The majority of professionals start as amateurs. They enjoy turning, progress, buy more equipment, need more space, sell some work. They evolve into professionals, frequently specializing in work for which there is some local demand. Alternatively there may be a specialty in which they desire to excel, and have to promote their sales over a wide area, even internationally.

You can opt to start as a professional by becoming apprenticed or by working for a professional for a period. I would recommend at least two years.

Another option is to take a tertiary course, but suitable ones are few and far between. Tertiary woodwork courses usually include some turning, as do some design, industrial arts, and arts courses. Such courses are insufficient on their own—to build your accuracy and speed of production to a viable level you need to put in many hours on the lathe.

Chapter Three

LATHES AND ASSOCIATED EQUIPMENT

This book assumes that your desired expenditure on equipment is a reasonable minimum – a noble but elastic brief.

Your neighborhood toolstore is an unlikely source for woodturning equipment. You should visit one or more specialist woodturning suppliers or obtain their catalogues. Few though will carry the full range of available brands and models. Consult the advertisements and equipment reviews in your national woodturning and woodworking magazines. Discuss equipment with other turners. You are more likely to buy wisely if you are well-informed.

When you buy turning equipment you are taking a chance and making a commitment. You know your situation now, but can only make an informed guess about your turning future. Why limit your future turning choices by opting for restricted-purpose equipment?

Your minimum, starting, basic equipment is:

1. A woodturning lathe.
2. Turning tools. Their choice is discussed in section 4.12.
3. Tool-sharpening equipment: a bench grinder and/or a linisher, a grinding jig, a dressing stick if you will be using a grinder, and hones. Sharpening is detailed in sections 4.9 to 4.11.
4. A Jacobs chuck on an arbor with the same Morse taper as your tailstock ram.
5. Some basic measuring equipment.
6. Appropriate dust protection equipment.

These items are discussed in this and succeeding chapters. There are many other items which you could buy now or in the future. Some will make certain operations more efficient rather than making new operations possible. In general wait until you have the need and know that an item will be worthwhile.

3.1 YOUR LATHE

A quality wood lathe should last for many decades with reasonable maintenance, and is unlikely to become obsolete. You should buy the best lathe that you can reasonably afford bearing in mind your anticipated usage.

Lathe Types

The usual lathe capacity is about 36 in (900 mm) between centers (figure 3.1).

Longer-than-standard beds are needed by architectural component turners. Long- and extendable-bed lathes are available. Alternatively you can fit a new headstock to an old, flat, metal-working lathe bed; or buy a headstock, tailstock, and banjos which you fit onto long, wood or steel bed sections (figure 3.2).

I recommend you buy a lathe which allows outboard turning if you are right-handed (figures 3.3 and 3.4). It will allow you to mount larger-diameter faceplate and bowl turnings. More importantly you will not be forced to adopt the inferior tool presentations or awkward body positions which inboard bowl hollowing dictates. A facility built into or attached to your lathe's stand is more convenient than a freestanding toolrest stand unless you are intending work of huge diameters. The swivelling-headstock alternative (figure 3.5) is currently fashionable. It is cheaper because you don't need both left- and right-hand-threaded faceplates, chucks, and inserts. It is more convenient for cupchuck hollowing because you don't have to lean over the bed. It also does not restrict your tool presentations for bowl hollowing. However the swivelling headstock has disadvantages: the toolrest can flex when cantilevered away from the bed, the diameters of workpieces may be unduly limited, and a right-handed turner's arm positions are less natural.

Miniature lathes are cheaper, portable, and often of high quality (figure 3.6). Their low center height and any lack of an outboard facility will again force inferior tool presentations for some cuts. Small work can readily be done on a standard-sized lathe, so do not unnecessarily restrict your options. If room is an insoluble problem, a short bed lathe (figure 3.7) is a better but heavier and dearer alternative. Special-purpose bowl lathes are also available, but the common beginners' vision of turning only bowls is unnecessarily restrictive.

Lathe Construction

Woodturning involves rotating dynamically-unbalanced workpieces at high speed. Your lathe should be as heavy, rigid, and absorbing of vibration as possible. The material which traditionally and still gives these benefits is not vibration-transmitting steel, but cast iron. Its cementite crystals are insulated from one another by free graphite. The best lathes therefore have cast-iron beds, headstocks, and tailstocks.

Cast-iron beds are a major cost component, in part because of their high machining costs. Lathes with heavy and rigid steel bar, tube, or rectangular-section beds are a cheaper, but still recommendable, choice.

Stands

The stand supports the lathe bed, and usually carries the electric motor, transmission, switching, and any outboard-turning facility. It may also incorporate dust extraction, cupboards, and a tool tray. Ideally the motor should be protected from dust and shavings so that its cooling is not impaired. It should be able to be locked in position; its

distance from the headstock spindle being varied using a sliding or pivoting mounting.

Most lathes are available for mounting on your own stand. Other options are open, fabricated steel-section stands, cabinet stands (figure 3.1), or bolt-on, cast-iron legs. Making your own stand can be very time consuming and surprisingly expensive, so if a manufacturer's stand is rigid and heavy or lends itself to having these desirable properties improved, for example by weighting and cross-bracing, opt to buy your stand.

The tailstock and banjo(s) (figure 3.1) are mounted on and slide along the bed. The bed should allow them to slide freely, and be locked securely in any desired position.

A gap in the bed immediately to the right of the headstock (figure 3.1) permits larger-diameter disks to be turned inboard. It is rarely big enough to allow optimum tool presentations. If too long it limits banjo positioning.

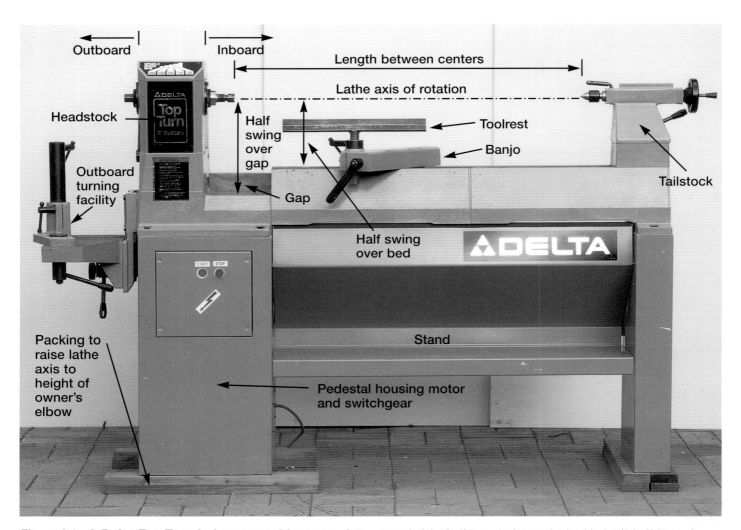

Figure 3.1   A Delta Top Turn lathe on a cabinet stand. Its center height (half its swing) over the bed is 8 1/8 in (207 mm), and its length between centers is 38 in (965 mm).

Figure 3.2 Conover lathe components, made in Ohio, USA, allow you to build a lathe of any length using wood or steel bed sections which you supply.

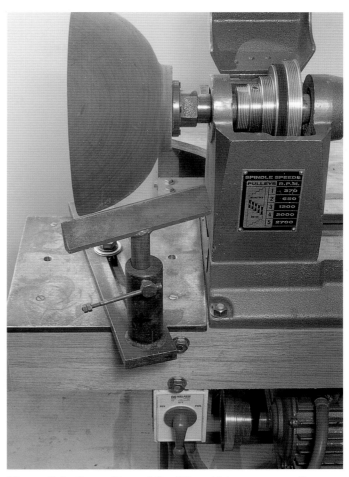

Figure 3.4 An outboard facility which you can easily copy. The top bearers of the wooden stand extend to the left past the headstock of this Australian-made Woodfast MC908 lathe, and support a l/2-in (13-mm) thick steel plate and a tall banjo. The banjo is locked in position with a bolt which threads into one of a couple of holes which are drilled and tapped through the plate.

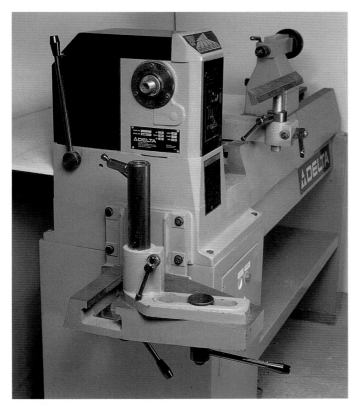

Figure 3.3 An outboard turning facility, that of a Delta Top Turn lathe.

Figure 3.5 A swivelling headstock, that of a Nova 3000. Nova lathes, made in New Zealand, are notable for their wide speed range, here from 178 to 3000 rpm in eight steps.

Figure 3.6 **The Carba-tec Mini lathe** has a center height of 3 in (75 mm) and a length between centers of 12 in (300 mm).

Figure 3.7 **The Vicmark VL 100 short-bed lathe** has six speeds, an outboard spindle nose, a center height of 4 1/2 in (115 mm), and a length between centers of 12 in (300 mm).

Headstocks

The headstock houses the headstock spindle which rotates the workpiece (figure 3.8). If its cast-iron or steel structure is too boxy, the positioning of your left wrist and forearm will be restricted.

The Headstock Spindle

The headstock spindle is housed in two bearings which are housed in the headstock structure. Normally the spindle's right-hand nose has a right-hand thread, and the outboard, left-hand nose has a left-hand thread. On all but the cheapest lathes the spindle should have a through hole which enables you to eject the drive center using a knock-out bar. This hole also allows vacuum chucking in which the workpiece is pushed by atmospheric pressure onto a suitable faceplate held on one spindle nose. Evacuation takes place through a special union (a rotatable seal) screwed onto the opposite nose.

You need to be able to lock the spindle to remove faceplates and chucks. A hexagonal or facetted flange is usually provided for this on the left of the right-hand spindle nose.

More-expensive lathes have an indexing facility which allows you to lock the headstock spindle at various orientations (figure 3.8). There is usually a sprung pin which can locate into holes (often 24) drilled at equal intervals around the largest pulley. It is used in radial drilling and in carving, especially when flutes or reeds have to be regularly spaced around a turning's periphery.

There are four main ways to mount a workpiece so that it is driven by the headstock spindle:

1. *Between centers*   The workpiece is called a *spindle* when its grain lies parallel to the lathe axis. (figure 3.7). The workpiece's left-hand end is usually driven and located by a drive center (figure 3.8) which has a slowly-tapered shank which pushes into the hole with the same taper (the *swallow*) in the inboard end of the headstock spindle. The right-hand end of the workpiece is located and pushed to the left by a tail center similarly held within the swallow in the left-hand end of the tailstock ram (figure 3.10). In small and miniature lathes the swallows' taper will be Morse No. 1, in most standard-sized lathes it will be the larger Morse No. 2. Morse tapers taper at about 1 in 20 and are therefore self-gripping.
2. *Inboard by a faceplate or chuck*   The workpiece can be screwed to a faceplate, or gripped by the screw or expanding or contracting jaws, etc. of a chuck (figure 3.9). The faceplate or chuck is itself screwed onto the threaded right-hand spindle nose.
3. *Outboard by a faceplate or chuck*   See figure 3.4.
4. *In the headstock-spindle swallow*   See figure 7.2.

Varying Lathe Speed

You need to be able to vary the rotational speed of your lathe's headstock spindle to safely turn different sizes and types of workpiece. How you choose the speed is discussed in section 4.7

Stepped pulleys (figure 3.5) provide the cheapest way to vary the lathe speed and are more than adequate for most uses. Flat Poly-V belts enable a larger speed range than do simple V-belts, and can transmit more torque than flat belts. The more speeds the better – some lathes have eight. To change speeds the motor has to be hinged or slid towards the headstock spindle. The belt should only connect pulleys which are in line – do not run the belt diagonally.

The lathe speed is lowest when the driving belt passes over the largest pulley on the headstock spindle. You can easily calculate your lathe's speed from:

Lathe speed = Motor speed x $\dfrac{\text{Diameter of pulley used on motor spindle}}{\text{Diameter of pulley used on headstock spindle}}$

Increased speed ranges and/or continuous speed variation can be obtained using intermediate lay shafts, pulleys which are adjustable in diameter, motors with multiple windings, and mechanical or electrical variable-speed systems. In general, mechanical speed variation is more noisy and slower to operate, electrical speed variation results in significant power loss at low motor speeds. The advertising boast that electrical speed variation gives constant torque is true; it also means that the motor's power output is proportional to the motor's speed.

Most lathes have a single on/off switch mounted at the left-hand end of the lathe. Extra flexibility can be added by installing double-switching, an emergency stop, or a clutch. Knee or foot operation is sometimes seen for these. Melvyn Firmager recommends a foot switch for hollow turning because of the likelihood of needing to switch off while still holding the tool with both hands.

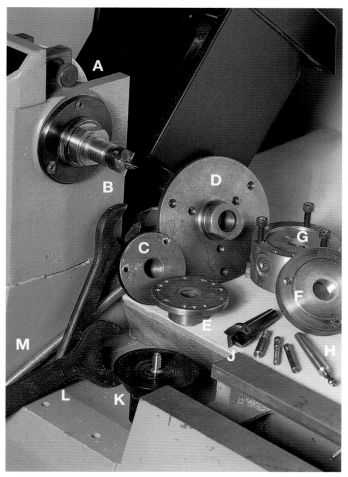

Figure 3.9 Accessories which are mounted into the headstock spindle swallow or are screwed onto its externally-threaded nose(s).

A is the indexing knob. Drive centers, **B**, are usually four pronged and have a central spike which should project 1/8 to 1/4 in (3 to 6 mm) depending on the size and hardness of the workpiece and the diameter of the drive center (several different diameters of drive center are available). **C, D** and **E** are faceplates. **E** has had further holes drilled for holding axially-grained hollow turnings. Faceplate **F** has been specially machined and is the backing plate for the Axminster scroll chuck **G. H** is a mini drive center from Bob Chapman Woodturning Accessories in England. **J** is a drive center which accepts any of the three cylidrical pins: it is used to center and drive workpieces such as lamp stems which have earlier been axially bored. The Glaser screwchuck **K** is shown in use in figure 7.4. Two spanners **L** are supplied with the Top Turn lathe. They mate with the flats on the headstock spindle above and on the bosses of accessories to allow the accessories to be loosened. **M** is the knock-out bar used to eject accessories with tapered shanks and arbors from the headstock and tailstock swallows.

Figure 3.8 A Delta Top Turn headstock showing its five-stepped pulley and indexing facility. A No. 2 Morse taper drive center is held in the spindle swallow. The right-hand spindle nose is threaded 1 in x 10 tpi (threads per inch) right-hand. The indexing facility is a sprung pin housed in the red block which you can locate into any of the 24 equally-spaced holes in the face of the adjacent pulley.

Tailstocks

Tail centers, tapered drill tangs (figure 5.4), and tapered chuck arbors can be mounted in the Morse taper swallow in the tailstock ram (figure 3.10). A handwheel (the larger the better) is used to forward and retract the ram. Older tailstocks usually have a self-ejecting mechanism to eject tail centers, etc. Newer tailstocks more often have an open hole through the ram and require you to eject with a knock-out bar. The open hole allows you to bore the workpiece through the tailstock using a suitable, hollow tail center. Some tailstocks have both facilities.

The ram should be locked in position when spindle turning or it will tend to vibrate to the right and allow the workpiece to fly out. Similarly the locking of the tailstock onto the bed must not allow the tailstock to creep to the right. A camlock allows you to position and lock the tailstock and banjo quickly, but it needs to be properly adjusted and regularly cleaned and dry-lubricated.

It is important that the axes of the headstock and tailstock spindles are coincident and parallel to the bed. If not, accurate boring will be impossible.

Toolrests

The tied-underhand grip (figures 6.29 and 6.30) is the best for detailed turning. It requires a toolrest with a neat and constant cross-section (figure 3.11). Even the toolrests of some expensive lathes are unsuitable, and you may have to buy compatible toolrests of another brand of lathe or visit your local engineering shop.

A single toolrest between 12 and 16 in (300 and 400 mm) long will serve most purposes. You will need longer toolrests with two or more stems for architectural and furniture component turning. Their stems should be a touch undersize in diameter so that they don't jam in the banjos' stem holes. Short, cranked, and curved toolrests are also useful. Toolrests which allow projecting pins to be fitted are used in metal spinning and sometimes in hollow turning. Toolrest stems should not flex – 1-in (25-mm) diameter stems are advisable for standard-sized lathes.

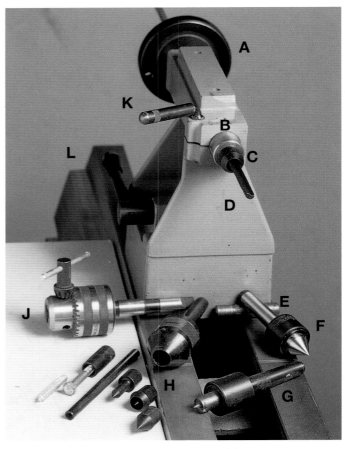

Figure 3.10 A Delta Top Turn tailstock and accessories viewed from the headstock.

The handwheel **A** at the rear moves the tailstock ram **B** to-and-fro. Mounted in the ram's swallow is a dead hollow tail center **C**, and passing through the ram and the center is a lamp-standard auger **D**. ("Dead" in connection with tail centers means without any internal bearings, "live" means with internal bearings and therefore free to spin). You remove the plug **E** from within the ram to allow augers to pass through. Replacing the plug restores the self-ejecting facility which automatically ejects a tapered arbor or shank when the tailstock ram is almost fully retracted. If the retraction does not happen it is usually because the tapered arbor's or shank's minimum diameter is too large. **F** is a cone live tail center. **G** is a cup or ring live center. **H** is a Nova multi-function live center; the accessories in front house in the Nova center's tapered swallow. **J** is a Jacobs chuck on a No. 2 Morse taper arbor. Lever **K** locks the ram. Lever **L** locks the tailstock to the bed.

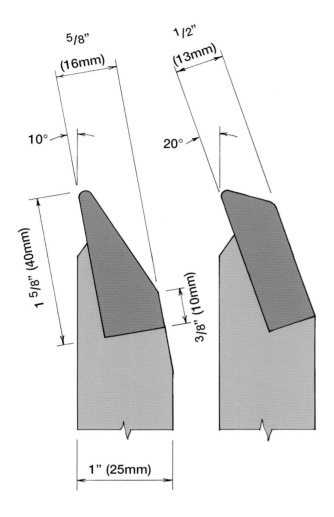

Figure 3.11 Preferred toolrest cross-sections. You should use toolrests with a smaller cross-section if you have small hands. The cross-section should be constant along the full length of the toolrest. The toolrest stem should be neatly welded to the horizontal section of the toolrest, not housed in a gobby boss.

Banjos

I prefer to call the toolrest holder (figure 3.1) a banjo – it resembles the latter when viewed in plan. Its job is to hold the toolrest stem. You will need a second banjo for most long toolrests.

Lathes for Left-Handed Turners

If lathes are "handed", they are right-handed. For spindle turning there is no difference, except in parting off when left handers gain because they do not have to work crossarmed (figure 6.112). Inboard hollowing is awkward left-handed unless the headstock can be swivelled, but

then the toolrest and banjo have to cantilever excessively to the left of the bed. There is a strong case for left handers turning right-handed, particularly if they use the left-hand-dominant, tied-underhand grip, but it is not overwhelming. Some turners recommend ambidextrous turning, but I have never found the need. Yet, although I am definitely right-handed, I am readily able to turn left-handed.

Some left-handed bowl turners order lathes with right-hand outboard threads and reversing switches to make bowl hollowing more comfortable. You could go the whole way and have a fully left-handed lathe made, but I suggest that to turn right-handed for all or just the awkward cuts is the simplest solution.

3.2 LATHE ACCESSORIES

New lathes are usually supplied with: a shortish toolrest, a drive center, a live tail center, and a right-hand faceplate. Depending on your budget and turning intentions, you should buy as soon as possible:

1. A live tail center if a dead center only was supplied. Unfortunately cheap ones, including those supplied as standard equipment with many wood lathes, seize within a short time.
2. One or more new toolrests if those supplied are unsuitable.
3. An outboard turning facility plus left-hand faceplate(s).
4. A screwchuck.
5. A cupchuck if you are not going to buy a multi-purpose chuck in the short term. I recommend a scroll type for your first and probably only multi-purpose chuck. The available options are detailed in section 7.1.
6. A Jacobs chuck on an arbor having the same Morse taper as your tailstock ram.

Faceplates

Threaded inboard and outboard headstock-spindle noses usually have right-hand and left-hand threads respectively. You can manage with one faceplate for each spindle nose, but it is handy to have more. Small faceplates of around $3^{1}/_{2}$ in (90 mm) diameter are generally more useful than large (figure 3.9).

Double-threaded faceplates which you can mount on either spindle nose are economic, but unscrew if you brake the spindle.

3.3 OTHER EQUIPMENT

Measuring Equipment

Figure 3.12 shows essential and optional measuring equipment, much of which you may already have. You should file the jaws of all calipers round (figure 3.13).

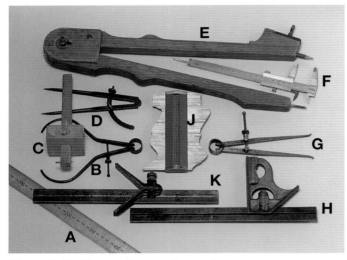

Figure 3.12 Measuring equipment.
    You will need from the start: a rule **A,** pencils, outside spring calipers **B,** a marking gauge **C,** dividers **D** (preferably wing not spring), normal or large compasses **E,** inside spring calipers **G,** and a square **H.** Vernier calipers **F** make small, detailed turning so much easier. Delay buying a Mimic **J** and center finder **K** until you need them.

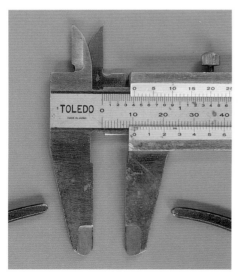

Figure 3.13 Rounded caliper jaws slip sweetly over the wood as it approaches the desired diameter. Vernier calipers with both inches and millimeters are particularly useful.

Wood Preparation Equipment

You can manage with hand tools and pay your lumber yard to do any special preparation. But you will want your own equipment as your involvement increases. What you need will depend on your turning preferences. For bowls and vessels: a petrol chain saw, an electric one for inside your workshop, an electric drill, and a bandsaw. For the turning of building and furniture components and treen: a bandsaw, table saw, jointer, thicknesser, drilling machine, jigsaw, and a self-centering center punch (figure 6.3).

3.4 YOUR WORKSHOP

In the workshop or area in which you propose to turn you will need a lathe plus some or all of:

1. A rack or similar close to your lathe for turning tools.
2. Turning-tool sharpening equipment close to your lathe.
3. Benchtop space.
4. Cupboards and drawers in which to store tools and equipment away from dust and chips.
5. Room and equipment for timber storage, seasoning, and working.
6. Ventilation and dust-extraction equipment. Heating also if the climate demands it.
7. Dust-free space and equipment for polishing, perhaps with its own filtering and extraction.
8. Good lighting.
9. Storage and racks for sheet abrasives.
10. Sufficient electrical power outlets.

Although we would all prefer a spacious, well-equipped workshop with an outside yard for processing logs (if you harvest your own timber), the beginner's norm is more likely to be a corner of an already overcrowded garage. But however grand or otherwise your workshop space, your layout should:

1. Help your projects to flow through the workshop. You should arrange your activity centres in the order: initial wood preparation, seasoning and storage, final wood preparation, turning and turning tool sharpening, assembling, finishing.
2. Give more priority and facilities to those activities you spend the most time on.
3. Allow for future expansion and changes in emphasis.

Lathe Installation

You really need a dedicated space for your lathe. Standard-sized lathes are barely portable and are best bolted down.

You need working room around a lathe. A lathe is a munificent source of shavings and dust, and if you turn green wood, of sticky, staining, rust-promoting sap.

You can install your lathe close to but not right against a wall or window. I suggest that the headstock spindle should be no closer to the vertical surface behind than 18 in (450 mm). Fit a wooden bench top just below the top of the bedways behind the bed. Allow 3 feet (1.0 m) at the right-hand end for removing the tailstock and for long-hole boring. Allow 5 feet (1.5m) at the left-hand end, and the same in front of the lathe. Chips, sap, and in-lathe polishing liquids are thrown out not just radially, but for up to 6 feet (2.0 m) in every direction. Use translucent plastic curtain to limit the spread of chips and sap.

Most lathes are installed with their axes too low. The ideal axis height is level with the point of your elbow when standing up straight. Bolt your lathe down, ideally onto a concrete floor. Level the bed along its length and across the top of the bedways with hard, not rubber, packers. Take care not to twist the bed when you bolt it down.

Ventilation and Dust Extraction

Wood dust does you no good. Especially when from species which are resistant to decay and insect attack, it can cause irritation, allergies, and respiratory ailments. The effects of exposure vary from person to person, but they seem to be cumulative and non-reversible. And it is the very fine dust which causes the problems. Wood dust can also spontaneously ignite. There is a need for information and balance. Fortunately the subject is receiving much more coverage in our magazines, and the first general book for woodworkers on the subject is out — *Workshop Dust Control* by Sandor Nagyszalanczy.

Turning does not create dust at one convenient spot, but widely and generously. You need access to the wood to turn and sand it. These factors prevent local extraction at the lathe being greatly effective. Plainly there is a need to properly filter the workshop air turners breathe, or to bring it in from outside. The occasional turner may find that a really good dust mask and good workshop ventilation will suffice. The serious hobbyist and bearded occasional turner should upgrade from the dustmask to a ventilated face shield (figure 6.6). The professional should consider dust extraction and filtration, ventilation, and a ventilated helmet. If you feel any ill effects from dust, you need to do something more.

Sap can also cause an allergic reaction. Wear protective waterproof clothing and wash as soon as possible after exposure.

Electric Power

You should consider having 3-phase power laid on if you want to use machines having motors larger than 2 hp (1.5 kW). Having this facility opens the potential to use industrial equipment, but for the hobbyist it is certainly not necessary.

Have an outlet for each machine – there's nothing more maddening than spending half your workshop time swapping plugs and messing with extension leads. Install extra power outlets for portable machines and adjacent to benches. Have an extra outlet handy to your lathe into which you can plug portable electric tools and a light for when cupchuck hollowing.

You should employ a licensed electrician to do all electrical installations and maintenance.

Lighting

Fluorescent lights minimize shadows, but still position them so that you are not working in your own shadow. As you get older your eyes' sensitivity to light drops, so don't skimp. Warm-white tubes are much more pleasant than green-tinted.

Install twin flourescents over the full length of the lathe, and for 3 feet (1.0 m) to the left if you have an outboard facility. You should have a light over each machine and your sharpening area.

Chapter Four

CUTTING AND TOOLS

Woodturning mesmerizes non-turners. Shavings fly off at great speed, profiles develop as if by magic, and the tool tip high on the wood is surely about to be buried and be flung back at the hapless turner. This chapter explains what happens at the tool tip and why the onlookers' fears are seldom realised; it then discusses the tools you will need and how to tune and sharpen them.

4.1 CUTTING WITH THE EDGE SQUARE TO THE APPROACHING WOOD

Your tool is said to be *cutting* when its tip rides high on the wood. When "cutting" is used in this sense it will be italicised. Figures 4.1 and 4.2 show *peeling*, the simplest form of *cutting* in which the tool's cutting edge is parallel to the lathe axis and the workpiece's grain direction.

Figures 4.3 to 4.5 illustrate the wood deformations, severance, and forces involved in peeling. When you correctly *cut* with a turning tool, its tip is stable, controllable, and responsive because the forces on the tool tip and on the whole tool are in balance and tend to work to retain that balance. This book is mainly about ensuring that you turn with these benefits.

The remainder of this first section then shows in figures 4.6 to 4.9 how the tool presentation influences the depth of cut.

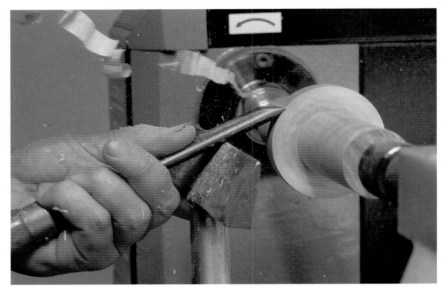

Figure 4.1 Peeling an upstanding rib on a spindle with a wide chisel sharpened square-across. The spindle's grain lies parallel to the lathe axis

Figure 4.2 A close up of peeling looking from the tailstock. The pencil lines radiate from the lathe axis.

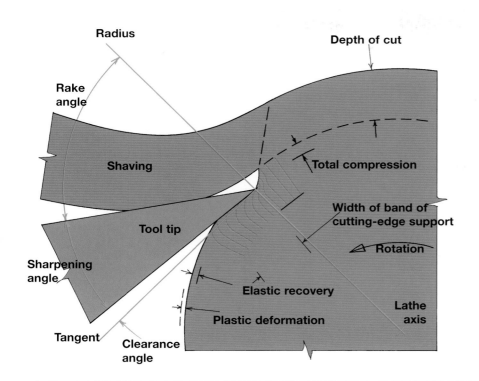

Figure 4.3 **The geometry of peeling.**

This diagram explains the situation in figures 4.1 and 4.2.

You need to become familiar with the concepts of *clearance, sharpening,* and *rake angles.* These terms allow the presentation of a cutting edge to a workpiece to be accurately described. You measure the three angles in a plane perpendicular to the cutting edge. Here the angles are measured in a vertical plane because the cutting edge is horizontal.

Here the *cutting* is with a 5° clearance angle. The shaving severs a minute distance ahead of and radially outside the cutting edge. The deformations which occur near the just-cut surface of the wood are indicated by the short, radial lines. There must be compression of the just-cut surface for it to support the cutting edge. After providing support, the just-cut surface does not spring back completely because the wood close to the surface has been plastically deformed. When this deformation is small it is called *burnishing,* when large it is called *crushing.*

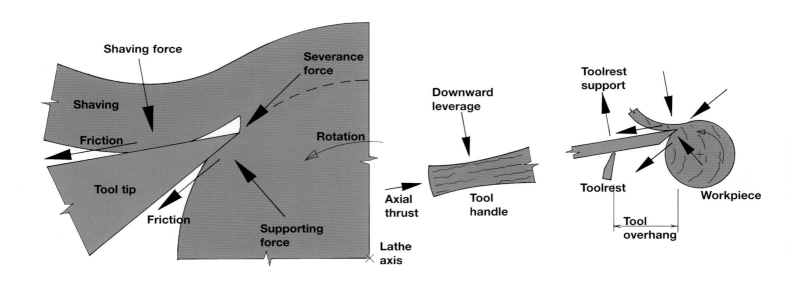

Figure 4.4 **The external forces on the tool tip peeling** at a large (55°) rake angle.

The shaving and supporting forces are approximately equal in magnitude in high-rake-angle *cutting.* They keep the tool tip in a stable equilibrium provided that you maintain a strong axial thrust on the tool. The magnitude of your thrust approximates to the sum of: the severance force needed to sever the shaving, the frictional force which slows the severed shaving, and the frictional force between the lower bevel and the just-cut surface. The forces acting on the whole tool during a peeling cut are shown in figure 4.5.

Figure 4.5 **The forces on a tool peeling** at a large (55°) rake angle.

You need to thrust strongly to achieve a large rake angle and minimum clearance. If you thrust too strongly, the cutting edge will rise up out of the wood and the blade will lose contact with the toolrest. But you need to maintain some contact between the tool and the toolrest to maintain tool control, and so need to supply a strong but just-sufficient thrust. When you supply such a thrust, you barely have to apply any leverage. You will also find it easy to move the tool over the toolrest because the upward force exerted by the toolrest is small.

Figure 4.6 Peeling with zero clearance. No shaving can be taken.

Figure 4.7 Peeling with about 2° clearance to take a fine shaving.
   The shaving and other forces acting towards the lathe axis must slightly exceed the supporting force acting in the opposite direction for the cutting edge to move towards the lathe axis. This photograph confirms that there must be a small clearance angle for this to happen and continue.

Figure 4.8   Peeling with about 12° clearance to take a thicker shaving than in figure 4.7.

To cut more deeply than in figure 4.7 you have to further increase the clearance angle. To achieve this you must present the cutting edge lower on the workpiece. This causes the radially-inward force on the tool tip to exceed the supporting force by a greater amount than in figure 4.7.

Figures 4.7 to 4.9 show that in cutting the width of the band of cutting-edge support is surprisingly narrow (usually less than 1/32 in (1 mm)). But it is not dangerously narrow, and is sufficient for large-rake-angle *cutting.* And you achieve large-rake-angle *cutting* by:

1. Sharpening your cutting edge to the smallest-practical sharpening angle, normally 25° to 30°.
2. Exerting the strong and correct axial thrust on the tool for the resulting clearance angle to be the minimum for your desired depth of cut.

This optimum *cutting* with minimum sharpening and clearance angles has six advantages over other presentations:

1. Because the tool appears sharper to the approaching wood, the surface finish is better.
2. You need to resharpen less often because there is less abrasion of the cutting edge.
3. You can take deeper cuts and thus remove wood faster.
4. You exert less energy because you thrust rather than lever.
5. You minimize the risk of losing control and can turn safely at longer tool overhangs by minimizing the downward forces on the tool tip and maximizing the supporting forces.
6. *Cutting* tends perpetuate its own stability. If for some reason the forces tending to force the tool deeper into the wood increase, as the cutting edge is forced deeper, the supporting wood is compressed more, and thus exerts a higher supporting force. Once the edge is forced down to a new balance, it stabilizes at a slightly-greater clearance angle and depth of cut.

Figure 4.9   Cutting with a small (30°) rake angle and a large (23°) clearance angle.

As the clearance angle increases it ceases to affect the stability of the tool tip. The rake angle has by then become the dominant factor. If the rake angle is greater than about 40° and you lose control, the shaving pushes the cutting edge deeper into the wood and there will be a serious catch. If the rake angle is less than about 40° when you lose control, the cutting edge will tend to be pushed down rather than deeper into the wood, and the catch will be less serious. This is perhaps a reason why sharpening angles of 45° are so commonly recommended for *cutting* tools. Certainly tools with such large sharpening angles catch less catastrophically, but this barely-positive reason does not compensate for the many disadvantages of small-rake-angle cutting.

If you cut with a small rake angle and especially with considerable clearance, you will find that compared with large-rake-angle cutting:

1. The surface finish is worse.
2. Your tools become blunt more quickly.
3. You have to exert greater leverage because the shaving is deflected and slowed more.
4. You cannot confidently use longer tool overhangs. If you present the edge at an overhang which would be considered relatively short for large-rake-angle *cutting,* say 1 1/2 in (40 mm), you will feel that you have to fight to retain control of the tool. Not only are the downward forces greater, the supporting force becomes more horizontal and is therefore less effective in supporting the cutting edge. This likelihood that you will lose control is far greater when you turn the cylindrical periphery of a radially-grained disk cut from a plank because of the adverse grain directions.
5. The rate of wood removal is low. You "rub" the wood off because you dare not thrust strongly enough to achieve and maintain the great depth of cut which is necessary for stable cutting at a large clearance angle.

4.2 CATCHES

Catches (or dig-ins) are the major problem for beginners (figure 4.10). They happen so quickly. They also often happen when a cut seems to be going well. This second characteristic confirms that many catches result not from gross errors, but merely because you allow your tools' presentations to stray a little from the ideal.

To *cut* a particular thickness of shaving most efficiently you need to apply the edge with the corresponding minimum clearance angle and the corresponding thrust. The converse is also true. If you present an edge with a particular clearance angle, the edge will attempt to take a shaving of the corresponding thickness. Similarly if you allow the clearance to increase during a cut because you reduce your axial thrust along the tool, the edge will attempt to take a correspondingly-thicker shaving. If the shaving thickness in either case is greater than you are expecting, the force you are applying will be insufficient to force the edge through the wood to sever the thick or thick-ening shaving, and the edge will be forced backwards. As the edge is forced backwards, the clearance angle increases. So therefore does the corresponding thickness of shaving that the edge wants to cut. This situation rapidly builds on itself, you lose control, the wood takes over, and a catch or a dig-in results. As the wood is typically rotating at between 5 and 50 revolutions-per-second, your reaction time is far too long to allow you to react in time once the conditions for a catch are present.

4.3 PRESENTATION WITH SIDE RAKE

In practice you will rarely choose to cut with the edge square to the approaching wood because a better surface finish results if you skew the edge, that is present it with *side rake* (figure 4.11) without increasing the rake angle. As you increase the side rake, the cutting action changes from peeling towards one of cutting away an upstanding shoulder. An edge presented with side rake acts in three ways to improve the surface:

1. It makes the cutting action more complex and more gentle.
2. It effectively decreases the sharpening angle of the cutting edge as seen by the approaching wood (figure 4.12).
3. It reduces the clearance angle needed for a particular depth of cut. Figures 4.6, 4.7 and 4.8 demonstrated that you have to increase the clearance angle to increase the depth of cut when peeling. When planing a cylinder as in figure 4.11, the cutting edge's distance from the lathe axis remains constant and the edge cuts away an upstanding shoulder. The clearance required is therefore tiny, but still reduces with increasing side rake.

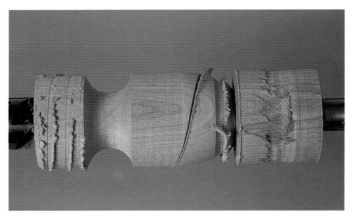

Figure 4.10 Three common catches (or dig-ins): *left,* at the start of a coving cut with a detail gouge; *center,* while rolling a bead with a skew; *right,* when planing with a skew.

Figure 4.11 Planing a cylinder with a skew chisel edge presented at 45° side rake. You measure side rake from a line at 90° to the wood's velocity.

Unfortunately you cannot continue to improve the surface finish by continuing to increase the side rake. Although the subsurface damage represented in figure 4.13 continues to decrease, the macro-cut surface tends to become increasingly rippled. For example, if you gradually increase the side rake while continuing to traverse the cutting edge along the wood at the same speed:

1. The profile cut during each workpiece rotation seen in longitudinal section increases in curvature. The spiralled nature of the turned surface thus becomes more noticeable.
2. The proportion of the length of cutting edge actively cutting which is supported by the just-cut surface lessens (figure 4.14). This increases the likelihood of the cutting edge fluttering and affecting the macro-cut surface.
3. There is a shorter width of reference support between the profiles cut on successive workpiece rotations (figure 4.15). Reference support is caused by the overlapping of adjacent "cuts". As the reference support decreases, you are more likely to cut a radius from the lathe axis to the bottom of each profile which

varies from that you intend. Therefore if you want to turn a macro-cut surface freer from irregularities, you have to decrease the side rake or better slow the speed at which you traverse the tool along the wood.

In spindle turning about 45° side rake gives you the optimum combination of macro-cut surface rippling and subsurface damage. To increase reference support use the tool of the appropriate type which has the largest-suitable flute radius. (A skew can be thought of as having an infinitely-large flute radius).

In faceplate and bowl turning a side rake of 60° to 70° is preferred for finishing cuts because the radial grain directions are less cooperative and yield greater subsurface damage.

The large clearance angle peeling in figure 4.9 was controllable. But you are less able to lever off the toolrest and less friction is generated between the toolrest and the tool blade as you increase the side rake. Therefore excessive clearance becomes a more serious problem, and at high side rakes you will feel the tool stutter if you present the edge with only a little excess clearance.

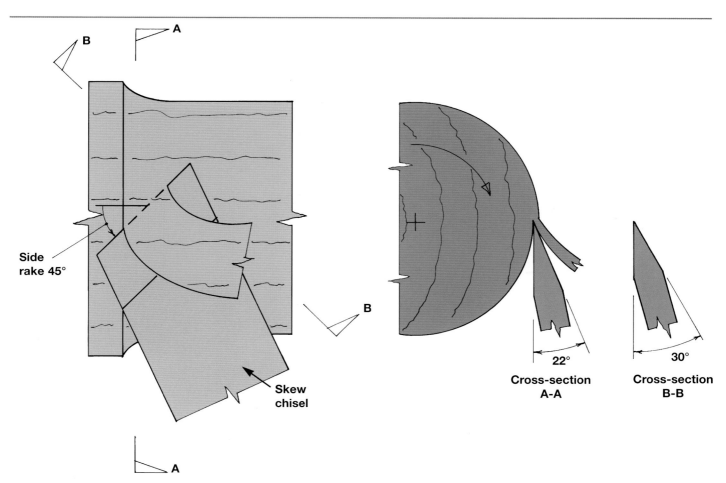

Figure 4.12 How side rake affects effective sharpness. Here increasing the side rake from 0° to 45° effectively increases the rake angle from 60° to 68° and makes the tool appear sharper to the wood.

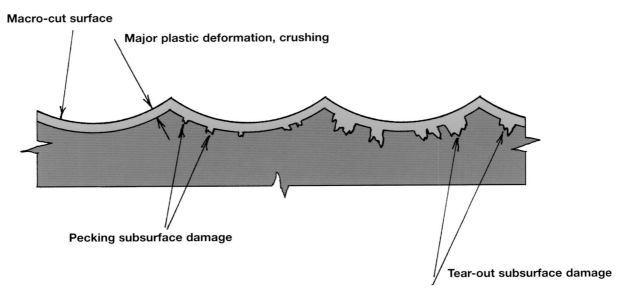

Macro-cut surface

Major plastic deformation, crushing

Pecking subsurface damage

Tear-out subsurface damage

Figure 4.13 Surface imperfections. The drawing shows a magnified longitudinal radial section through a turned surface. The upper scalloped line represents the macro-cut surface which would be left if no fibres were torn out, and if the just-cut surface sprang back completely after being compressed (see figure 4.3). The lower line represents the actual turned surface produced. The shaded area between the two lines represents subsurface damage of two types: plastic deformation resulting from compression, and tear-out of various magnitudes.

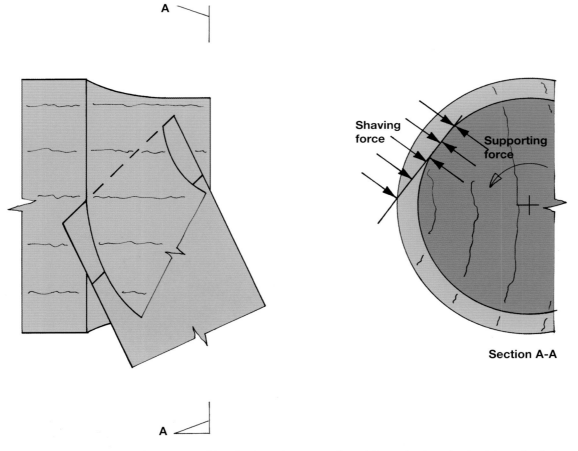

A

Shaving force

Supporting force

Section A-A

A

Figure 4.14 Side rake and support. Showing how the proportion of the active length of cutting edge being supported decreases with increasing side rake. It also decreases with increasing shaving thickness.

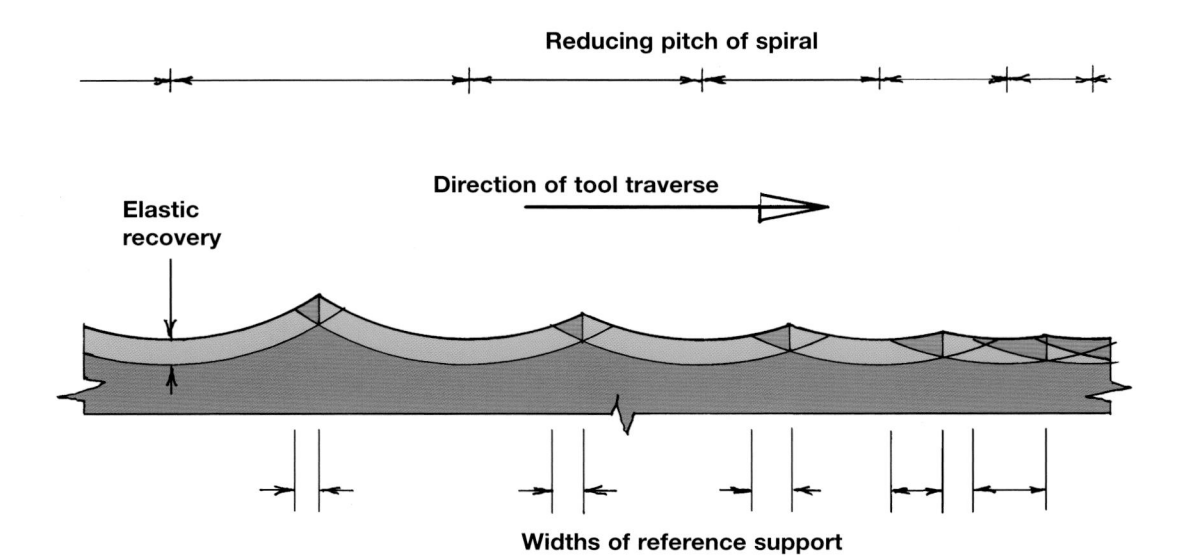

Reducing pitch of spiral

Direction of tool traverse

Elastic recovery

Widths of reference support

Figure 4.15 Reference support. This longitudinal section shows that the width of reference support increases as the speed at which the tool is being traversed decreases. Here the tool slows as it traverses to the right.

4.4 OTHER FACTORS AFFECTING SURFACE FINISH

Instep and Heel Support

Figures 4.7 and 4.8 showed that only a very narrow band of cutting-edge support is needed to stabilize the tool tip in the *cutting* presentation. Augmenting or replacing cutting-edge support by bevel-heel or instep support is harmful. When a cutting edge is presented with side rake, any heel or instep support is provided by wood surface exposed during an earlier workpiece rotation than that at which the cutting edge is cutting (figure 4.16). What makes this a problem is that a hand-turned surface is not truly circular. The radius from the lathe axis to say the bottom of a concave profile (see figure 4.13) may vary by up to 1/250 in (0.1 mm) in a single workpiece rotation. The workpiece surface is also rippled because it is spiralled. Therefore as a heel or instep follows the irregular surface cut during earlier workpiece rotations, a surface with greater irregularties results. This is because the cutting edge is further from the fulcrum of the toolrest than the instep or heel. There may be other factors too, but the result is that the tiny radial eccentricities of the wood surface build on one another rapidly on a workpiece rotating at between 5 and 50 revolutions-per-second. Not surprisingly the surface can soon show significant ribbing (figure 4.17)

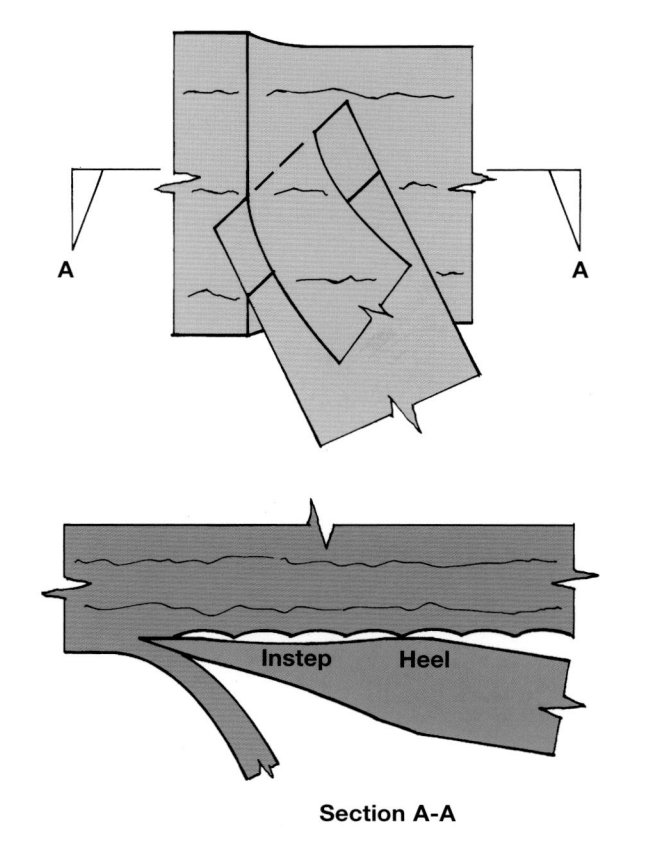

A   A

Instep   **Heel**

Section A-A

Figure 4.16 Planing with bevel-heel support. Figure 4.17 shows the noticeably rippled macro-cut surface which can result. When planing therefore keep the bevel heel just clear.

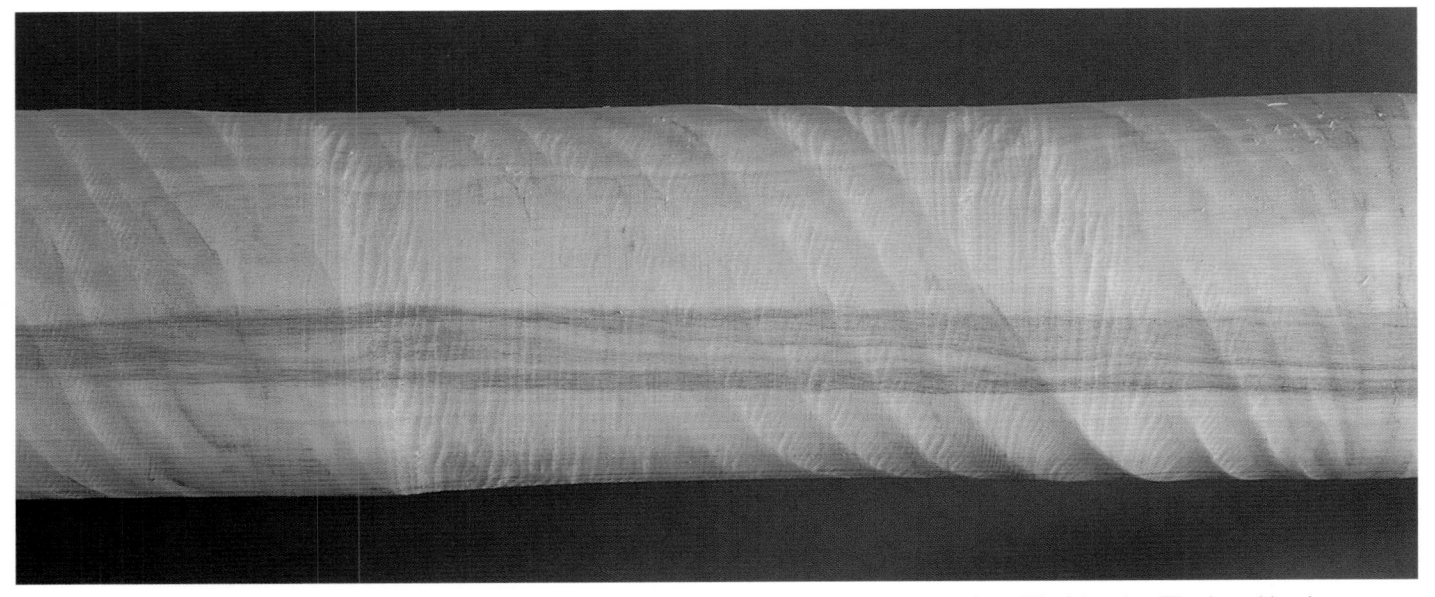

Figure 4.17 A ribbed macro-cut surface produced by planing with a skew presented at 45° side rake. The bevel heel was pressed against the wood throughout the traverse.

Grain Direction

In woodturning as in other woodworking specialties, you should work as far as possible with the grain. Figures 4.18 and 4.19 show the preferred directions of tool movement for workpiece grain directions parallel to and perpendicular to the lathe axis. However in faceplate and bowl turning you inevitably have to work against the grain twice during each workpiece rotation.

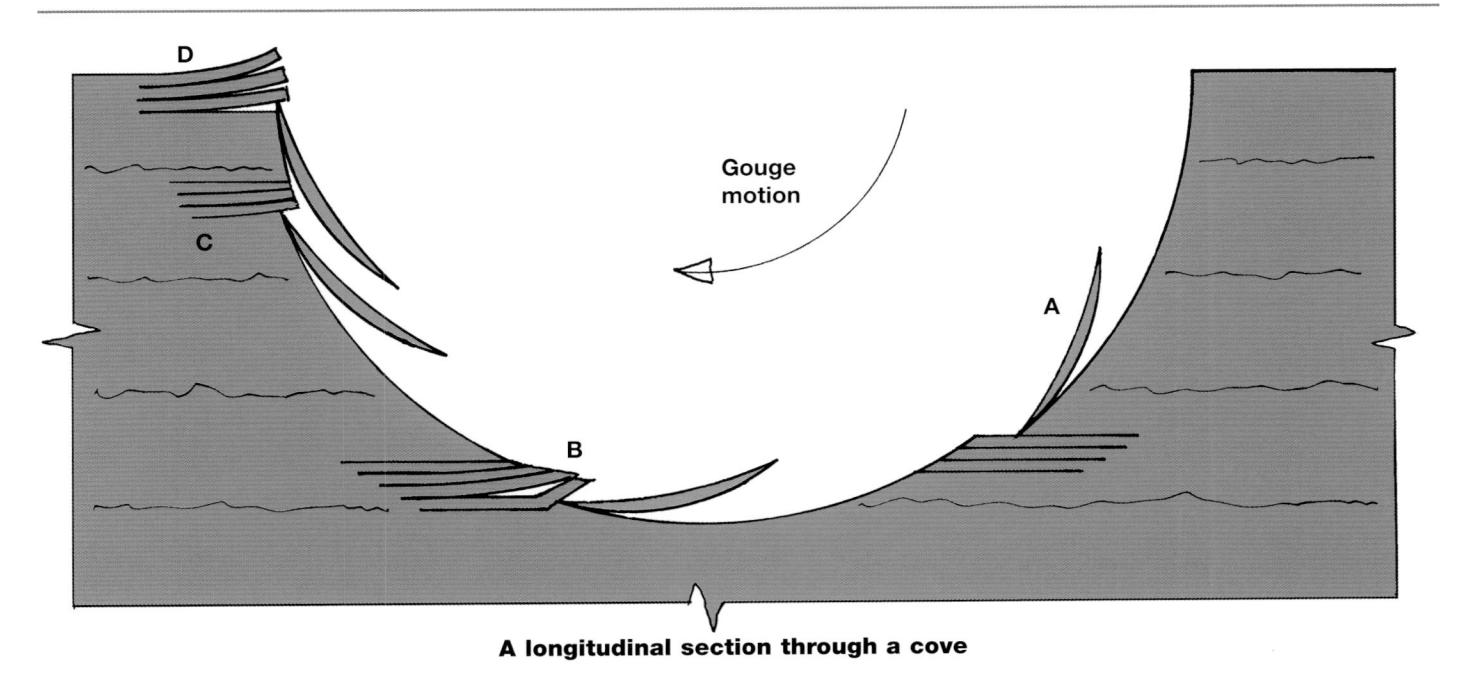

A longitudinal section through a cove

Figure 4.18 Cutting with and against the grain when turning a cove in a spindle.
At **A** the fibres being cut are supported by the fibres below. At **B** the fibres will tend to buckle. At **C** the fibres being cut receive less support than at **A**. At **D** the fibres splinter away.

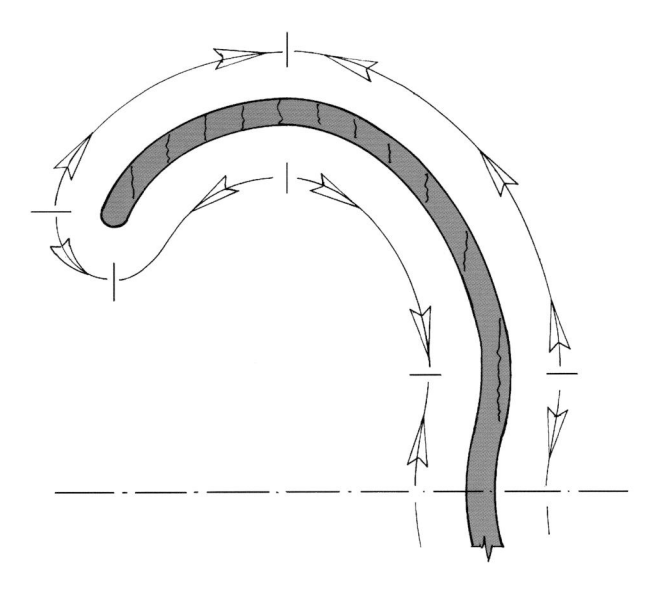

Figure 4.19 Cutting with the grain. A cross-section through a bowl turned from a disk cut from a plank. The cross-section is taken parallel to the grain. The arrows show the directions of tool movement which cut correctly "with the grain" in faceplate and bowl turning.

Depth of Cut

The depth of cut affects the degree of subsurface damage. A thin shaving is weaker and therefore less able to tear wood out from below the macro-cut surface. With a thick shaving the length and lever arm of the unsupported cutting edge shown in figure 4.14 increase. This will lessen control and is likely to result in a poorer macro-cut surface.

Speed of Traversing

The faster you traverse the tool tip along the wood surface, the more pronounced will be the spiral which a tool inevitably cuts (figure 4.20).

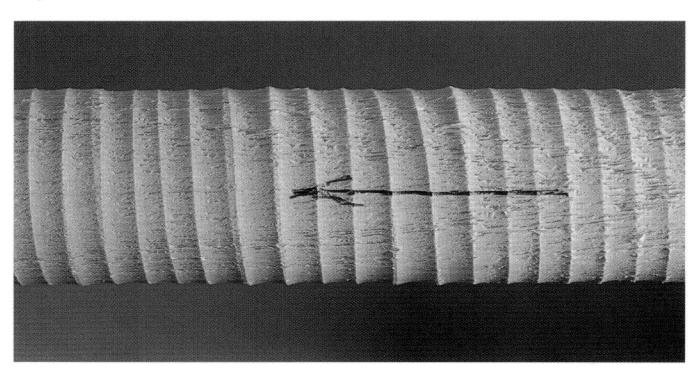

Figure 4.20 A grossly-spiralled macro-cut surface resulting from a fast tool traverse along a spindle rotating at a very low speed. The low lathe speed is largely responsible for the excessive subsurface damage.

Lathe Speed

Section 4.7 shows you how to determine the optimum lathe speed. If you use a lathe speed which is too low, you will produce an excessively-rippled surface because of the lack of reference support and the large pitch of the spiral which your tool cuts (figure 4.15). Using a low lathe speed also increases subsurface damage (figure 4.20) for two reasons:

1. The shaving will have less momentum and will therefore separate less readily.
2. Wood is weaker at higher temperatures. For example at 160°F (71°C) the loss in strength is from 10% to 50%. At low lathe speeds the temperature of the cutting edge will be lower, the adjacent wood's temperature will be raised less, and the wood will therefore fail less readily and less cleanly.

4.5 SUMMARY OF LARGE-RAKE-ANGLE CUTTING

When *cutting* you are likely to be roughing or finish-turning. When roughing your aim is to remove waste wood quickly and safely. When finish-turning your aim is to safely achieve the best-practical combination of minimum subsurface damage and minimum macro-cut surface rippling. In both situations:

1. Your tool should have the minimum practical sharpening angle, usually 25° to 30°.
2. You should present the edge at the minimum clearance angle corresponding to the shaving thickness you want.
3. You will need to exert a strong and appropriate axial thrust along the tool. Most of the problems beginners have stem from a failure to exert sufficient thrust.

For roughing you will use less side rake to maintain a large shaving cross-sectional area. You will also traverse the tool more quickly.

For a finishing cut you should traverse the tool slowly, and use a high side rake. You must take care to keep the clearance angle correct. Too much clearance and the tool will stutter, too little and the resulting bevel or instep contact will cause the tool to start to bounce with greater surface crushing, and rippling. You will be able to diagnose even a 1° departure from the ideal clearance angle by the feeling transmitted back through the tool and by how the cutting sounds. When cutting you should therefore be actively monitoring these sensations and adjusting your tool's presentation accordingly.

4.6 SCRAPING

Sometimes *cutting* is not possible due to tool-access restrictions. The most-common solution is to present a special type of tool called a *scraper* at a zero or small-negative rake angle. This presentation is known as *scraping* (figures 4.21 and 4.22).

Scraping has had a bad press in recent years. If you did woodturning at school you probably scraped because it was thought to be safe and need little skill. It is though an entirely-valid turning technique to use when tool access is restricted, or a very long tool overhang is unavoidable.

Scraping with side rake is called *shear scraping* (figure 4.23). Scraping and shear scraping are used in similar situations. Shear scraping will produce less subsurface damage but a more-rippled macro-cut surface. Shear scraping is sometimes preferred to *cutting* where the grain is contorted because it may leave less subsurface damage. Ask the wood if you are in doubt which technique to use: trial the alternatives and compare the surfaces.

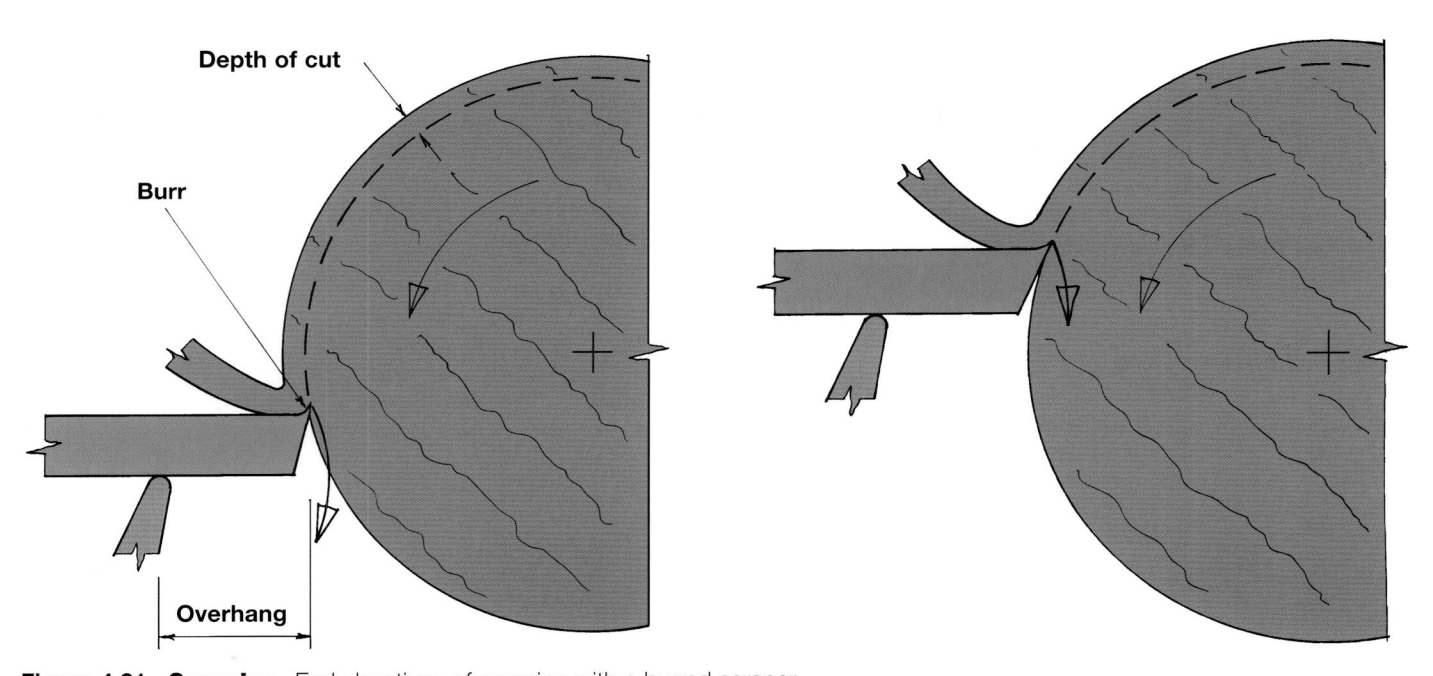

Figure 4.21 Scraping. End elevations of scraping with a burred scraper.

By increasing the sharpening angle of an edge presented at about 0° rake angle from the 30° used for *cutting* tools to 70° to 80°, the edge is strengthened without appearing any blunter to the descending wood. The simple, sharp edge formed by the meeting of the bevel and the tool's top face will leave a good surface on hard, crisp-turning woods. On more-typical woods, scrapers can still leave a good surface if the edge is sharpened so as to leave a burr. The burr imperfectly converts near-zero-rake-angle scraping into a form of large-rake-angle *cutting*.

The left-hand drawing shows that if you present a scraper with a small negative rake angle, the edge will free itself if you lose control. A serious catch can happen if you lose control when scraping at a small positive rake angle *(right-hand drawing)*.

Figure 4.22 Scraping, a close up.

Figure 4.23 Shear scraping with the stub of a wornout HSS gouge. The blade cross-section near its tip is semicircular, and therefore stable whatever the side rake.

You will find control easier if you drag shear scrapers. It is both normal and even unavoidable to shear scrape with *cutting* tools during some cuts in difficult situations.

4.7 LATHE SPEED

Shavings are cut away more readily and the surface finish is improved as you increase the lathe speed. But there are practical limits to the speed you can safely and comfortably use. The preferred speed for a given workpiece maximum diameter or thickness can be read from figure 4.24. This assumes that you have a heavy lathe and optimum conditions. Factors which should cause you to reduce your lathe's speed below the maximum in figure 4.24 include:

1. *The workpierce not being trued*. This occurs commonly with bowl blanks. Use a slow speed to true the blank, then increase the speed.
2. *Your lathe's weight and rigidity*. If your lathe is shaking, its speed is too high.
3. A *high wood density* means a hard as well as a heavy workpiece. Both factors may mean that a lower lathe speed is desirable. Also wood is not always of even density. A workpiece containing heartwood and less-dense sapwood will be unbalanced and need to be turned at a lower speed
4. *Workpiece slenderness*. In extreme cases you may need to reduce your lathe speed to 15% of the figure 4.24 value.
5. *If your workpiece is laminated or eccentrically mounted*.
6. *The presence of free silica in the wood*. Teak for example contains up to 1% of free silica grains which will rapidly blunt your tools. Use a lower lathe speed and take deeper cuts to prolong cutting edge life.
7. *If the wood is high in resin* you should sand at a slow speed to prevent heating the surface and inducing cracking.

If your lathe has a set range of speeds you will rarely be able to turn exactly at the figure 4.24 speed. Fortunately woodturning speeds are not critical and you will notice little difference if the speed is say 25% lower than the preferred. Also as most cuts traverse a range of diameters, there is little point in being too pernickety.

Some texts recommend different speeds for roughing, finish-turning, and sanding. I recommend that you generally use the same speed for the three operations, except, of course, if any of the seven factors listed above apply.

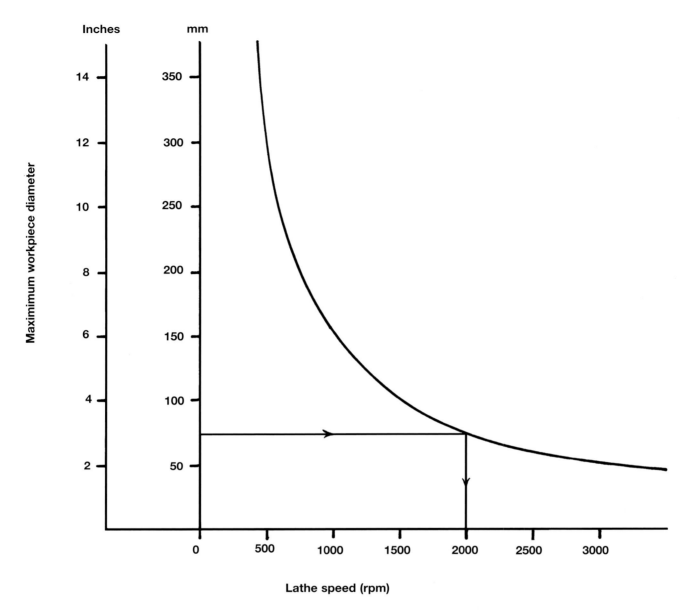

Figure 4.24 Lathe Speed. The maximum recommended speed for any workpiece diameter or thickness is represented by the curved line. It is based on a workpiece of 3-in (75-mm) diameter being turned at 2000 rpm. This is equivalent to a peripheral wood velocity of 26 fps or 7.86 mps.

4.8 INTRODUCING TURNING TOOLS

This section introduces turning tools: the types, the steels they are made from, their common design faults, and their tuning and sharpening.

A turning tool is similar in form to most woodworking chisels. It has a blade which has a particular cross-section, and a shaped and sharpened tip. The other end of the blade, the tang, is often narrower or tapered and is fitted into a handle. The handles are usually wood (section 4.13).

Most woodworking chisels are shorter than turning tools. Turning tools typically have blades 9 in (230 mm) long and handles 12 in (300 mm).

Tool Types

There are about ten types of turning tool, plus many variants. Most types are available in a range of sizes. The main types are introduced in figures 4.25 and 4.26. There are other tool types; some have little relevance to beginners, some have little relevance to any turner.

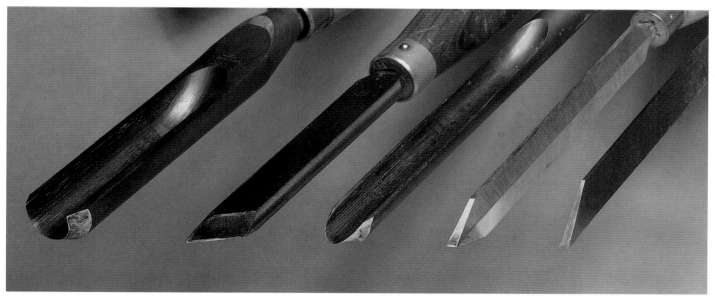

Figure 4.25 Spindle-turning tools. *Left to right:* P&N 30-mm roughing gouge, P&N 25-mm skew, P&N 19-mm detail gouge, Robert Sorby diamond-section parting tool, Henry Taylor fluted parting-off tool.

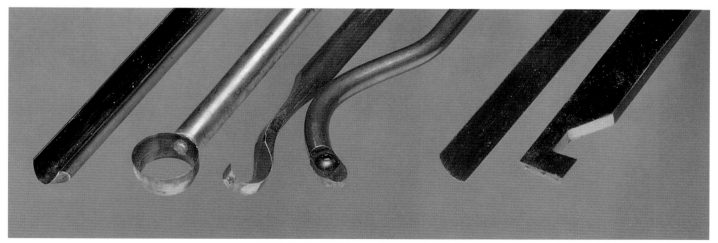

Figure 4.26 Bowl-turning and hollowing tools. *Left to right:* Henry Taylor Superflute bowl gouge designed by Roy Child, Robert Sorby ring tool, Kurt Johannson hook tool, Robert Sorby hollow-turning tool, Ashley Isles Reg Sherwin shear scraper, Henry Taylor side-cutting flat scraper.

Tool Steels

All tool steels are prepared for use by heat-treatment. The final operation in heat-treatment is tempering which is needed to toughen the very hard, brittle structure produced earlier by quenching. High-speed steel (HSS) is tempered at a far-higher temperature than carbon tool steel and so is far less likely to be softened during grinding or during very heavy turning. HSS is also more abrasion resistant than carbon tool steel and so holds an edge longer. HSS is therefore now the preferred blade material.

There are many different HSSs, each having unique percentages of alloying elements such as manganese, chromium, tungsten, cobalt, molybdenum, etc. Turning tools are manufactured from HSSs at the tougher end of the range, M2, M4 or T2 under the American Iron & Steel Institute's classification. Crucible HSSs, made by recombining atomized HSS particles, have even greater resistance to abrasion and are easier to grind. They are used only by a couple of American manufacturers, notably Glaser HiTEC Tools. Tungsten carbide is too brittle to be used for other than tips on scrapers. Do not use old files as they can shatter explosively.

Common Tool Faults

You can manage well with the heaviest tools sold by the reputable manufacturers. However in mid-1997 every maker's range includes tools which can be improved. Common faults are:

1. Blades which are too slender and which you can feel flex in normal use.
2. Sharp edges and corners not arrissed or rounded.
3. Uneven and badly-scored flute surfaces.
4. Blades which are too short. This is not a serious problem for amateurs who master the sharpening procedure which reduces blade lengths only by honing (figure 4.27). It means however that you have to take the left-hand grip partially on the handle for detailed turning for much of a tool's active life.
5. Tangs which are weak. Manufacturers seem to want to use the same ferrule and tang-hole size and cross-section for all their tools.
6. Poor heat-treatment. The hardening and tempering of HSS is complex and exacting, but only rarely will you buy a tool which will not hold an edge.

Tool Tuning

Turning-tool manufacturers don't always supply their tools as they should. Turners have to correct the faults which can be corrected by grinding and honing, a process I call *tuning*. But tool blades should not have to be tuned by their buyers to be made fit-for-use. It requires skills and equipment few beginners have. Turners should demand better from their suppliers, but be prepared to pay a little extra for tools which are sold as they should be.

Sharpening

Even in 1997, magazine articles, books, and tool manufacturers' catalogues promote sharpening angles of 45° and larger for turning tools used in *cutting* presentations. If you are unsure whether to accept such sharpening advice or this book's, sharpen a gouge or skew at 45°, use it, then try the same tool resharpened at 30°.

4.9   INTRODUCTION TO SHARPENING

Turning-tool sharpening was simple until the late 1970s. You manipulated your tool tips by hand on a rotating grinding-wheel rim and then honed them. (In *honing* you further refine the ground cutting edge by abrading it by hand with much finer-grained stones). Since those naive times, turning teachers and manufacturers have sought to help us to achieve a better edge more efficiently. They have also sought to deskill the sharpening process to aid hobby turners. The result? More choices, more expense, more complexity, more disputes, more understanding, and sometimes a lengthening of the time spent sharpening. This and the two following sections seek to distil the advances and eliminate the confusion.

Only with truly-sharp and properly- and consistently-shaped turning tools will you produce the best-possible surface finish and enjoy maximum tool control. And only with truly-sharp tools can you experience the sweet, singing feeling of clean cutting. A further advantage of consistent sharpening geometry is that you will soon be able to present your tools without having to make any preliminary presentational adjustments. The four processes needed to produce a properly-shaped and sharp cutting tool are:

1. Tuning the tool, refining the blade's manufactured cross-section and surfaces.
2. Grinding the tool tip as shaped by the manufacturer to the shape you desire. Each surface which you grind adjacent to the cutting edge is usually a bevel.
3. After each grinding, refining the edges of cutting tools by honing. You may then resharpen the edge several times by honing alone before having to regrind.
4. Regrinding the bevel(s) back to your desired shape once the tool has been honed several times and is again blunt (figure 4.27).

Scrapers are resharpened by honing if small, or grinding if large.

You should hone all *cutting* edges. Many turners do not agree, although there are signs that honing is again becoming fashionable. A honed edge is sharper and less jagged; it leaves a smoother surface, and is more durable. Your tools will also last far longer if their lengths are reduced by honing rather than by grinding.

The chisels used by cabinetmakers and joiners are typically sharpened as in figure 4.28. Figures 4.7 to 4.9 showed that only the bevel surface immediately behind the cutting edge is normally in contact with the wood. Therefore the cabinetmakers' bevel in figure 4.28 should suit woodturners. It doesn't for three reasons:

1. You need to precisely align the band of cutting-edge support by eye for some cuts. You can sight clearly along the two honed bands of the turners' bevel in figures 4.27 and 4.28, but would find it difficult to sight along the cabinetmakers' single microbevel.
2. You automatically hone at the correct sharpening angle with a turners' bevel by reciprocating your hone while keeping it in constant contact with the cutting edge and bevel heel.
3. You need to grind a cabinetmakers' bevel at a 5°-smaller angle than a turners' bevel to achieve a cutting edge with the same honed sharpening angle. This weakens the tool tip.

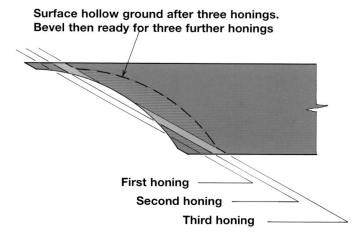

Surface hollow ground after three honings.
Bevel then ready for three further honings

First honing
Second honing
Third honing

Figure 4.27 The ideal regrinding and honing process
for resharpening turning-tool cutting edges. (The amount of
hollow grind is exaggerated).

After a regrinding, the surfaces which intersect to form the
cutting edge are honed. Once the edge becomes blunt (and
once you have experienced a sharp edge you will have no
trouble in recognizing a blunt one), hone again. After about
three honings the widths of the honed bands on the hollow-
ground bevel(s) would make further honings too slow, so you
regrind rather than hone again. Ideally when you regrind you
should leave just-visiible bands of honed surface. Your tool is
thereby shortened only by honing, and lasts a long time. This
process also minimizes grinding time, and the possibility of
heating the tool tip above its steel's tempering temperature and
thus softening it.

If you grind on a wheel which is too small in diameter, you
will produce bevels with too much hollow grind and a greater
tendency to break off. Use 8-in (200-mm) or larger diameter
wheels for average-sized turning tools.

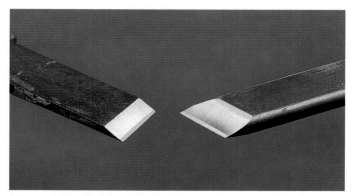

Figure 4.28 Cabinetmakers' and turners' bevels. *Left,*
the bevel of a cabinetmakers' chisel with one honed surface or
microbevel; *right,* the upper bevel of a woodturners' skew chisel
with two honed surfaces.

4.10   SHARPENING EQUIPMENT

For shaping, tuning, and sharpening turning tools you can
use a double-ended electric bench grinder. It should take
8-in (200-mm) diameter wheels, 1-in (25-mm) wide or
wider. You will also need a wheel dresser to dress away
glazed grains of abrasive and embedded steel from your
grinding wheel rim(s) and to true them. The cheapest and
most versatile dresser is a dressing stick (figure 4.29). A
multi-point diamond dresser is the best if you want to
produce a flat rim. Although grinding on grinding wheels
has long been the norm, a linisher, an abrasive-belt grinder
for metal (figure 4.30), and an expanding linishing wheel
(figure 4.31) are both superior alternatives to grinding
wheels because:

1. Belts grind quicker and cooler.
2. You do not dress or true abrasive belts, so it's goodbye
   to the clouds of choking abrasive dust dressing creates.
   Also, steel is less likely to become embedded in a
   belt's surface because of its slippery coating and
   because the belt flexes as it passes over the wheels.
3. Aluminum oxide is the abrasive most-commonly glued
   onto belts. Silicon carbide reacts with steel at higher
   temperatures and is therefore unsuitable. There are
   more-aggressive abrasives such as seeded-gel
   aluminum oxide, but these *superabrasives* are more
   costly. Grinding wheels made of them would be too
   expensive for we occasional users. But these superabrasives are affordable on belts where the volume and
   therefore the cost of the abrasive is so small.
   Superabrasive-coated belts are becoming more available. For example, you can now buy belts coated with
   seeded-gel aluminum oxide.
4. The abrasive on a belt is in a layer one grain thick. The
   grains can therefore be orientated on the belt to
   maximize grinding efficiency.
5. The diameter of the surface on which you grind is
   constant. This makes it far easier to accurately and
   repeatably set the desired grinding angle for each tool.

You can buy a linishing machine, or a machine with a
grinding wheel on one end and a linisher on the other, or a
linishing attachment which fits onto one end of a double-
ended bench grinder (figure 4.30). The last two are particularly useful for turners because of the facility to both belt
and grinding-wheel grind. Abrasive-coated belts are available in standard lengths and widths, or can be made to any
size by specialist suppliers. A linisher though is expensive.
An expanding linishing wheel gives all the advantages of a
linisher except that of a long, flat, grinding surface at a
fraction of the cost.

A belt running away from you tends to drag the tools
with it and make accurate grinding impossible. You therefore have to grind with the belt running towards you which
is not quite as safe. Because there is a slight risk, wear eye

and face protection, reject any belt with even just a tiny tear, use belts with cloth not paper backing, and mount the belt so that grinding tends to close the scarf joint not pry it open.

You will need in addition to a bench grinder and any belt-grinding equipment:

1. One or more grinding jigs to speed and improve the quality of your tool grinding (figures 4.32, and 4.55 and 4.56).
2. A fine-grained, flat hone for honing skew chisels, parting tools, and similar (figure 4.33).
3. One or more slipstones or convex hones (figure 4.34).
4. Eye and preferably face protection.

If you decide to specialize in bowl turning you should consider investing in the equipment needed to produce convex bevels—a grinding wheel into which you dress a concave rim (figure 4.35), and a buffing wheel (figure 4.36).

Figure 4.29   Dressing a grinding wheel. The dressing stick is, a 1-in x 1-in x 6-in (25-mm x 25-mm x 150-mm) long stick of coarse aluminum oxide. The grinding wheel is composed of 38A aluminum oxide mounted on an 8-in (200-mm) bench grinder.

You should true your grinding wheel rim when it is not flat, square, or does not run true. You should dress it when it shows glazed grains and embedded grey-colored steel like the undressed left-hand half above. Truing and dressing are usually combined and should yield a flat, white (if 38A aluminum oxide), and matt rim which will grind quickly and coolly.

Figure 4.30   A Multitool linisher made by P.A. Products of Sydney attached to an Abbot and Ashby 8-in (200-mm) bench grinder. The grinding jig is a prototype Darlow linishing jig. Its scale is especially large so that its user can set grinding angles very accurately..

Tools are best ground on this linishing attachment's idling wheel because its driving wheel is well below 8 in (200 mm) in diameter. If you have a linisher with both wheels too small, the solution recommended by Leonard Lee in his excellent book *The Complete Guide to Sharpening* is to fit a convex, hard wood platen onto your linisher's flat steel platen.

It is slightly better if the wheel you grind over is not toothed. Some linishers and linishing attachments incorporate a sanding disk larger than the adjacent wheel which prevents the wheel rim being fully used for tool grinding.

Figure 4.31   A slotted linishing wheel patented and manufactured by Linishall in Sydney, Australia with a Darlow linishing jig.

The teeth on this linishing wheel become more radial as the grinder accelerates, and effectively increase the wheel diameter so that it grips the 2-in (50-mm) wide belt.

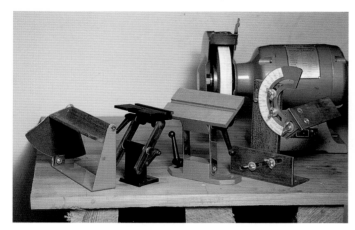

Figure 4.32 Platform grinding jigs. There are many brands. The black jig *(centre-left)* is a Canadian Veritas Grinder Tool Rest; the green jig is marketed in Australia by Carba-Tec and is available internationally.

The platform of the Darlow linishing jig on the left has an angle cross-section which helps the user keep the tool blade in full contact with the platform. The Darlow Jig on the right is designed for use with grinding wheels. It compensates for wheel wear and variations in tool blade thickness, and allows any required grinding angle to be set without templates in seconds.

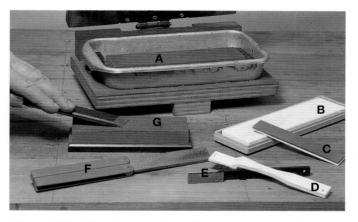

Figure 4.33 Flat hones. A is a Norton aluminum oxide, fine-grained India bench stone. The very fine-grained white bench stone **B** and the very fine- and fine-grained, double-sided slipstone **C** are manufactured by Spyderco in seeded-gel aluminum oxide. **D** and **E** are plastic-handled, flat hones by 3M. The green-handled hone **F** and the red bench stone **G** are both by Diamond Machining Technology (DMT). The green DMT hones are very-fine grained, the red are fine grained. For honing turning tools I prefer the red.

You need a flat hone for skew chisels and parting tools. If you already have a fine-grained bench stone or need one for other sharpening, you can use it for your turning tools. If you want to buy a flat hone just for your turning tools, I suggest a small, fine-grained diamond hone. Opt for one where the diamonds are bonded to a substantial metal plate – where the diamonds are bonded to foil, the foil can tear long before the diamonds are worn. Small, flat diamond hones are also handy for resharpening the small scraping tips common on shear scrapers and hollow-turning tools.

Bench stones are usually kept immersed in a light mineral oil such as kerosene or in water according to type or preference. The India stone **A** at the back is in a freezer tray. The tray is glued into a lidded box which is free to slide along the lathe bed and is therefore always handy. The main job of the honing fluid is to prevent the steel "shavings" bonding to the abrasive. Water promotes rust, oils stain wood and are harmful if absorbed into your skin. With a flat hone there is little risk of your skin coming into contact with the fluid, but you should use water in prefer-ence to an oil when you hone with a slipstone whatever the hone manufacturer's recommendation.

Because you will hone often, you will need to flatten a conventional bench stone every few weeks when it is worn hollow. Do this by rubbing the stone on glass with a slurry of coarse abrasive. If you don't want to be bothered with this, buy a stone which wears very slowly such as diamond or seeded-gel aluminum oxide. These two abrasives also cut faster than the common aluminum oxide, but are more costly.

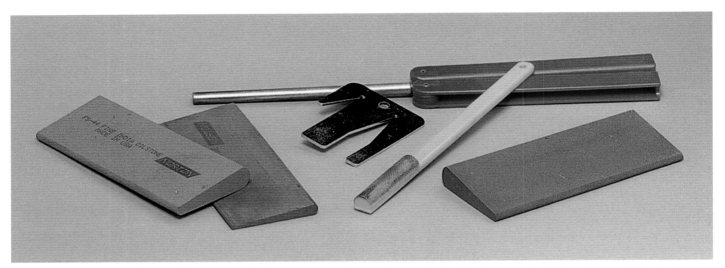

Figure 4.34 Convex hones. The orange aluminum oxide and grey silicon carbide slipstones are by Norton. The red-handled diamond file is by DMT. The yellow-handled curved hone is by 3M. In the center is a Hatfield Tip used for checking sharpening angles.

The slipstones pictured have the ideal geometry for honing gouges. These hones provide convex surfaces of constant curvature for honing flutes, and flat surfaces for honing bevels. And when you hone with them you apply pressure directly over the contact area between the hone and the gouge. They are most-commonly available in aluminum oxide and silicon carbide. I prefer silicon carbide because it cuts faster and its recommended honing fluid is water.

Currently there is no superabrasive hone for gouge flutes which is correctly shaped. If you use one of the curved diamond hones with a projecting handle or a round or rat-tail diamond file, you are liable to dub over the edge. You can use a slipstone for the flute and a separate, flat, superabrasive hone for the bevel, or rehone only the bevel using a flat hone. I hope that a diamond slipstone will be introduced soon.

Figure 4.35 Grinding a convex bevel on a Robert Sorby 3/4-in (19-mm) bowl gouge on a concave-rimmed grinding wheel.

It is easy to hollow a grinding wheel's rim with a dressing stick. The radius of the concaveness should be about 1 in (25 mm). To grind a convex bevel you have to align the gouge blade not square to your grinder's axis, but at an angle. You then axially rotate the blade about this angled axis. You will find it easier to grind the right-hand half of the bevel (looking from the handle) on the right-hand side of the rim and vice versa. You can increase the convexity of the bevel by increasing the angle between square to the grinder's axis and the tool blade.

You can also grind detail gouges more evenly by the rotate-and-thrust method in a concave rim than on a flat rim. The sharpening action remains exactly as shown in figures 4.52 to 4.54, still with the detail gouge positioned square to the grinder's axis.

Figure 4.36 Buffing on a hard felt wheel. The outer guard has been temporarily removed.

Buffing in this context is grinding with a very fine-grained abrasive. You have to charge the wheel rim with buffing compound, very fine-grained abrasive in a wax matrix in stick form. Explain your usage to your supplier so that you get the best formulation. During buffing the compound is thrown off the wheel, so you may need to fit an additional guard.

The buff's rotation should tend to pull the tool tip away from you. You should therefore buff from behind a conventional bench grinder. You will be able to buff more precisely if you use a toolrest—a primitive one will suffice. Take care not to dub over the edge (increase the sharpening angle) by having the handle too high.

You can dress a felt wheel with an old saw blade or by power sanding with a coarse grit.

Grinders

With slowly-rotating, water-cooled grinders such as the Tormek there is no risk of overheating carbon-tool-steel cutting edges. When used with accurate jigs such grinders are not too slow for resharpening, although they remove metal too slowly to reshape tool tips in a reasonable time. But with HSS tools the risk of affecting the steel's temper steel is tiny if you use accurate jigging with grinding belts or wheels of a suitable specification. Turners therefore prefer high-speed dry grinding.

If you buy a new bench grinder it will usually have fine- and coarse-grained grey grinding wheels. If you dress them prior to and frequently during each use they will just do. However they are too hard for fast, cool grinding. It is far better to use the grinding wheels specially formulated for tool steel. Their preferred specification for the Norton brand is 38A 80 - H 8 V BE. (Other brands use related specification codes). In this specification which is printed on the wheel's paper label:

1. 38A refers to a white aluminum oxide which is harder but more friable and therefore grinds faster and cooler than the common grey abrasive.
2. 80 refers to the grain size of the abrasive. The larger the number, the finer the grain size.
3. H is the grade, the strength of the bonding together of the grains. The later the letter in the alphabet, the harder the bond. The grey wheels usually supplied as standard on grinders often have an N or P bond.
4. 8 is a measure of the openness of the wheel's structure.
5. V denotes a vitrified bond, and BE also relates to the bond.

This ideal wheel specification should, but may not, be readily available—turners remain a neglected market. The penalty of having to use the usual grey form of aluminum oxide, 60 or 100 grit size, or an I or J bond is not too serious if you keep your wheel rims in good condition by frequent dressing.

A cracked grinding wheel can disintegrate explosively. Before using a new wheel, inspect it visually. Then suspend the wheel by its center hole and tap it lightly in several places. If this does not produce clear, metallic ringing sounds, reject the wheel. Stand aside for a couple of minutes when you first run a new wheel. Grinding wheel manufacturers produce booklets on grinding and safety which are well worth reading.

Sharpening Jigs

Each time you dress a grinding wheel you decrease its diameter. Accurate resharpening on a grinding wheel can therefore only be achieved by frequently resetting the grinding jig platform from an accurate template, or by following the geometry described in figure 4.37. Figure 4.38 shows the patented Darlow Jig which uses this figure 4.37 geometry to ensure accurate regrinding. This jig is not in manufacture in 1997.

Figure 4.39 shows the usual type of template used to set platform grinding jigs. Such templates are not fully accurate as figure 4.37 shows. The Darlow Template (figures 4.40 and 4.41) overcomes the usual template deficiencies by using the figure 4.37 geometry.

Grinding on an abrasive belt reduces the problems of accurately and quickly setting platform sharpening jigs because the diameter of the grinding surface is constant. But to gain full advantage and to resharpen as described in figure 4.27, you must be able to set the grinding platform accurately. The Darlow linishing jig shown in figures 4.32 and 4.43 gives both accuracate and fast resetting.

There is a second type of sharpening jig which sharpens gouges by a process I call *fanning*. These were developed for sharpening detail and bowl gouges (figures 4.55 and 4.56).

There are other types of grinding jig. When choosing a jig consider how accurate the alternatives really are, how quick they are to use, whether they will accommodate shortened blades, and what tool types they can and cannot be used for.

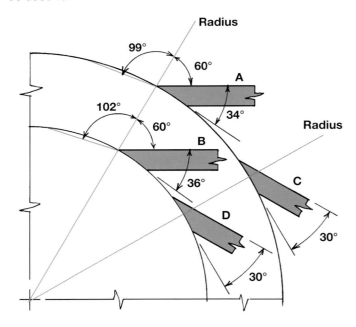

Figure 4.37 Grinding wheel sharpening geometries.
This side elevation shows a quarter of the rim of a new grinding wheel, and the rim after it has been dressed many times. **A** and **B** illustrate that the grinding angle varies if you set your grinding jig platform using a conventional template like that shown in figure 4.39. In **C** and **D** the centre of the bevel lies on a radius and the sharpening angle is set from that radius to the center of the thickness of the blade. Using this method the grinding angle is correct whatever the tool's blade thicknesss and however much the wheel has been dressed.

Figure 4.38 The Darlow Jig uses the ideal geometry of **C** and **D** in figure 4.37.

The upper part of the jig slides in the sloping slot in the angle-sectioned base to compensate for wheel wear. The jig incorporates a mechanism for rapidly resetting the upper part of the jig in the correct postion in the sloping slot after you have redressed the wheel. You set the required grinding angle on the annular scale. The platform slides to adjust for the tool's blade thickness—you set the projecting width of the red band to half the blade thickness.

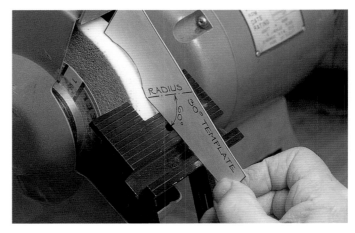

Figure 4.39 Setting a tilting-platform grinding jig (here a Veritas Grinder Tool Rest) with the common form of home-made template. This is difficult to do accurately.

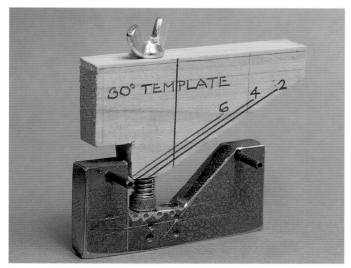

Figure 4.40 The Darlow template is designed to be easier to use than the figure 4.39 type of template. It is also fully accurate as it uses the **C** and **D** geometry in figure 4.37. This design needs a separate wooden section for each grinding angle. This first prototype shows the scars of alteration.

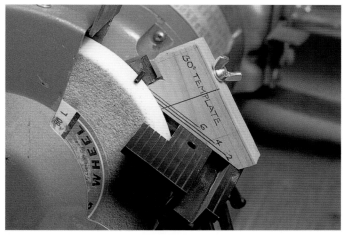

Figure 4.41 Using the Darlow template to set a platform jig.

You first rest the two pins on the wheel rim. Secondly, with the wing nut screw the wooden section down against the spring. Do this until the intersection between the radius and the line representing half the blade thickness is level with the wheel rim. Finally lock your jig's platform when it is flat against the bottom edge of the template's wooden section.

4.11 THE MAIN TURNING TOOLS AND THEIR PREPARATION FOR USE

Roughing Gouges

Uses   You use a roughing gouge for: roughing spindles from a square cross-section down to a cylinder; and for roughing and finish-turning cylinders, long curves, pins, spigots, and tapers. A roughing gouge is preferred to a

skew for finish-turning when the grain is non-axial. Roughing gouges can be used with calipers to set diameters.

Sizes   The geometry of roughing gouges is shown in figure 4.42. The overall width is usually between 1 and 2 in (25 and 50 mm). Wider, shallower gouges are preferred for larger, longer work such as veranda posts. Widths narrower than 1 in (25 mm) are available for miniature turning.

Faults   Roughing gouges commonly have: weak tangs which are liable to bend or snap, flutes which are not an arc of a circle but "V"- or "U"-shaped in cross-section, edges which are rounded or incorrectly angled, and flute angles greater than 170°. The last two faults make roughing away from a pommel (exercise 6.6) more difficult.

Tuning   The smoothness and evenness of any gouge's flute surface where it intersects with the bevel affects the quality of its cutting edge. You should therefore smooth and polish the flute using the slipstone edge with the largest-suitable radius. You can also polish the flute using a narrow felt or cloth buffing wheel dressed with buffing compound, but take care not to dub over the cutting edge.

If necessary grind the edges back to reduce the flute angle (figure 4.42). Also make the angle between each edge and the adjacent band of flute a little less than square. Both operations are best done on a linisher, but with care can be done on a grinder.

Sharpening   The grinding of roughing gouges on a grinding jig is described in figure 4.43.

Freehand grinding is now largely obsolete even for professionals due its uncertain accuracy and the development of improved grinding jigs. But the approach is the same for any cutting tool you have to grind freehand. You can support the gouge entirely in your hands, or rest the blade or your forward hand on the grinder's toolrest. The tool will be easier to axially rotate if you hold it within your fingers and thumbs rather than into your palms. to grind a roughing gouge place its bevel heel onto the grinding wheel rim. Gently raise the handle until the sharpening angle is correct, or, when regrinding, you feel the whole bevel instep come into contact with the grinding wheel rim. Slowly rotate the blade alternately clockwise then counterclockwise until a new bevel at the correct sharpening angle is formed, or,whwn regrinding until the previously-honed bands are almost ground away. At this stage sparks will start to climb over the top of the cutting edge. Throughout regrinding you should not press the tool tip down onto the wheel, the tip's own weight is sufficient.

After grinding, you should hone. You hone all gouges in a similar way (figures 4.45 and 4.46).

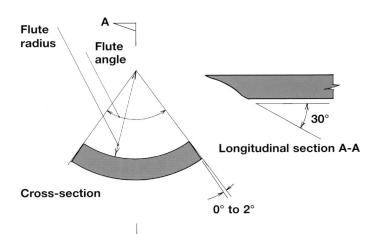

Figure 4.42 **Roughing-gouge geometry.**

Figure 4.43 **Regrinding a roughing gouge on Linishall linishing wheel using a Darlow linishing jig.**

A roughing gouge is one of the easier woodturning tools to grind. Set your jig's grinding (sharpening) angle to 30°. Keep the gouge's axis square to grinder's axis and the blade in full contact with your grinding jig's platform while you slowly rotate the gouge alternately clockwise and counterclockwise. Your aim is to grind the full length of the cutting edge straight and square in plan. The pressure of the bevel against the abrading surface should be light—even so regrinding should only take a few seconds because of the thinness of the layer of steel you have to remove. If more prolonged grinding is required, take care not to heat the steel above its tempering temperature. For carbon tool steel that temperature is reached when the oxides which form on the steel surface reach a light straw color (figure 4.44). For HSS it is unwise to let the steel approach red heat. You should swish carbon tool steel tools in water every few seconds to cool them. Manufacturers recommend that HSS tools should be allowed to air cool because rapid cooling causes fine cracks to form.

Figure 4.44 **The oxide colors which form on the surface** of steel as it is heated give a useful guide to the steel's temperature. The tool tip is more likely to be overheated if ground on a wheel which needs dressing like the one shown.

Some of the colors and the temperatures they form at are: dark blue, 300°C (572°F); light purple, 275°C (527°F); very dark yellow, 250°C (482°F); and light straw, 225°C (437°F).

Figure 4.45 **Honing the bevel of a roughing gouge.**

Grip the slipstone at its near edge, top, and far edge with your thumb, first, and other fingers respectively. Place either of the slipstone's flat faces against the bevel heel. Tilt the slipstone forwards until both the gouge's heel and cutting edge are in contact with the flat face. Then reciprocate the slipstone briskly while continuing to keep both the heel and the toe of the bevel in contact with the slipstone's flat face. To hone all the cutting edge, alternately rotate the gouge clockwise then counterclockwise while you reciprocate the slipstone. You will find it easier to axially rotate the gouge if you locate the end of its handle in the hollow at your left hip.

Figure 4.46 Honing the flute of a roughing gouge.
Use the slipstone edge with the largest-suitable radius.
Reciprocate the slipstone while rotating the gouge alternately
clockwise and counterclockwise. Do not allow more than a third
of the slipstone's length to project past the cutting edge or there
is a high risk of dubbing over the cutting edge.

Skew Chisels

Uses   You use skew chisels in spindle turning to: plane
cylinders and long curves, V-cut and roll beads, square
shoulders, cut the ends of pommels, and part off.

Sizes   Skews are available in widths up to 2 in (50 mm),
with 1 in (25 mm) being the most popular size. The
geometry of skews is shown in figure 4.47.

Faults   Skew chisels' blades are often too thin. I recommend a 5/16-in (8-mm) thickness for a 1-in (25-mm) wide
chisel. Oval cross-sections are fashionable but inferior to
rectangular. Skews' long and short edges should be
semicircular so that they slide more easily along toolrests
and do not damage them. Semicircular edges also allow
you to cut very small beads without having to traverse the
blade backwards.

Tuning   Manufacturers should not leave flat edges on
skews. You can just arris the corners. (An arris is a quarter
round with the radius of a pencil lead or a little larger). It
is better though to grind, hone and polish the edges to a
semicircular cross-section. A linisher is far easier to use for
this than a grinder.

Sharpening   Grinding is shown in figure 4.48, honing in
figure 4.49.

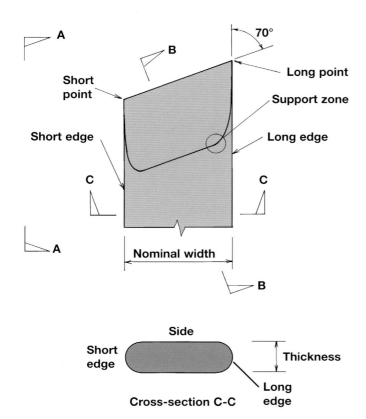

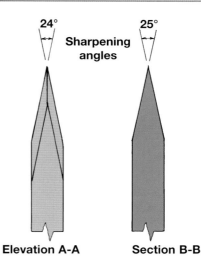

Figure 4.47 The geometry of the skew chisel.
    When planing concave profiles or cutting them with the short
point you may have to bear the supporting zone on the wood. If
the work warrants it, smoothing this area will lessen subsurface
damage.
    A cutting edge which is convex in side elevation is a popular
alternative to the usual straight one. There is little to choose
between them. The included angle at the long point for a
convex edge should remain at 70°; the included angle at the
short point should not be increased by more than 15°.

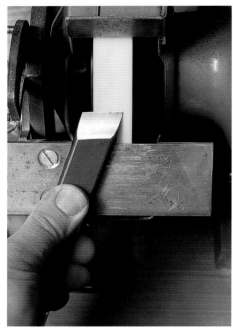

Figure 4.48 Grinding a skew chisel on the flat rim of a grinding wheel.
Set your jig's sharpening angle to 12 1/2°. Grind first one bevel, then invert the blade to grind the other. Keep the cutting edge parallel to the grinder's axis to retain the 70° angle at the long point. When grinding, traverse the blade to-and-fro across the wheel to equalize wear.

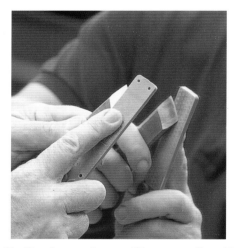

Figure 4.49 Honing a skew with a very fine DMT diamond hone photographed in front of a mirror. By keeping the hone in contact with both the cutting edge and the bevel heel, you retain the sharpening angle produced by grinding.
You can hone a skew on a bench stone (figure 4.33). Place the bevel heel on the stone, then gently lift the handle until you feel that both the heel and the cutting edge are in contact with the stone. You then make short forward and backward movements of the skew, taking care to keep both the heel and toe in continuous contact. I keep the movements brisk and short, about 1-in (25-mm) long, to minimize the possibility of altering the sharpening angle.

Detail Gouges

Uses You can use detail gouges to: cut coves, ogees, and convex profiles on spindles; hollow cupchuck and faceplate turnings and bowls; and cut details in faceplate and bowl turning.

Sizes Although it would be logical to designate detail gouges by their flute radiuses, detail gouges are sized by a width—which width varies according to the manufacturer. Detail gouges with correct cross-sections are available in widths to 3/4 in (19 mm). Their geometry is shown in figure 4.50. What I call hybrid gouges in figure 4.50 are sold under various titles by different manufacturers. Most hybrid gouges are unstable when cutting at steep gradients.

Faults Gouges machined from round bar often have dangerously-sharp edges along the tops of their flanges. Smaller sizes are unnecessarily slender. Flute surfaces are sometimes scored and uneven.

Tuning You may need to smooth and polish the flute, and grind and/or hone down the sharp flange tops. Most smaller sizes of detail gouge are too slender. The slenderness of such blades can be improved by shortening them. But until manufacturers produce properly stiff small detail gouges, buy a bowl gouge with a suitably-small radius at the base of its flute and sharpen it like a detail gouge.

Sharpening There are two basic grinding methods for detail gouges: the *rotate-and-push*, and the *fanning*. There are also idiosyncratic variations which I shall not attempt to cover. Different methods give different tip geometries (figure 4.51). Currently you can only perform the rotate-and-push method freehand, although you should use a platform grinding jig to establish the sharpening angle under the base of the flute. Figures 4.52 to 4.54 show you how to grind by the rotate-and-push method, and achieve the nose geometry of the middle gouge in figure 4.51.

You will find it more difficult to grind freehand by the fanning method than the rotate-and-push. But you can now replicate and improve on freehand fanning with the Glaser grinding jig (figures 4.55 and 4.56) and other similar descendent grinding devices.

You hone detail gouges in the same way that you do roughing gouges (figures 4.45 and 4.46).

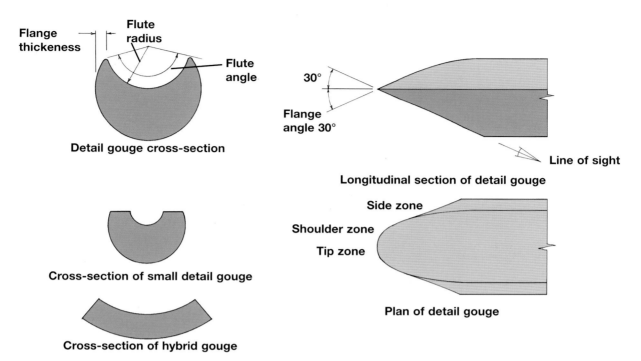

Figure 4.50 **Detail gouge geometry.** A detail gouge has three zones on the cutting edge. Each has distinct uses which will be described in later chapters.

Once the blade width drops below 3/8 in (10 mm) it becomes too flexible for safe, normal use. Small-fluted detail gouges should therefore have blades similar to the cross-section shown. The other alternative of grinding a shallower flute increases the stiffness but also increases the size of the movements you have to make with your right-hand when cutting coves.

Hybrid gouges are unstable when you cut coves with them because they do not have a semicircle of steel beneath the bottoms of their flutes.

Figure 4.51 **Different detail gouge nose geometries** ground on three P&N 3/4-in (19-mm) detail gouges: *top,* produced by the rotate-and-push method, keeping the blade fully in contact with the grinding platform through the grinding of the tip and shoulder zones; *middle,* produced by the rotate-and-push method with the gouge blade being pushed axially forwards and starting to lose contact with the front of the grinding jig platform during the grinding of the shoulder zone; *bottom,* produced by fanning with the Glaser grinding jig at the recommended setting for a detail gouge.

The top nose has the same sharpening angle (measured in longitudinal section) through the tip and shoulder zones—this is the ideal sharpening for cutting coves. The middle nose has a smaller sharpening angle along the shoulder zone and longer shoulder and side zones. It is probably the most versatile sharpening. The fanning method gives even smaller sharpening angles back from the tip; longer shoulder and side zones; and bevel sides which are concave in cross-section in the shoulder and side zones, not convex as with the rotate-and-push method. This bottom nose geometry is excellent for faceplate turning.

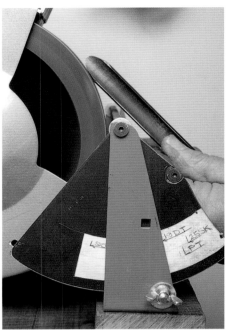

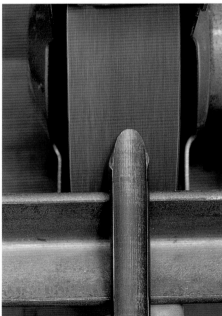

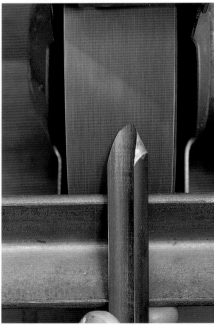

Figure 4.52 Starting to regrind a detail gouge by the rotate-and-push method.

The grinding jig has been set to 25° to provide a reference for grinding the tip zone. You should have the blade in full contact with the platform at the start of grinding. Keep the blade's axis square to the grinder's axis throughout the grinding.

This plan shape of tip is known as a ladyfinger.

Figure 4.53 The blade has been axially rotated about 20°. The gouge has been pushed forwards a little, and is about to lose contact with the front edge of the grinding jig platform.

If you wanted to grind the top nose in figure 4.51 you would keep the gouge blade in full contact with the your grinding jig platform while grinding the whole of the shoulder zone.

Figure 4.54 About to reverse the action. The blade has been rotated 90° counterclockwise. Depending on how high your gouge's flanges are, you may rotate it a little more to blend in the bevel. The nose has been pushed up the wheel to its maximum extent. Once this gouge presentation is reached, you reverse the process, then repeat it in a transposed fashion to regrind the right-hand half of the bevel. To regrind a gouge you may repeat the grinding cycle several times. As with all regrinding, the pressure of the tool onto the wheel should be light.

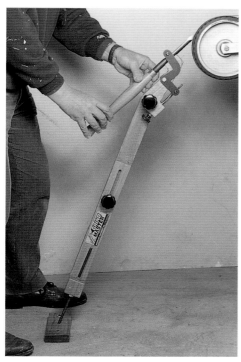

Figure 4.55   Grinding the tip zone of a detail gouge
using the Glaser grinding jig aligned square to the grinder's axis
in plan.

This jig looks more complicated than it really is. It comes with
full and clear instructions which make it simple to set up and to
use.

Figure 4.56   Starting to grind the side zone on the left-
hand side of the nose using the Glaser jig.

You pivot the jig up to 90° clockwise then 90° counterclockwise in plan, repeating the cycle as often as necessary.

Parting Tools

Uses   You use parting tools (figure 4.57) in spindle turning
to remove waste, set diameters, and cut spigots. They cut
parallel-sided grooves with flat bottoms. I do not recommend parting tools for parting off because their crude
action tends to lift the left-hand end of the workpiece up
unexpectedly.

The beading-parting tool (a parting tool with a square
cross-section, typically 3/8 in x 3/8 in (10 mm x 10 mm), is
a compromise and an inferior alternative to a parting tool
and a skew.

Sizes   Parting tools have deep, narrow blades and short,
straight, horizontal cutting edges. The most-common
blade cross-section is a rectangle. The diamond-like cross-
section shown in figure 4.57 is slightly less likely to be
grabbed by the wood at long overhangs. Although widths
up to 1/2 in (13 mm) are available, 1/4 in (6 mm) is the
most useful. If you need a narrower one, I suggest you buy
a narrow parting-off tool in preference.

Faults   You often rock a parting tool to provide clearance.
Also because its bottom edge is narrow, you will not always
present a parting tool to the wood with its sides vertical,
and may need to correct its presentation during the cut.
Both actions are made more difficult if the edges are not
semicircular or at least arrissed.

Tuning   You should arris the corners; or better grind and
hone the top and bottom edges semicircular .

Sharpening   You grind and hone parting tools with a 30°
sharpening angle in the same way that you do skews,
except that you keep the blade square to the grinder's axis.
Take care to keep the cutting edge at the widest part of
parting tools with a diamond cross-section.

Parting-Off Tools

Uses   Parting-off tools (figure 4.57) cut narrow, parallel-sided grooves with convex bottoms. They can be used with axially- or radially-grained workpieces. They are used to part (separate) the finished part of a workpiece from the waste part which remains held in a chuck or on a center. Parting-off tools are also used to divide a workpiece into two parts.

A parting-off tool's upper bevel should be flat in cross-section, its lower bevel should be shallow-fluted. If you flute the upper surface, there is more risk of losing control because the bevel's edges a more likely to catch. If the flute in the lower bevel is deep rather than shallow, the tool will cut less freely.

Fibres are often pulled out along the lathe axis when you part off axially-grained turnings. If you grind and/or hone the flute so that the right-hand cutting point is a touch shorter than the left-hand, when you part off a tiny bobbin of wood is left on the turning which you can trim off to leave an unblemished surface.

Sizes   Widths are 1/4 in (6 mm) or narrower.

Tuning   You should round or at least arris the bottom edge of the tool. Do not do this to the 3/4-inch (20-mm) length nearest the tip of those tools which have a fluted bottom edge.

Sharpening   In general you only grind or hone the flat upper bevel. If you have a suitable convex hone you can hone the fluted surface.

Figure 4.57 Parting and parting-off tools. *Left to right:* a P&N 6-mm parting tool, a P&N 6-mm parting tool converted into a parting-off tool by grinding and honing a shallow flute in its lower bevel, a Robert Sorby 5-mm Diamond parting tool, a Henry Taylor Roy Child parting-off tool, a Robert Sorby 2-mm parting-off tool, and a Robert Sorby cranked parting-off tool.

Scrapers and Shear Scrapers

Uses   Scraping was introduced in section 4.6. Scrapers and shear scrapers (figure 4.58) are most-commonly used where access for cutting tools is difficult or impossible. Example one: hollowing cupchuck and hollow turnings; turning chucking recesses; and for rough- and finish-turning bowls and faceplate work, especially on near-radial surfaces. Shear scraping produces less subsurface damage than flat scraping, but usually leaves a more uneven macro-cut surface.

Sizes   Scrapers can be up to 2 in (50 mm) wide. Shear scrapers are narrower. Scrapers less than 5/16-in (8-mm) thick may flex at longer overhangs.

Faults   The corners along the bottom faces of scrapers and shear scrapers should be arrissed so that they will slide freely.

Tuning   You should arris the bottom corners. Polishing the top face will improve the edge which the tool can take and help the shavings to escape.

Sharpening   Flat scrapers are often bought square-ended, and are then ground to the desired plan shape by the turner (figure 4.59). Turners tend to buy a new scraper when they need a new plan shape to save time-consuming and expensive reshaping.

Most scraping tools are now HSS. The burrs on carbon tool steel are not as durable.

Larger scrapers are traditionally sharpened by grinding their bevels at about 70° to 80° to their top faces. This produces a burr which you can feel, which is effective, but which is barely visible. Some turners advocate ticketting in which you produce a larger burr by plastic flow (figure 4.60).

Shear scrapers are sharpened similarly to flat scrapers, but as they should be used at negative rake angles, you can grind their sharpening angles at 80° to 90°.

Some scrapers, shear scrapers and hollow-turning tools have small scraping tips. To give them a reasonable life, hone their bevels with a fine diamond hone rather than grind them. The loss of or reduction in the size of any burr is not a significant problem.

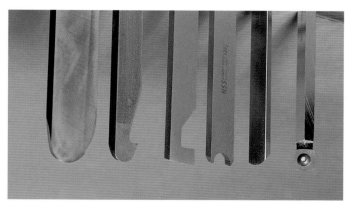

Figure 4.58 Flat and shear scrapers. *Left to right:* a P&N 25-mm scraper originally supplied with a square end, a Robert Sorby HSS-tipped round side-cutting scraper, a Henry Taylor diamond side-cutting scraper, a Robert Sorby bead-forming scraper, an Ashley Isles Reg Sherwin shear scraper, and a Robert Sorby 45° shear scraper.

Figure 4.59 Grinding a scraper on a Linishall linishing wheel.

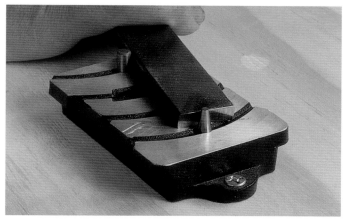

Figure 4.60 Ticketting a burr on a Veritas Scraper Burnisher.

Hook and Ring Tools

Uses   Both tools are used for hollowing, especially for finishing cuts where gouge access is restricted such as in the bottoms of deep bowls.

Hook tools have long been neglected in the English-speaking turning world, perhaps because their lives are perceived to be very short. In earlier times turners lived alongside blacksmiths or had toolmaking skills. When the hook was worn away it was a simple job for the turner or his colleague to forge a new hook on the same carbon-tool-steel blade. Now hook and ring tools are best considered as finishing tools.

The ring tool was first developed for hand turning in Tasmania by Vin Smith, and is a variation on the hook tool.

Faults   Chatter, rapid and noisy vibration of the tool tip, is the most common problem and is caused by a shaft which is too slender and therefore flexes. As hook and ring tools are used to cut concave surfaces, the outside surface of the hook or ring which bears to provide the cutting-edge support should be convex. If it is concave you bear the heel which results in an inferior surface. Having an outside surface which has one or two flats simplifies sharpening and manufacture, but will cause excessive clearance where the curvature of the wood's surface is high.

Tuning   You can make the outer surface of the hook or ring convex by carefully grinding it in a slightly concave grinding wheel rim. An intermediate stage would be to reduce the size of any flats.

Hook tools are rarely in HSS, ring tools usually are. Because such tools are often subjected to torsion, buy them unhandled. You can then make your own thick, rough-surfaced handles which will help you resist torsion better than the smooth, smaller-diameter handles supplied by manufacturers (figure 6.99).

Sharpening If the cutting edge has an adjacent flat surface on the outside of the hook or ring, wipe a hone around it keeping the hone flat on the flat. Otherwise hone only the inner bevel of the hook or ring. For rings use a round cross-sectioned hone—I suggest a diamond file. You can use an edge of a slipstone for a hook tool.

If you ever need to grind the inside of the hook, use a small rotary stone in a Jacobs chuck or a chainsaw grinder.

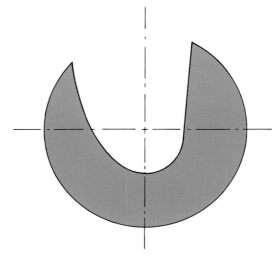

Figure 4.62 Bowl gouge blade cross-sections. *Left,* the preferred cross-section; *right,* this flute is too "U"-shaped and its sides too straight.

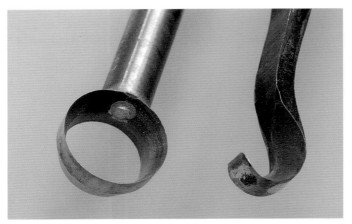

Figure 4.61 A ring tool and a hook tool. *Left,* a Robert Sorby HSS 1-in ring tool; *right,* a Kurt Johannson hook tool.

Bowl Gouges

Uses Bowl gouges are used to turn bowls and suitable profiles on faceplate turnings. Bowl gouges sharpened with special tip geometries are sometimes used inside hollow turnings.

Sizes The overall diameters of bowl gouge blades go up to 1 in (25 mm) The geometry and sharpenings of bowl gouges are shown in figures 4.62 to 4.65.

Faults There is no standard cross-section for bowl gouges, but the consensus would be that some have flutes which are too narrow and flanges which are too straight in cross-section (figure 4.62).

Tuning Soften the top edges if they are sharp, but do not materially reduce their height. Smooth and polish the flute if it is scored or uneven.

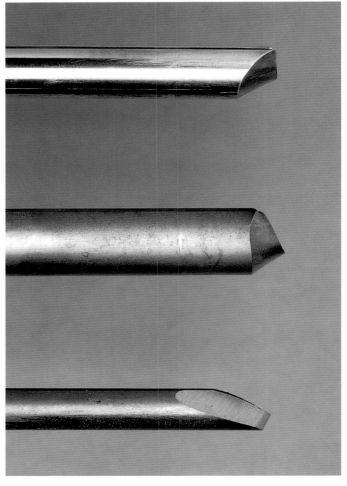

Figure 4.63 The three basic sharpenings in side elevation. *Top,* the square-across; *middle,* the ground-back; *bottom,* the swept-back.

Sharpening and Tool Selection

You can turn bowls with detail gouges, but bowl gouges are preferred in most situations. Bowl gouges have higher flanges on which you can sharpen longer cutting edges. They have non-circular flute cross-sections which allow you to select the most-suitable cutting edge curvature for a particular situation. And you can present bowl gouges sharpened with larger flange angles so that they both cut and scrape at the same time on different parts of the cutting edge.

Although there is wide disagreement on how to best sharpen bowl gouges, the alternatives boil down to those in figures 4.63. I prefer the square-across and the ground-back profiles. The swept-back profile is fashionable, but limited in its usefulness. These three basic sharpenings are then complicated by variations in sharpening angle, whether the bevel is concave or convex, whether the cutting edge is honed, and whether the sharpening is symmetrical or not. The confusion is partly because you can achieve apparently similar cutting success from a spectrum of different sharpenings.

Tool access is another complication. The tool you would ideally use near a bowl's rim is unlikely to be suitable to turn the bottom of the inside because there the rim would prevent you presenting the tool's edge at near-zero clearance. There are other restricted access situations. If you chuck a bowl by its base to turn its outside, the headstock limits the tool presentations you can use.

Bowls are usually turned from disks cut from planks. As a disk is turning, its grain direction relative to a cutting edge is continually changing. Because of the greater tendency for subsurface damage with the adverse grain directions, it is better to use a higher side rake for finish-turning bowls than the 45° used in spindle turning.

Early in turning a bowl you rough turn. You want to remove waste wood quickly with safety and control, and want to be able to work at long overhangs so that you don't have to keep moving the toolrest.

When roughing, having the flanges ground back enables you to retain some side rake at long overhangs. You also want to be able to take thick cuts. If you try taking a thick hollowing cut with a detail gouge, the shaving doesn't separate and blocks the tool's progress. The bowl gouge's smaller flute radius at the base of its flute and its projecting lower flange enable the gouge to scrape away the shaving after it has been partially severed.

When finish-turning it is better to aim for a surface with minimum subsurface damage, even if this leaves a slightly-uneven macro-cut surface. The surface with minimum subsurface damage looks better if unsanded, and requires less sanding (figure 5.7). To minimize subsurface damage you want a thin shaving, a small sharpening angle, minimum clearance, and a high side rake. To minimize rippling you want a long horizontal component of cutting edge support, a wish which conflicts with that for a high side rake. You can help satisfy both desires if you can achieve a long band of cutting edge support. For this the curvature of the cutting edge should be close to that of the surface which it is cutting.

You expect to need several types of tool for spindle or cupchuck turning. Yet there is a common expectation that you only need one main tool, a bowl gouge, to turn bowls. You can make do with one, supplementing it with spindle- and cupchuck-turning tools, but this is not always ideal. Also your choice of bowl-turning tools and their sharpening should be influenced by the shape and size of the bowls you wish to turn, by the chucking procedure(s) you will use, and by how many special bowl-turning tools you propose to buy. However rather than descend further into the can of worms of bowl-turning tool theory, I recommend you buy a HSS ring or hook tool and one or two bowl gouges.

The ring or hook tool will probably be a ring tool as HSS hook tools are rare. For small bowls choose a ring or hook diameter of around 1/2 in (13 mm); for larger bowls prefer a larger size. By having a ring or hook tool you will not need to shear scrape nor adopt coarse sharpening angles for your bowl gouge(s). Instead of a ring or hook tool you could use a capped hollowing tool (figure 10.7), but they can clogg with radially-grained workpieces.

If you buy one bowl gouge you should sharpen it as shown in figure 4.64. This sharpening is good for roughing and finish-turning on both the insides and outsides of bowls. If you buy two bowl gouges you can divide the functions. I recommend one gouge for roughing and one for finish-turning (figure 4.65).

You can grind square-across, ground-back, and similar noses easily on a platform jig. Because you are using these gouges to *cut*, you should hone their edges in the usual way. The swept-back nose is best achieved using a fanning jig such as the Glaser. How to produce convex bevels was described in figures 4.35 and 4.36.

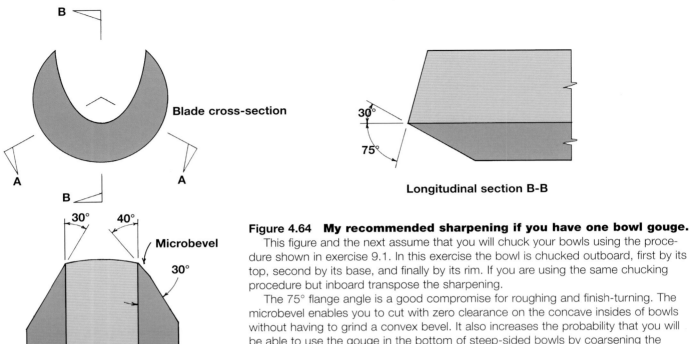

Blade cross-section

Longitudinal section B-B

Plan section A-A

30° 40° **Microbevel** 30°

Figure 4.64 My recommended sharpening if you have one bowl gouge.
This figure and the next assume that you will chuck your bowls using the procedure shown in exercise 9.1. In this exercise the bowl is chucked outboard, first by its
top, second by its base, and finally by its rim. If you are using the same chucking
procedure but inboard transpose the sharpening.

The 75° flange angle is a good compromise for roughing and finish-turning. The
microbevel enables you to cut with zero clearance on the concave insides of bowls
without having to grind a convex bevel. It also increases the probability that you will
be able to use the gouge in the bottom of steep-sided bowls by coarsening the
sharpening angle. You can easily grind this microbevel by increasing the setting of
your jig by 10°. The microbevel's width should not be wider than a quarter of the
bevel's total width, and it should run along just one half of the cutting edge.

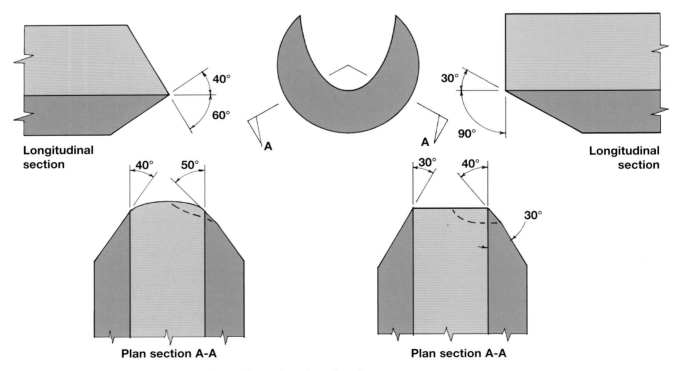

Longitudinal section

Plan section A-A

Plan section A-A

Longitudinal section

Figure 4.65 My recommended sharpenings if you buy two bowl gouges.
The left-hand gouge is for roughing, the other for finish-turning. The smaller sharpening angles of the finish-turning gouge may
prevent you *cutting* the whole inside of a bowl, but this is not a disadvantage, if as recommended, you also have a hook or ring tool.

Hollowing and Hollow-Turning Tools

Uses   Hollowing tools can be used to hollow axially and radially-grained turnings. Hollow-turning tools are primarily used to hollow hollow turnings, especially where the access is more restricted. The choice and use of hollow-turning tools are detailed in chapter 10.

Faults   The most common fault is too slender a shaft. Hollowing tools similar to ring tools can share the same fault.

Sharpening   Scraping tools have small tips and should be sharpened by honing their bevels. Those similar to gouges or ring tools are sharpened in similar ways to those tools.

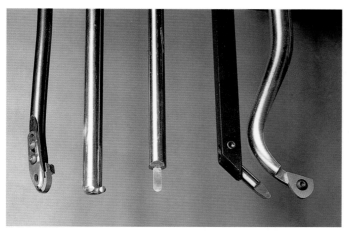

Figure 4.66 Hollowing and hollow-turning tools. *Left to right:* a Woodcut Mighty Midget, a Melvyn Firmager angle tool, a straight hollow-turning tool by David Ellsworth, a Crocodile hollow-turning tool by Bierton Craft Turnery, and a Stewart System reversible hooker.

4.12 RECOMMENDED SET OF TOOLS

What tools should you buy to start turning? Those listed below will allow you to complete all the exercises in this book and tackle a wide range of other turnings.

For spindle turning:
Roughing gouge, 1 1/4 in (32 mm)
Skew chisel, 1 in (25 mm)
Detail gouge, 1/2 in (13 mm)
Parting tool, 1/4 in (6 mm)

For cupchuck turning (in addition to the spindle-turning tools):
Scraper, 1 in (25mm)

For bowl turning (in addition to the above):
One or two bowl gouges, about 5/8 in (16 mm)
HSS ring or hook tool

For hollow turning (in addition to the above):
One or more hollow-turning tools. Their choice is discussed in chapter 10.

The above list is the minimum required. Purchase additional tools when you need them. General recommendations for extra tools are:

Larger and smaller detail gouges
A wider and a narrower skew
A narrow parting-off tool
More scrapers as required
A shear scraper
An extra bowl gouge if you bought only one

4.13 TOOL HANDLES

Woodturning tools usually have wooden handles (figure 6.99). You should buy your first tools already handled. You can buy just the blades of most brands of tools, and make and fit your own handles. As tools are more easily selected if they have distinctive handles, this is a sensible option. Making and fitting handles is described in exercise 6.5.

A typical wooden tool handle is about 12 in (300 mm) long. You may make a handle larger or smaller according to the blade size and the tool's anticipated usage.

Tool manufacturers' handles are sanded and polished, and most turners prefer them this way. Where a tool will tend to be twisted by the forces on its tip, it is better to have its handle larger in diameter and with a rough surface. Similarly, use a long and heavy handle on a tool which will have large downward forces coming onto its tip. These two situations are common in hollow turning. The handles for hollow-turning tools are discussed in section 10.3.

Chapter Five

DESIGN, WOOD, AND WORKSHOP PRACTICES

This chapter covers those subjects which I wish to introduce rather than detail, or which don't slot logically into the chapter sequence.

5.1 DESIGN

Technique has its own challenges and rewards, but is a means to the end of manifesting a design. As you progress in turning, your focus should shift from technique to other areas of turning, especially to that of design.

Design, even when restricted to woodturning, is a mighty and complex subject. I shall merely introduce it and name some of the common profiles used (figures 5.1 and 5.2).

What is the secret to becoming a good designer? There isn't one. Some turners have the advantage of an inborn feeling for shape and proportion, but this alone is not sufficient. Every turner needs to continually aquire design knowledge, become more critical, and practice design, particularly through exploring alternatives. Design formulae such as the Golden Mean and the Fibonacci Series are greatly overrated as design aids, their main role being to explain the success of designs which were often produced without their aid.

Traditional turning designs are still popular, but many recent designs in traditional styles have failed because their designers lacked a real understanding and knowledge of the area. Modern turning design is less detailed than traditional. "S"-shaped and assymetrical profiles are spurned in favour of the purely geometric spheres, cones, and cylinders. But failure is again common for the same reasons, and/or because a crude, subtractive approach is taken—"All you have to do is eliminate the twiddly bits."

The pre-turning design process includes finalizing the equipment and techniques you will use and preparing the gauges to set out the turnings. By using gauges you will more faithfully replicate your design intents. Freehand doodling on the lathe may be more tempting, but it rarely succeeds because the only turning equivalent of the eraser is to start again with a fresh workpiece. Designing with pencil and paper before you turn is the most efficient option. It encourages rather than stifles creativity. You are much more likely to succeed if you clarify your design intents and how you will achieve them before you switch on your lathe. And you are still free to modify a design while you are turning it.

When designing a turning you often have functional dictates to satisfy. You have to make the design compatible with the available wood, your turning equipment, and your level of turning expertise. You have to clarify and incorporate your aesthetic and communicative intents for the design. You need to explore, decide, and compromise. You have to decide how you want those who will experience your design in the future to react to it.

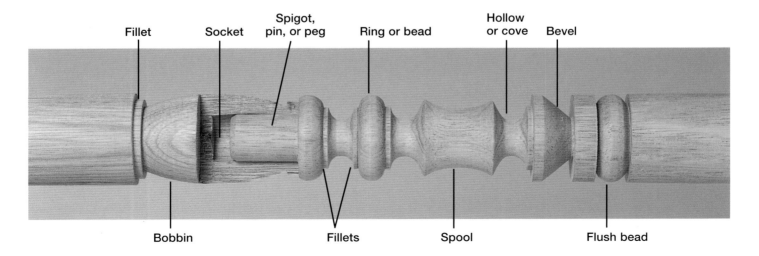

Figure 5.1 Common spindle details.

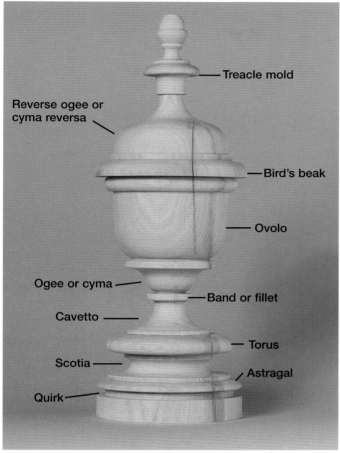

Figure 5.2 Common molding profiles. The treacle mold and bird's beak have concave undercuts.

Labels in figure:
Treacle mold
Reverse ogee or cyma reversa
Bird's beak
Ovolo
Ogee or cyma
Band or fillet
Cavetto
Torus
Scotia
Astragal
Quirk

5.2 WOOD

Solid wood will be your main working material, although you can hand turn many others. It continues to be desirable due to its relative cheapness, useful physical properties, and wide availability. For us its beauty, individuality and tactility are paramount. But these benefits come at a price—it is a contrary material. It stains, distorts and cracks. It cannot be cast, forged, or welded, and has to be shaped by carving processes.

Naming Woods

The plants which yield wood of usable dimensions are almost exclusively trees. A tree type which can reproduce itself exactly is a *species*. The number of tree species in the world is unknown, but it runs to tens of thousands. Each species has a Latinized two-word botanic name. *Quercus palustris* (figure 5.3) for example is the botanic name of the pin oak. The first word of the binomial nomenclature denotes the *genus*. *Quercus* is the original Latin name for an oak tree, was therefore chosen as the genus name, and is common to all the 450 oak species. The pin oak commonly grows in bogs in its native America. It was therefore given the species name *palustris*, Latin for "boggy". The derivations of these botanic names is a fascinating area of taxonomy, the classification of species. Non-Latinized names are used far more commonly; many species have one or more local or common names, and commercial species have standard trade names. Tree species are also divided into hardwoods and softwoods, a division based on how they reproduce rather than on the working properties of their woods.

Structure and Properties

Both woody and soft-tissue plants are largely composed of cellulose fibres built up from cells, but in woody plants these fibres are bound together by lignin. (It is the thermoplastic nature of lignin which allows wood to be reshaped by steam bending). Woods also have medullary rays, very noticeable in some species such as oaks, barely visible in others.

Woods' properties vary because of differences in their cell structures and compositions. Particular species are characterized by the presence of different extractives, volatile substances which give smell, colour, and insect and rot resistance. Some woods, for example teak, contain significant amounts of tool-blunting silica.

The appearance and qualities of a particular piece of wood are due to:

1. The species of the parent tree, its age and where it grew, and any damage or attack the living tree sustained.
2. Where in the tree the piece grew. Wood taken from the straight, vertical, large trunk of a mature forest-grown tree will be more stable than that from a young, solitary tree. Wood from butts, crotches or burls will be usually be more ornate than the trunk wood. Wood near the surface may show a strong color contrast between the sapwood and heartwood.
3. The care and treatment given to the wood after the parent tree's death or felling.

Beginners are frequently disappointed when a woodturning distorts or cracks. The reason is usually that the wood was not fully seasoned. Living wood is fully saturated with water held both between the cells and within them. Once a tree is felled or dies, its wood starts to lose moisture. A thin sliver would rapidly dry to the equilibrium moisture content—when wood contains this percentage of moisture it is seasoned and no longer seeks to expel or attract water to or from the surrounding atmosphere.

Wood has to lose about 90% of its moisture to season. It

also has to shrink, the percentages of shrinkage varying with the species. Wood does not shrink uniformly: sapwood shrinks more than heartwood; radial shrinkage is less than circumferential; and there is no shrinkage parallel to the grain. Unfortunately the moisture does not flow freely out of the wood during seasoning, and moisture-content gradients result. These and other factors combine to make seasoning a difficult and not always successful process.

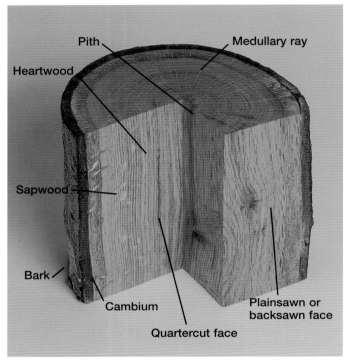

Figure 5.3 Wood features shown in a small log of pin oak *(Quercus palustris).*

This log's end grain shows growth rings which are a product of the tree's annual life cycle. Tree growth is rapid in the spring. As the season progresses growth slows, and denser and often darker wood is produced until growth ceases during the winter.

The pith is the upward path of the growth tip. A tree increases in girth by the following process. The sapwood conducts nutrient-laden sap upwards to the leaves during the growing season. Green-colored chlorophyll in the leaves absorbs energy from sunlight and promotes photosynthesis in which water from the sap and carbon dioxide from the air react to yield sugars, starches, amino acids, and oxygen. The transformed sap then flows down the very thin cambium layer which produces new cells of bark on its outer side and sapwood on its inner side. Nutrients are conducted radially by the medullary rays. On the quartercut face the rays appear as pale blotches, on end grain as pale lines radiating from the pith, and on the plainsawn face as dark lines.

The sapwood of this log is narrow and grey. In the living tree the sapwood is pale. Once the tree is felled fungi attack this nutrient-rich and extractive-deficient wood causing blue stain.

The heartwood was once sapwood which now just provides structural support.

5.3 DRILLING IN THE LATHE

Stand a lathe up on the right-hand end of its bed and it resembles a drilling machine. A lathe might lack a table, but does allow you to rotate the workpiece.

The headstock and tailstock axes must align well. Misalignment will cause oversize holes and chatter. Wear in the bed and tailstock will increase misalignment.

Drill Chucks

Most smaller drilling machines have Jacobs chucks on the ends of their spindles. A lathe has a Morse taper swallow in the right-hand end of its headstock spindle which will grip the matching taper on a Jacobs chuck arbor or tapered drill shank. The workpiece then has to be pushed axially towards the headstock to be drilled. More commonly the Jacobs chuck or tapered drill shank is held in the tailstock ram, and fed into the workpiece which is rotated by the headstock spindle (figure 8.6).

Drill Types

Figure 5.4 and table 5.1 detail the commonly-used drills. Cutting edges may be carbon tool steel, HSS, or tungsten carbide. To avoid softening carbon-tool-steel edges don't run the lathe too fast and feed at a comfortable rate. You can overheat bits by not feeding while the lathe is running, and by not clearing the chips frequently. The latter leads to a rapid build in frictional heat, to the jamming of the bit in the hole, and shortly afterwards to possible damage to the workpiece, to equipment, and to the driller. When the safe recommended turning speed for a workpiece is different from the speed recommended for the drill, use the lower.

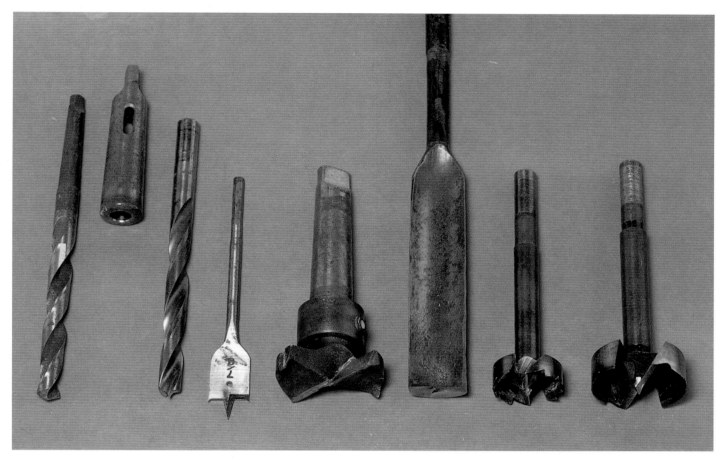

Figure 5.4 Drills used in woodturning. *Left to right:* a twist drill with a tapered shank, a 1 to 3 Morse-taper sleeve, a brad-point-sharpened twist drill, a spade bit, a boring bit with tungsten-carbide cutters and spurs, a lamp-standard (shell) auger, a sawtooth bit, and a Forstner bit.

A sleeve enables a Morse-tapered shank to be mounted in a larger Morse-tapered socket or swallow. Not shown are a tapered drift which you hammer into the slot in the sleeve to eject a shank, and an extension socket which allows you to mount a tapered shank in a swallow with a smaller Morse taper.

A brad-point sharpening gives a cleaner entry and hole in wood than the standard twist drill tip.

Spade bits are not recommended for boring into end grain. Always stop the lathe before starting to withdraw a spade bit.

A Forstner bit allows you to drill a hole which does not descend squarely from a surface.

No drill is self-centering. Drills which use a high component of tip steerage have a greater tendency to run off line than lamp-standard augers which steer themselves by being held in line within the wall of the hole they have just bored. Long twist drills which are both tip steered and held in alignment by their shanks can jam when the tip starts to veer.

Gun drills (not shown) have superseded lamp-standard augers for high accuracy, high speed, high volume, long-hole boring. Gun drills are tungsten carbide tipped, much dearer than lamp-standard augers, and require compressed air to be blasted through their hollow shanks and tips to clear the chips. They do not have to be withdrawn during boring.

TABLE 5.1

Drill type	Diameter inches	Diameter mm	Recommended speed rpm
HSS twist and brad-point	1/8 to 3/8	3 to 10	3000
	1/2	13	2300
	3/4	19	1550
	1	25	1150
Spade	All sizes	All sizes	2500
Lamp-standard auger	1/4 to 1/2	6 to 13	1000
Sawtooth and Forstner	3/8	10	1000
	1/2	13	750
	3/4	19	500
	1	25	400
	1 1/2	37	250
	2	50	200

Drilling Procedures

There are two main procedures, plus others which are used less often.

Short workpieces are mounted in the headstock spindle swallow, on a faceplate, or in a chuck. The drill is held in the tailstock ram. The workpiece is rotated at a suitable speed and the drill is fed in using the tailstock handwheel (figure 8.6).

Long workpieces are bored similarly, except that their right-hand ends need to be axially located, especially if the rotational speed of the workpiece relative to the drill needs to be high. There are three ways to locate the right-hand end: by a dead or live, hollow tail center mounted in the ram of a tailstock which allows an auger to pass through it (figure 3.10); by a hollow center which can be mounted in the banjo; by a steady; or by a home-made, hollow, intermediate "tailstock". If you are making lamp stems, axially bore them first. You then mount them for detailed turning using a cone tail center and a drive center which has a suitably-sized cylindrical pin, not a spike-shaped one (figure 3.9).

Short, small-diameter holes can be bored into the ends of long workpieces by mounting the drill in the headstock spindle swallow. Hand-hold the workpiece's left-hand end while you feed it to the left using the tailstock handwheel. The concentricity of the hole is unlikely to be high. It is wise to use a low lathe speed. This procedure is shown in exercise 6.5.

You can mimic a drilling machine by mounting a drill in the headstock spindle swallow and supporting the workpiece on a table which fits into the banjo or better slides along the bedways.

Boring into the side of a turning is achieved by using a post which fits into the banjo stem. The post can be hard wood or metal. It should have a horizontal hole of the same diameter as the required hole(s) drilled through it at lathe axis height. Commercial equivalents are available with interchangeable bushes. If you need a ring of holes, space them using the indexing attachment or make pencil marks around the periphery of a faceplate to mimic one. Alternatively you can drill holes into the sides of spindle blanks or finished turnings away from the lathe.

5.4 SANDING

You sand for two reasons:

1. To remove any surface defects left after turning.
2. To prepare the surface for finishing by eliminating any visible scratches left after removing the surface defects, and by creating a surface of, as far as possible, uniform absorption.

Coated Abrasives

Only two abrasives are of importance. Aluminum oxide is a tough, pale-brown abrasive. Silicon carbide is a sharper, harder, and more friable blue-black abrasive. It does not last as long, but leaves a less-scratched surface. It is therefore preferred for the final sanding where an especially-fine surface is required.

Abrasive grits are graded by number. The smaller the number, the coarser the grits. The commonly-available and useful sizes for turners are: 60, 80, 100, 120, 150, 180, 220, 260, 320, 400, 500, and 600. The scratches left by one grit are efficiently sanded away by the next-finest grit in the series. If you leapfrog grits, you will tend to leave scratches in the surface. Many suppliers sell abrasive cloths and papers in small quantities. This makes it feasible for the hobbyist to have a full range of grit sizes.

Abrasive grits may be glued onto paper or cloth (figure 5.5). Very thin and flexible cloth backings have recently become available and are suitable for all but the finest sanding. Abrasive cloths are dearer but more economical than abrasive papers because the bond between the grit and the cloth backing is far more durable. Very-fine grits are usually available only in silicon carbide, bonded to a paper backing with waterproof glue, and sold as wet-and-dry paper.

Coated abrasives are available with the grains deposited tightly together (*close coat*) or with space between (*open coat*) Open coat is better for turning as it clogs less. Some papers are stearate-coated, also to reduce clogging.

Abrasive papers are available in C or the thinner A weight. The A weight is better as it will conform to detailed profiles better, and creases well to sand where there are abrupt changes in direction. Abrasive papers need to be kept dry, but they can be too dry and be inflexible (figure 5.6). Modern papers are less likely to curl and are less affected by moisture than those of twenty years ago.

Sanding Methods

Sanding is slow, boring, dusty, and expensive. You should do as little as possible. First, aim for the best possible off-the-tool surface. Second, sand only when you need to. Third, sand efficiently. I for example don't sand or finish tool handles; and I leave most bowls with an off-the-tool surface.

Efficient sanding results from starting and ending with the appropriate grit sizes. If you start with too coarse a grit, you sand needlessly. If you start with too fine a grit, you have to sand for too long with the first grit, or change to a coarser grit once the ineffectiveness of your first choice becomes apparent. As a guide, start spindles with 120 to 150, faceplate turnings with 60 to 100. If the turning is to be clear-finished go to 320: if it is to be stained and clear-finished go to at least 400.

Sanding will abrade softer wood more than hard, and will therefore tend to destroy the circularity you achieve off-the-tool. With woods with annual rings, the harder autumn growth will be left higher, giving a wavey feel to the surface. Sanding is effective in removing projections, but slow at eliminating subsurface damage where thickness has to be removed over an area (figure 5.7).

Most in-lathe sanding is done with the paper or cloth hand held. You can also power sand, and this is commonly used in bowl turning and on the outside of radially-grained hollow turnings.

Figure 5.6 Pulling a coated abrasive over an edge makes it more flexible.

Figure 5.5 Sanding materials.
The SIA cloth at the rear is especially thin and flexible. The 11 in x 9 in (280 mm x 230 mm) standard-sized sheet of brown wet-and-dry paper is face down. The whitish, aluminum oxide, A-weight, stearate-coated paper shows how you should prepare paper or cloth for hand sanding. Both are usually used in the form of a twice-folded sheet, the size of that sheet being a quarter that of a standard-sized sheet. This gives two sanding edges and three sanding faces. (Reverse the folding to expose the third face).

For power sanding use an electric drill and/or an angle drill, ideally with a side handle, reverse, and variable speed. Foam sanding pads of various diameters can be mounted into the drill chuck. The pads are Velcro faced to receive cloth-backed disks which are available in a full range of grit sizes.

A rippled surface without subsurface damage

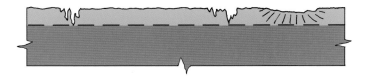

A plane surface with tear-out and crushing

Figure 5.7 Sanding compared. The volumes of wood which have to be sanded away to remove projections and subsurface damage are colored green. Comparison shows that less wood has to be sanded away from a rippled surface than from one with subsurface damage.

5.5 FINISHING

It must be wonderful to work in a material like glass which is self-finishing. Wood alas is assumed not to be, and the time and effort demanded for some finishes exceeds that expended on the turning.

There is no agreement on the ideal appearance of finished wood, perhaps because there is no natural precedent. You rarely see wood in nature, you see bark. And when you do see wood in nature it is weathered, splintered, charred, or rotted. The gloss or satin finish on a man-made, often plane, surface is an entirely artificial concept. Perhaps we have become too demanding of shine, too intolerant of a little temporary grubbiness, too impatient to allow a patina to develop through use. Do we need to polish or even sand everything?

When choosing the material(s) and procedure for finishing a turning, you should consider:

1. What gloss level you want. The higher the gloss, the more imperfections show.
2. The protection you want against water, weather, solvents, abrasion, etc.
3. What equipment you have both to apply the finish(es) and to exhaust or ventilate your polishing area.
4. Should the pores be filled?
5. Can you achieve a dust-free finishing and finish-drying environment?
6. Will food be near or in contact?
7. Should the finish be easily repairable?
8. How much expense and effort you are prepared to put into the finishing.
9. Is it important that the wood's colors not be altered, say by using a tinted finish? Do you want to modify them by staining, or cover them by an opaque finish such as paint?
10. Should the finish set hard?
11. Does the finish raise the grain?
12. If your procedure requires sanding between coats, can you do this in the lathe?
13. Does the new finish have to match an existing one? What about future color changes in both?
14. Exposure to air and light causes wood and finishes to change color. In general, the initial brilliance fades, darkens, yellows, or browns into an effect which is different rather than inferior.
15. Is the wood soft and absorbent or harder and less absorbent? Softer woods are less suited to non-setting finishes.
16. The protection a finish gives is related to its film thickness and to its absorption into the wood. Slow-setting, less-viscous finishes are absorbed more deeply and leave a thinnner and less obvious surface skin. Long-term they can give more protection.
17. Whether a finish can be buffed or worked to increase its gloss and eliminate imperfections.

Whatever finishing material(s) and procedure you select, try it on scrap wood of the same species first.

Almost all polishing materials are to some extent bad for us. We may be affected by breathing their vapors or through skin contact. The effects tend to be cumulative. Occasional use outside may be virtually harmless, whereas frequent use in an unventilated space will seriously harm your health. Note the cautions on the cans, and wear vinyl gloves. The accelerating trend to finishes with lower proportions of toxic solvents is an encouraging development.

Finishing is frequently described in the relevant magazines and has its own extensive literature. This section therefore ends by describing a few finishing options to get you started.

1. If the finish is just to liven the colour, rub in an edible vegetable oil. Waxing on top will give an imperfect seal. Waxing alone on more porous woods leaves a patchy surface.
2. Turners' friction polishes are quick to use and give a good shine on small items in hard woods. Use vinyl gloves or the alcohol solvent will cause deep and painful cracks in your fingertips.
3. Dipping in Scandinavian oil gives a brown-tinted, low-sheen finish on harder woods.
4. If you want more build and gloss than Scandinavian oil gives, use Danish oil which is again usually brown-tinted. It is sanded between coats.
5. For a non-tinting clear finish use white shellac, two-part polyurethane, or clear nitrocellulose (sometimes called melamine) laquer. Nitrocellulose laquers are popular with in-lathe finishers because they dry rapidly. They usually need thinning. A final wire woolling or very fine sanding followed by waxing and buffing is commonly used.
6. One-part polyurethane is widely available, but too treacly to be absorbed into the wood unless thinned with about 20% of mineral turpentine or thinner. Brush it on, wipe any surplus off with a rag when absorption stops, allow to dry, sand, and recoat. Repeat this process as many times as required. Adding a few drops of linseed oil makes the polyurethane more workable.

5.6 SAFETY

You can injure yourself with any woodworking machine. A woodturning lathe may be one of the least potentially harmful, but to minimize the risk of injury you should:

1. Know what actions are likely to be unsafe.
2. Develop safe working habits and an awareness of the importance of safety.

You are entirely responsible for your safety when working at home. If you are learning woodturning as an employee or in a school, your employer or the school has a duty to provide safe conditions and insist on safe practices. That does not mean that you cease to have any responsibility for your safety. Even if you can shift the legal blame, that will not undo the inconvenience, injury, pain, and health damage which might result.

Personal Safety

1. Loose clothing and long hair can become caught. Take preventative measures.
2. Tools sometimes fall from your lathe. Wear sturdy shoes.
3. Keep wood chips out of your clothing by wearing a smock or coat with a close-fitting collar.
4. Contact with wood can be a problem. Some species with high levels of extractives can cause dermatitis. Avoid them rather than wear gloves or use barrier creams. The problem of wood dust was discussed in section 3.4.

Workshop Safety

1. Keep your workshop clean and tidy, and its floor clear.
2. Ensure that the floor is not slippery.
3. Provide sufficient working area around each machine.
4. Ensure that machines are properly guarded.
5. Stack materials safely.
6. All electrical work should be performed by professional electricians, and should be properly maintained.
7. Disconnect the power before working inside machines.
8. Maintain a first-aid kit and know how to use it. Keep details of the nearest doctor and hospital prominent.

Safe Procedures

1. Ensure that the wood is free of defects which could cause it to split in the lathe. Fault-free wood gives a clear sound when tapped; cracked wood sounds dead.
2. Check the lathe speed, that the wood is securely held and clears the toolrest, and that lockings are properly but not thread-stripping tight before switching the lathe on.
3. Stand aside when you switch the lathe on so that if the wood flies out you won't be hit.
4. The tool should be supported on the toolrest before being presented to the wood.
5. Keep your hands away from the rotating wood unless you have a sound reason to feel or support it. Some turners feel the wood after almost every cut, a habit both dangerous and timewasting.
6. Ensure that wood being bandsawed cannot tip, or be grabbed and rotated by the blade.

Chapter Six

SPINDLE TURNING

Spindle turning is the most useful form of turning. Chair and table legs, handles, stair balusters, stems, columns; you see them everywhere. Spindle turning is also the best form of turning to learn first. The wood is readily mounted in the lathe, and is unlikely to fly out being held at both ends. Because the grain is parallel to the lathe axis there is no turning against the grain. And once you have achieved competence in spindle turning you will find it easy to become competent in the other turning specialties.

This chapter is in the form of a series of graded exercises. By following them you will be able to teach yourself spindle turning's basic techniques. Exercises 6.1 to 6.4 (shown in figure 6.1) take you through the most-important basic cuts. You then learn the remaining basic spindle-turning techniques in exercises 6.5 to 6.7 through turning the items shown in figure 6.2.

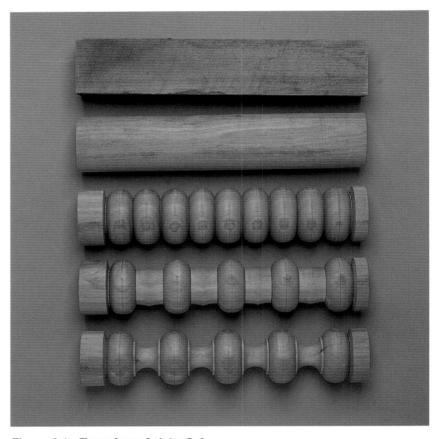

Figure 6.1   Exercises 6.1 to 6.4.

Exercise 6.1   You learn to rough a square cross-section, *top,* down to a cylinder, *one from top,* with a roughing gouge, and then refine the surface by planing it with a skew.

Exercise 6.2   From the cylinder left after exercise 6.1, you learn to turn a row of beads, *middle,* using V-cuts and rolling cuts with a skew chisel.

Exercise 6.3   You again use the skew chisel, but cut away alternate beads to produce the workpiece *one from bottom.*

Exercise 6.4   You cut into the cylindrical sections left after exercise 6.3 to produce fillets and coves between the beads, *bottom.*

These exercises are the most important in this book. Once you are competent in them, you will find that competence comes easily in every other turning cut and technique. If you are coming back to turning after a spell, a few minutes practicing this series will quickly restore your former speed and assurance.

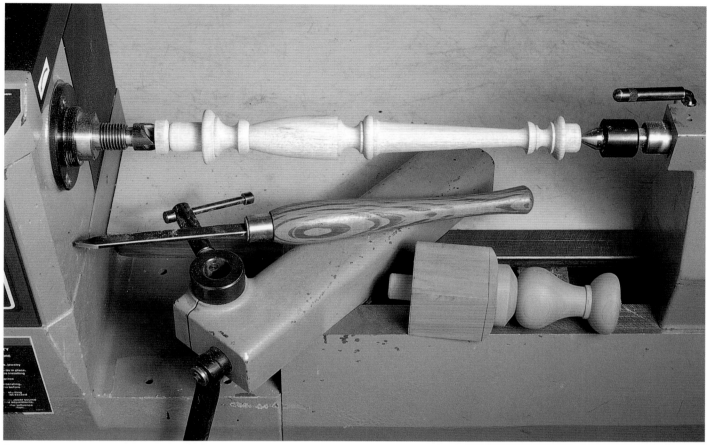

Figure 6.2 Exercises 6.5 to 6.7 show you how to turn a tool handle, a short leg, and a hatstand shaft.

These later exercises add new cuts with the roughing gouge, skew, and detail gouge to the skills you have already learnt. You will learn to use a parting tool and calipers. You will also learn how to transfer a design onto a turning and produce that design, and how to best order the different cuts.

EXERCISE 6.1   ROUGHING AND PLANING

Techniques taught	Mounting a spindle blank in the lathe The overhand grip Roughing from a square cross-section to a cylinder of the largest-possible diameter Planing a cylindrical surface
Tools needed	Roughing gouge Skew chisel 1-in (25-mm) or wider
Workpieces	Square cross-section of 2 to 3 in (50 to 75 mm) thick, length about 2 in (50 mm) shorter than your standard toolrest, grain running lengthways.

There are five parts in this first exercise:

Preparing the workpieces (figure 6.3).
Mounting the workpieces in the lathe (figures 6.4 and 6.5).
Taking your stance (figure 6.6).
Gripping the tool correctly (figures 6.8 and 6.9).
The roughing and planing cuts (figures 6.7 to 6.24).

The roughing and planing cuts are easy to master, yet they rarely are. Many turners have no definite roughing procedure and present the cutting edge too low on the workpiece. They then carry these shortcomings through to the rest of their turning. So take care with this exercise and set yourself on the right road.

Figure 6.3 Marking and punching workpiece ends.

You should inspect and prepare a workpiece before mounting it into the lathe. Doing this for all the workpieces in a batch before you start any turning is more efficient than inspecting, preparing and turning each piece in turn. Reject any workpieces with visible cracks or loose or large knots. You can test for hidden cracks by tapping the workpiece on your lathe—if cracked it will sound "dead".

You can mount the workpiece more quickly and accurately if you first mark the centers of its ends. You then press or hammer small conical holes at these points for the driving and tail centers to locate into.

To mark the centers *(left)* use a marking gauge set to exactly or approximately half the workpiece thickness—in the latter case it will be easy to judge the center of the small quadrilateral formed by the four scribed lines. In the slower and less-accurate method shown center, you draw diagonals with a pencil.

To form a conical hole you can press in an awl similar to the blue-handled ex-screwdriver, or tap in a punch. Only with the hardest woods or with lathes with very flimsy beds should you need to resort to drilling holes for the centers' pins, sawing grooves to locate the prongs, or hammering in the driving center outside the lathe with a soft-faced hammer.

You can make an automatic centering punch *(middle and right)* out of steel and/or wood. The sides of each square recess are best approximately 15% greater across than the workpiece thickness you commonly expect to use in it. To punch a center, introduce the workpiece end into the recess, twist the workpiece so that its corners jam against the recess sides, and tap the top down onto the center pin (with your hand is suffi-cient for soft woods). You can make a hand-held version to offer up to the ends of very heavy or long workpieces.

Figure 6.4 Locating the left-hand end of a workpiece onto the drive center—the first stage in mounting a workpiece in the lathe.

Before you mount a workpiece in the lathe, check the lathe speed, and if in doubt change it. Err on the low side of that recommended in section 4.7. Move the toolrest sufficiently away from the lathe axis so that it will not interfere, and retract the tailstock ram into the tailstock body to within 3/8 in (10 mm) of the maximum.

Locate the workpiece's left hand-end by pushing its punched hole onto the driving center's center pin with your right hand. Your left hand meanwhile supports the left-hand end of the workpiece.

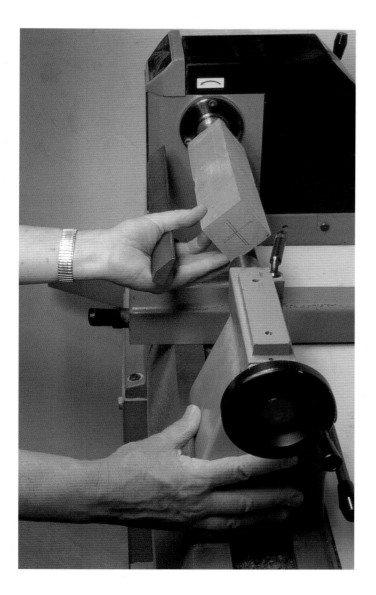

Figure 6.5 Bringing up the tailstock to locate the workpiece's right-hand end.

After locating the workpiece's left-hand end, move your left hand to support the right-hand end of the workpiece. With your right hand move the tailstock to the left until its tail center locates into the punched hole in the right-hand end of the workpiece. Lock the tailstock to the bed. Wind the tail center to the left until the drive center's prongs firmly engage, then lock the tailstock ram.

Next position the toolrest. Its ends should project at least 1 in (25 mm) past the ends of the workpiece. When you rotate the workpiece by hand its corners should clear the rest by 1/4 to 1/2 in (6 to 13 mm). You should angle the banjo's neck square to the lathe bed in plan to minimize the possibility of hitting it with your tool tips as you swap tools.

There is no absolute relationship between the height of the top of the toolrest and the height of the lathe axis (which should be at elbow height). The top of the toolrest would commonly be positioned about 1/4 in (5 mm) below the lathe axis, but its ideal height depends on several factors. If using a lathe that is too low for you, raise the toolrest and vice versa. The toolrest should be a little higher when turning large-diameter workpieces. If your tools are unusually heavy in cross-section, the rest needs to be a touch lower. The governing factor is your comfort at the lathe.

You do not need to keep moving the toolrest forwards to minimize tool overhang for any of the exercises in this chapter because:

1. There is no need. You can work safely and comfortably at overhangs exceeding 2 in (50 mm) if you exert sufficient axial thrust.
2. Longer overhangs allow you to see the top and bottom of the workpiece to compare diameters and judge blurring and tapers.
3. At short overhangs you will feel constricted and cannot use the preferred tied-underhand grip introduced in exercise 6.2.
4. You may move the toolrest forwards with the lathe running — a risky practice.

Before switching on recheck the lathe speed, the workpiece mounting, and the banjo and toolrest positions. Move well to the safe, switch side of the workpiece. Switch on with your right hand if the switch is on the left so that if the workpiece is tossed out you are not hit. If the lathe vibrates noticeably, switch off. The lathe speed is too high, something is loose, or the workpiece is unbalanced. Correct the problem and restart the lathe. Once the workpiece is rotating safely, wait a while to become accustomed to the speed before you start roughing if this is your first time at a lathe.

Figure 6.6 **The ideal stance for spindle turning.**

You should be relaxed, upright, and at ease, with both arms comfortable. Do not raise your left elbow. Your left upper arm should hang down close to your body. Do not crouch. You will be cramped if you stand too close to the lathe. Stand too far away and you have to stick your buttocks out and lean forwards, a sure recipe for a sore back. Your ankles must be parallel to the lathe bed to allow you to sway and shuffle parallel to the lathe axis. You cannot make these movements from the more-natural one-foot-back stance without falling over.

Accidents with lathes are rare, but are most likely when you are learning. Reread the safety section 5.5, and wear a protective face shield or ventilated helmet—here a Racal Dustmaster Mk II.

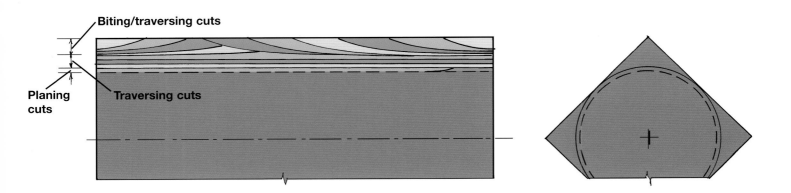

Biting/traversing cuts

Planing cuts

Traversing cuts

Figure 6.7 Roughing a square to cylinder involves biting/traversing cuts, traversing cuts, and planing. The diameter of the resulting cylinder should usually be only a touch less than the thickness of the square.

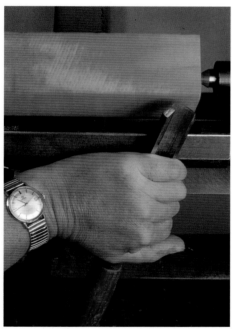

Figure 6.8 **Starting the first biting/traversing cut** of a series using the overhand grip.

Figure 6.9 **The bevel heel is bouncing on the workpiece corners,** but cutting has not yet started. The cutting edge is being slowly drawn down and backwards under control.

If you ram a roughing gouge into the center of a workpiece, you may split off long, large splinters or cause some other mishap. You are likely to lose control of your roughing gouge if you attempt to cut towards and into the end of a rotating square. The corner of the gouge nose which first contacts the wood is likely to be unsupported as it penetrates, and large splinters are likely to be levered off. To avoid these risks, start roughing by taking a series of cuts working back from one end (the right-hand end if you are right-handed). The best cuts to use are lengthening biting/traversing cuts. They are shown in detail in figures 6.7 to 6.17.

There are two basic, best left-hand grips in woodturning: the *overhand,* and the *tied-underhand.* You only use the overhand in this exercise as it is preferred for cuts requiring long tool traverses along the toolrest. With the roughing gouge's flute facing up, take a shaking-hands or tennis grip with your right hand towards the back end of the handle. Place the blade on the toolrest as shown in this figure with the tip well clear of the wood, and place your left hand on top of the blade, before presenting the tool to the wood. With the overhand grip your thumb should ride on, not under, the blade because otherwise it can get trapped between the tool blade and the toolrest in some faceplate-turning cuts. Do not press down on the blade or it will be harder to move on the toolrest.

When starting all *cutting* cuts, present the cutting edge a little too high on the wood to take a shaving. You must also have the tool blade on the toolrest, if not the rotating wood will grab the tool tip and slam the tool blade down onto the toolrest with a loud bang.

If you are right-handed, start the first cut about 1in (25 mm) in from the right-hand end of the workpiece. If you are left-handed you will prefer to start cutting towards the workpiece's left-hand end.

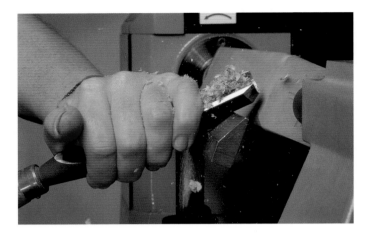

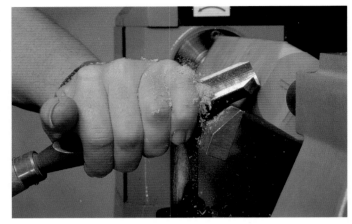

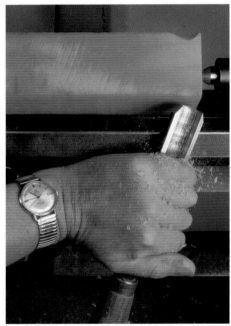

Figure 6.10 Cutting has just started. The shaving is being taken at the base of the flute. The blade should be angled 10° to 20° to the right in plan so that the right-hand section of bevel does not block the tool's progress. The flute should point about 20° clockwise from the vertical. Keep exerting a strong axial thrust with the handle low so that the clearance angle is the minimum for that particular depth of cut. The object of roughing is to cut away the waste quickly. Take strong, deep cuts. The roughing gouge is a tool you can be a bit rough with.

Figure 6.11 Completing the first biting/traversing cut. The cut has been deepened and the tool traversed to the right.

Figure 6.12 Halfway through the second biting/traversing cut.

Start the second and each succeeding cut about 1 1/4 in (30 mm) to the left of the start of the previous one, and traverse and deepen it through to the workpiece's right-hand end. Continue to deepen and traverse only until the area being cut is almost cylindrical. As this stage approaches the workpiece's top and bottom edges will cease to look blurred.

Figure 6.13 Starting the third biting/traversing cut.

Figure 6.14 Completing the third biting/traversing cut.

If you continue this series of biting/traversing cuts, starting each one to the left of the previous one, the final cut will be risky. The unsupported right-hand corner of the gouge nose may be grabbed by a corner of the left-hand end of the workpiece. To avoid this, start a second series of biting/traversing cuts near to the workpiece's left-hand end (figures 6.7, and 6.15 to 6.17). Each cut starts to the right of the previous one, and traverses through to the left-hand end of the workpiece.

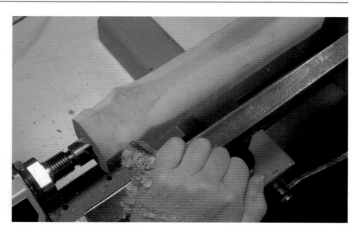

Figure 6.15 Taking the first biting/traversing cut to the left. The blade is now pointing to the left in plan and its flute faces about 20° counterclockwise from vertical.

Figure 6.16 Taking the second biting/traversing cut to the left.

Figure 6.17 Taking the last biting/traversing cut to the left.

Figure 6.18 Starting the first traversing cut from the left. The blade is pointing to the right.

After removing the corners, start long traversing cuts, alternatively from one end to the other. You can now safely start these cuts into the ends of the workpiece and run the gouge through to the other end. As you approach a true cylinder make these traversing cuts slower and shallower, take the cut more on the gouge flanges (but keep the corners exposed), and increase the side rake towards 45°. These three actions will improve the surface finish. Cutting on the flanges also uses edge not blunted by the impacts of the wood during the earlier biting/traversing cuts.

Figure 6.19 "Planing" with a roughing gouge. Run the striking part of your left hand along the toolrest during traversing cuts to produce a truer cylinder.

Finish-turn the cylinder with slow roughing gouge traverses when the workpiece's grain is not straight and axial. Otherwise you should plane it with a skew chisel (figures 6.22 and 6.24).

Figure 6.20 The stance at the start of the traversing cut from the left shown in figure 6.19. Start each traverse with your weight on your left leg.

As you traverse the tool to the right, sway to the right keeping your right arm in an unchanging position relative to your upper body. If this were a long spindle you would use a series of slightly overlapping traverses, the end of each traverse being reached when you can sway no further without the risk of losing your balance. Shuffle parallel to the lathe axis between each traverse.

Figure 6.21 The stance at the completion of the traversing cut from the left started in figure 6.20.

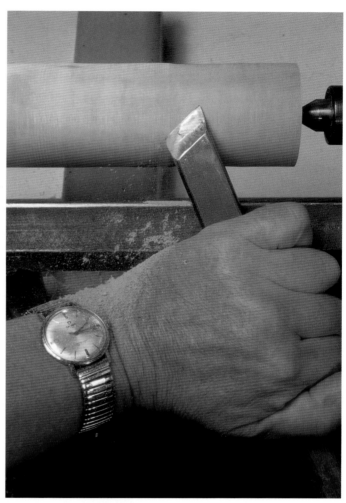

Figure 6.22 Starting a planing cut to the left again using the striking part of the hand to guide the tool. Because planing is cutting away an upstanding shoulder, there should be almost no clearance and the bevel heel should be almost touching the wood. The optimum side rake is 45°.

Do not start a planing cut into the end of the workpiece because you are likely to lose control. Instead start the cut 1 in (25 mm) or so in from the end. Then traverse through right to the other end. You cut away the waste left (in this case at the right-hand end) when you traverse back (see figure 6.24).

If you plane with the short point, the wood will tend to rive leaving an inferior surface. If you attempt to cut with the long point, the point will be pushed backwards, the blade will be banged down onto the toolrest, and a spectacular catch will result. Plane therefore with both points out of the wood. For better control take the cut nearer the short point than the long. In areas where the edge is planing against the grain there will be tear-out and the cutting will feel and sound rough.

Do not raise the toolrest for planing cuts. Instead bend your knees.

Figure 6.23 Checking whether there are any flats left.
As the workpiece approaches a cylinder, its top and bottom edges will cease to look blurred. Even when the bottom of the workpiece looks crisp, there may still be small flats remaining. Testing for flats with your hand underneath the toolrest and workpiece is safe because your fingers are trailing. Feeling with your hand on top is dangerous.

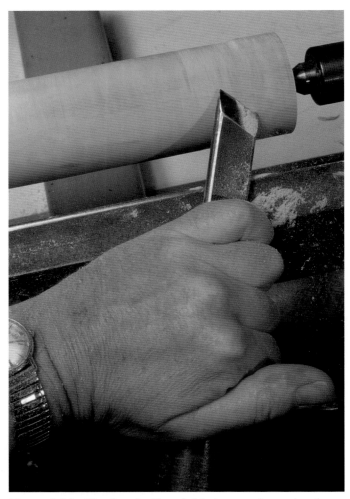

Figure 6.24 Planing to the right. I am again running the striking part of my hand along the toolrest to smooth the cut.

EXERCISE 6.2   SYMMETRICAL V-CUTTING AND BEAD ROLLING

Techniques taught	Making and using a simple pencil gauge The tied-underhand grip V-cutting Bead rolling
Tools required	Wide skew chisel Rule and pencil
Workpieces	The cylinders turned in exercise 6.1

In this exercise you will learn to V-cut and roll a row of near-semicircular convex profiles called beads into the surface of a cylindrical workpiece with a skew chisel (figure 6.25).

Bead rolling has the unjustified reputation of being the most difficult cut in turning. It is though an exacting cut which when improperly executed usually results in a spectacular spiral catch (figure 6.25). Even the best turners occasionally get one, but as the reasons for such a loss of control are well understood and readily overcome there is no need to become too concerned.

The figures which describe this exercise are in three groups:

1. Figures 6.25 to 6.27 introduce the exercise.
2. Figures 6.28 to 6.40 describe the tied-underhand grip and the preparatory V-cuts.
3. Figures 6.41 to 6.64 describe the rolling cuts. The first four figures show the actions of both hands during rolling. The next five figures follow the cutting edge in close up as it rolls. A sequence of figures then shows rolling as you would see it. The final figure looks at the problems turners have with rolling cuts.

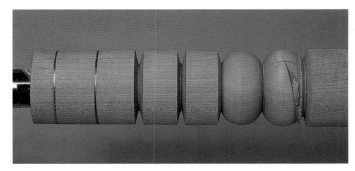

Figure 6.25 A workpiece illustrating the V-cutting and bead rolling process, and a spiral catch.
Left to right: lines have been pencilled on the rotating cylinder at the intended cusps where adjacent beads are to touch; "V"-sectioned grooves which define the cusps have been cut with V-cuts made with a skew's long point; and rolling cuts with a skew's short point have been used to form two beads. The right-hand bead is marred by a spiral catch.

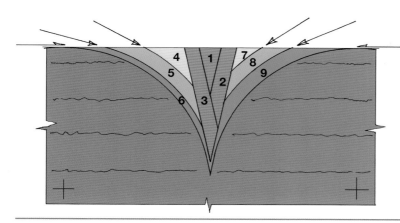

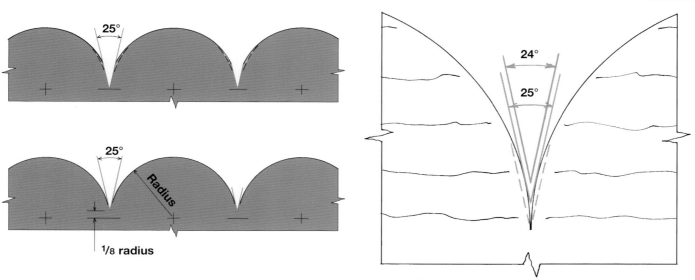

Figure 6.26 The geometry of V-cutting and bead rolling.

Cuts **1**, **2** and **3** are V-cuts. They are not ignorant pokes into the wood. They:

1. Define the positions of the bottoms of the beads along the spindle.
2. Define the depths of the beads.
3. Remove waste, creating space for the rolling skew to move into and for its shavings to escape.

You therefore need to V-cut with precision if the dependant beads are to have the desired profiles.

Cuts **4** to **9** are rolling cuts. The cutting edge inclination at the start of each rolling cut is defined by its upper arrow.

Figure 6.27 The geometry of beads.

The minimum angle that you can cut at the cusp between two adjacent beads using a skew is a touch less (24°) than the skew's sharpening angle (here 25°). You should therefore halt your V-cutting short of the final bottom of a cusp to minimize crushing at the bottoms of the adjacent beads. You can then cut the whole of the beads' surfaces with rolling cuts.

As the sides of adjacent beads spring upwards at half your skew's sharpening angle from the vertical, the beads cannot be truly semicircular. You have to choose whether to make your beads' heights half their widths (*top left*), or whether to make your beads a little shallow but keep their profiles truly round (*bottom left*).

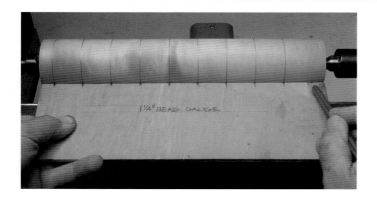

Figure 6.28 Marking out the cusps of the beads from a pencil gauge.

A pencil gauge is the most common means of transferring a design to a workpiece. Use thin plywood about 4 in (100mm) wide—too narrow and you can lose the gauge between the toolrest and the workpiece. Short grooves projected to the gauge's top edge are made with a three-cornered saw file to guide your pencil point. I recommend a bead width of about 1 1/4 in (30mm) for this exercise because it requires you to make lengthy movements of the chisel along the toolrest during the rolling cuts.

Use the cylindrical workpieces remaining from exercise 6.1. Mount each into the lathe as shown in figures 6.5 and 6.6. Your toolrest's position should be unchanged from that used for exercise 6.1. Switch on the lathe, hold the pencil gauge lightly against the workpiece, and mark the positions of the cusps by sliding your pencil point forwards along the filed grooves.

Figure 6 29   About to take the tied-underhand grip.

After marking out the bead cusps, your next task is to learn the grip for turning details.

First position the skew with its long edge resting on the toolrest. The blade should be at 90° to the lathe axis in plan, resting on its long edge with its sides vertical. Take the shaking-hands (tennis) grip with your right hand towards the back of the handle. You can extend your forefinger along the handle if you wish.

Bring your left hand up under the tool blade. Position your forefinger beneath the toolrest and your palm so that the blade lies along the lifeline, the major crease in your palm nearest your fingers. Then close your fingers and thumb so that the blade is gripped into your palm.

The tied-underhand is the best left-hand grip for detailed turning. It is "tied" because your forefinger goes below the toolrest to grip its bottom or back; and "underhand" because your hand is under the tool blade. Your tool and hand are thus tied to the toolrest. Your left hand can therefore be active in powering and controlling the forward, backward, sideways, and rotational movements of the tool blade. Traditionally these movements were the preserve of the more remote right hand, but the replacement of wooden toolrests by smaller cross-sectioned steel rests enabled the tied-underhand grip to be developed in the 1920s in Auckland, New Zealand or in Sydney.

With the tied-underhand grip you share power and control between your two hands. The sharing varies according to the type of cut and its forcefulness, but in most the left hand should dominate.In the inferior "untied"-underhand grip, which is still commonly taught, the right hand always dominates.

Figure 6.30   The tied-underhand grip.

The tied-underhand grip will feel strange at first. You will tend to grip far too tightly which will restrict your hand and wrist movements. Your grip should be active but relaxed, tightening only when you need to exert greater force.

During cuts you continue to hold the blade into your palm, while manipulating the tool with your left wrist and forearm, and right hand. The tip pad of your forefinger grips the toolrest's bottom edge or the rear face. If you attempt to grip too far up the rear face of the toolrest and/or the toolrest section is too deep, or you have your thumb flat on the blade rather than arched, the vee between your thumb and forefinger will get jammed against the toolrest and prevent free left-hand movement.

Figure 6.31 A sloppy version of the tied-underhand grip. Holding a tool between your fingers and thumb lessens the need for proper left-wrist- and forearm-powered movements, but it also lessens control.

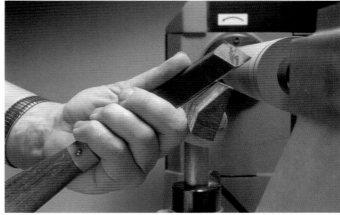

Figure 6.32 Starting a first V-cut.

V-cuts are made with the long point because it will penetrate far more deeply than the short point. For example, in softish woods you should only need three V-cuts for a bead height of about 5/8 in (15 mm).

Keep the blade square to the lathe axis in plan and the sides vertical throughout the cut. V-cuts should be crisp, rhythmic, forceful, swing-pushes powered mainly by your right hand. If you start the long point too high on the wood, the wood will thrust the tool back towards you and splinter out the surface. If you start the cut too low it becomes a push. This first V-cut does not remove wood, it squashes it along each side of the vee and raises feathering along both edges of the vee.

Figure 6.33 The completion of a first V-cut.
During a V-cut you should swing-push the long edge down through about 30° until it points at the lathe axis. You should then withdraw the tool from the wood. Swinging the long edge lower will not deepen the cut. From comparing figures 6.32 and 6.33, you will see that that the tool has barely moved forwards during the cut, and that it is the downwards swing which gives most of the penetration. You also need to keep the power on through to the end of a V-cut to maximize its depth.

Figure 6.34 Starting the second V-cut, here from the left.
You can take the second V-cut to the right or to the left of the first. If a bead is an isolated one high enough to require three or more V-cuts, take the second one on the bead side of the first.

A second V-cut (from the left) is similar to a first except that:

1. The long point first penetrates the wood immediately to the left of the left-hand feathering.
2. The blade should remain at 90° to the lathe axis in plan and be tilted about 5° counterclockwise throughout the cut. In practice the blade sides will tend to become more vertical during the cut.

Figure 6.35 Completing the second V-cut.
As in figure 6.33, swing-push the long edge down until it points at the lathe axis.

Figure 6.36 Starting the third V-cut, here from the right.

As with the second V-cut, the blade should start and remain square to the lathe axis in plan. The long point should first penetrate the wood a touch further outside the right-hand feathering than it did outside the left-hand feathering in the second V-cut. Again the blade should be axially tilted about 5°, but clockwise.

You alternate the third and any successive V-cuts from the left and right. Present the long point so that it first penetrates the cylindrical surface of the wood about 1/32 in (1 mm) outside the rim of the vee groove. Perform these later V-cuts as you did the second and third.

Figure 6.37 Completing the third V-cut.

As discussed in figure 6.27, a bead's shape is affected by the depth of your final V-cut. You also define the bead's lateral extent with your final V-cut. The more V-cuts you require to define a bead, the more likely the bottom of the vee is to wander. Therefore when accuracy is critical and the bead is high, or you want its side to be steep, use the offset V-cutting method described in exercise 6.6.

Figure 6.38 The starting presentation for a very deep V-cut from the left.

The blade is still square to the lathe axis in plan. If you had the the handle further to the left so that the blade pointed somewhat from left to right, you would cut a wider vee which would leave an undesirable flat on the side of a bead on the left of the vee. The blade is tilted about 5° counterclockwise so that the cutting edge points to the bottom of the cut you are making. You should not attempt to change this blade tilt during the cut, although it may tend to steepen.

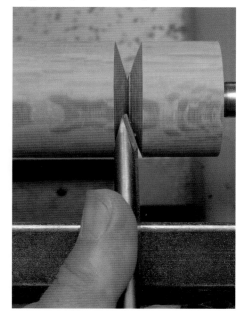

Figure 6.39 The correct completion of the deep V-cut started in figure 6.38.

The blade is still square in plan and has moved along the toolrest to the right. The blade still has some counterclockwise tilt.

Figure 6.40 Common mistakes in V-cutting.

Common mistakes with V-cutting include: **A**, prolonging the follow-through chars the sides of the vee without significantly deepening the cut; **B**, the cutting edge above the long point may catch on the rim of the vee if you attempt to lever the the shaving out; **C**, you cut too wide a vee if you angle the blade in from the side in plan, and thereby chop the side off the intended bead; and **D**, taking too thick a cut will leave a wide ruff level with the bottom of the previous V-cut.

Other mistakes are: being jerky, ponderous or timid; giving up early in the cut; giving the blade too much axial tilt so that the cut does not deepen the vee as much as it should; and attempting too thin a cut which can lead to the long point wandering into the vee prematurely.

Rolling Cuts

To achieve a successful rolling cut you have to:

1. Keep the active part of the cutting edge (ideally the short point) cutting with the correct near-zero clearance angle.
2. Cut the desired profile while leaving a surface with minimum rippling and burnishing.

To achieve these two simple aims you have to co-ordinate five very simple component actions; you have to:

1. Axially rotate (roll) the blade typically between 30° and 95°
2. Traverse the contact point between the short edge and the toolrest along the toolrest. Usually this traverse will be to the right for a clockwise roll and vice versa. But when cutting a tiny bead with a thick skew the direction of traverse may have to be reversed.
3. Alter the angle of the blade from behind square to the lathe axis in plan to square, or even to past square.
4. Thrust the blade axially forwards. (You could have to draw the blade backwards if you have the toolrest very high).
5. Raise the handle to lower the cutting edge.

Bead rolling resembles changing gear in a manual car while turning a corner. The latter's component actions involve operating and moving the gear lever, clutch, steering wheel, and an indicator. Each action is ludicrously simple in isolation, it is their successful coordination which demands sustained practice.

It is usually best to cut right on the short point throughout each rolling cut. If you use the long point, the cutting is more visible, but the surface left will be more porous and rippled because the shaving is being cut upwards and because the long point receives less reference support. You can totally plane a bead, taking the shaving with the short point exposed, but because the shaving is far wider you will have to thrust much harder. A useful method for wide, shallow beads is to start by planing. You then gradually thrust the tool forwards so that the shaving moves down to the short point towards the end of the cut. This procedure is called a slide cut, and the more common type is detailed in exercise 6.6.

Figures 6.41 to 6.50 are intended to give you an overview of bead rolling. Figures 6.51 to 6 64 then show the sequence for cutting a "semicircular" bead.

After you have completed a row of beads, if your workpiece diameter allows, rough the workpiece back to a cylinder and cut a second row. Practice beads until you can cut a couple of rows consistently, confidently, and without a catch. Competence at this exercise means that you will be able to present any cutting tool with confidence.

When you are feeling competent and confident with 1 1/4 in (30 mm) diameter beads, repeat the exercise with rows of equal beads of different diameters.

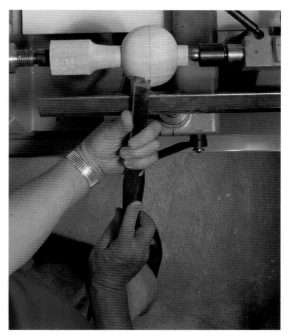

Figure 6.41 Skew and hand positions at the start of a final clockwise rolling cut. Your right hand should be in a strained position, anxious to help. Grip the tool blade into your palm and keep it there throughout the cut. Your left upper arm should hang down vertically. Through a series of rolling cuts your left elbow should barely move.

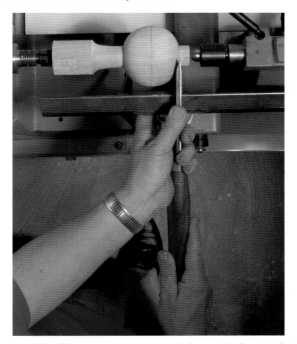

Figure 6.42 Skew and hand positions at the end of a final clockwise rolling cut. You should have traversed the blade along the toolrest, rotated the blade 90°, and retained the short point at minimum clearance. You should have rotated your right hand into a relaxed shaking-hands position.

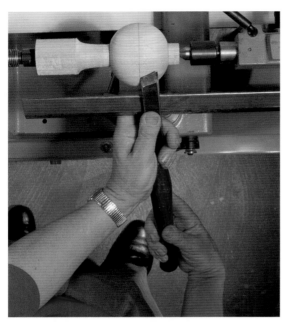

Figure 6.43 Skew and hand positions at the start of a final counterclockwise rolling cut.

Most turners find the counterclockwise roll less natural than the clockwise. The back of your left hand should point to the left. Have your thumb pad on top of the top side of the blade. If you have your thumb pad partially on the short edge, your skin is likely to get pinched during the rotation. Flex your left forefinger, ready to power and control the traverse of the blade along the toolrest to the left.

Your right hand should be in a strained position because you should not have altered your right-hand grip.

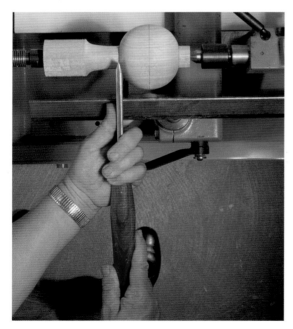

Figure 6.44 Skew and hand positions at the end of a full counterclockwise rolling cut. Thrusting with your left forearm and the hingeing your left wrist pulls your hand down and under, and forces the blade to rotate.

Figure 6.45 Starting a final rolling cut. This and the following five figures show the path of the cutting edge in close up as it performs a full roll.

At the start of the cut the short edge is angled less than 5° behind square. This presents the end of the cutting edge (the short point) to the wood. If your have the handle more to the right you will be attempting to cut with end of the blunt short edge. The cutting edge is tilted about 1° clockwise from horizontal. If the short point is sharp it will pick up a shaving at even this low inclination.

Figure 6.46 A quarter of the way through the roll.
The blade is still a touch behind square, and has therefore been traversed along the rest as it has been rotated clockwise. The short point is still high on the wood at minimum learance. Thrust with your left wrist and forearm and pull with your forefinger to power the cut. You should feel that your left hand, not your right, is in control. Once you become confident, you should not watch the short point but the profile being cut. Take the cut very slowly, the short point is not going to melt! By taking the cut slowly you allow enough time to coordinate the five simple, component movements listed earlier. You also need the time to monitor and respond to the changing bead profile.

Figure 6.47 Halfway through the roll.

Figure 6.48 Three quarters through the roll.

Figure 6.49 Completing the roll on the right-hand side of a bead as if the bead is one of a row.

The tool tip is positioned as it would be at the bottom of the cusp between two adjacent beads. The blade is square to the lathe axis in plan, and the cutting edge is vertical. To penetrate as deeply as possible, the grinding marks at the short point should point to the lathe axis. During the cut slow the traversing of the blade along the toolrest while continuing to roll at the same rate.

Figure 6.51 Starting a first rolling cut to the right (cut **4** in figure 6.26). The blade is angled about 2° behind square in plan and its sides are tilted at about 35° to the horizontal.

If you present the skew with the cutting edge inclined too steeply you will cut a bead which has the profile of an inverted vee (a "Gothic" bead). If you present the cutting edge too low on the workpiece, its clearance angle is excessive. To prevent these two common faults start with the blade sides more horizontal than they should be, and with the short point too high on the wood. You can then draw the blade back and down under control. As soon as the short point starts to take a shaving, start the rolling cut. If the blade sides are too flat, axially rotate the blade at the start of the rolling cut to correct the presentation. As you become more competent, you will automatically reduce the size of these safety margins until they are almost imperceptible.

Take your right-hand grip first. Rest the skew on its short edge with its sides vertical. Take a shaking-hands grip, just like that you used for V-cutting. You then retain this grip for all the rolling cuts, whether for just a half bead or for a series of beads. Because your right hand will be strained at the start of each rolling cut, it will want to rotate the skew into an unstrained, comfortable orientation.

Your left-hand grip should be the tied-underhand (see also figures 6.29 and 6.30). One version is used for clockwise rolling, a different version is used for counterclockwise rolling. For clockwise rolling, arch your left thumb and grip the skew's long edge with the pad at your thumb's tip. Extend your forefinger along the bottom edge of the toolrest so that you can grip with its tip pad to pull your hand and the tool along to the right.

Beginners will find it helpful to mark where to start each rolling cut. The preferred equally-spaced marks on the right-hand bead lead to each pair of left and right rolling cuts being thinner than the preceding pair (see figure 6.26). If you roll using the marks on the left-hand bead, your rolling cuts will be of equal thickness.

Figure 6.50 At the completion of a 95° rotation.
When you want the short point to cut truly vertically at the end of a rolling cut, you have to rotate the cutting edge about 5° past the vertical. The bevel in contact with the bead also has to be perpendicular to the lathe axis: to achieve this you have to traverse the blade further along the toolrest than square in plan.

Figure 6.52 The completion of cut 4.
You axially rotate the blade and traverse it along the toolrest by thrusting to the right with your forearm, hingeing back your wrist, and pulling with your forefinger. By swaying to the right you can keep your right hand comfortably close to your body and move the skew's handle to the right so that the blade becomes almost square in plan.

Figure 6.54 Completing cut 5.

Figure 6.53 Starting cut 5, a second rolling cut to the right.
Your hand and tool positions are similar to those in figure 10.51 except that the blade is flatter.

Figure 6.55 Starting cut 6, a third rolling cut to the right.
The sharp short point is taking a shaving even though it is tilted at only about 1° above horizontal.

Figure 6.56   Halfway through cut 6.

Figure 6.58   Starting cut 7, a first rolling cut to the left.
   Your left-hand grip should be the counterclockwise-rolling version of the tied-underhand. Your right wrist should be hinged backwards as shown in figure 6.43.

Figure 6.57   Completing cut 6.
   The blade is square in plan and its sides are vertical. At the end of the cut the grinding marks at the short point should point at the lathe axis. If you lever the short point lower, the bevels will crush the wood on both sides of the cusp.

Figure 6.59   Completing cut 7.
   Counterclockwise rolling demands that you exert a very positive pull forwards and under with your left wrist. You will have to force yourself to do it. As in all rolling cuts, your right hand is a minor partner.

Figure 6.60   **Starting cut 8, a second rolling cut to the left.**

Figure 6.62   **Starting cut 9, a final rolling cut to the left.**

Figure 6.61   **Completing cut 8.**

Figure 6.63   **Completing cut 9.**

Figure 6.64   The two most-common bead faults. *Left,* a Gothic bead; *right,* a spiral catch.

A Gothic bead results from starting a cut with the skew's sides inclined too steeply. This faulty presentation often then causes a catch later in the cut as explained in points 3 and 4 below.

The reason for the fearsome reputation of the skew is that the slightest error seems to result in the dreaded spiral catch. The causes are simple and fixable:

1. A poor starting presentation with the cutting edge too low on the wood (see figure 6.51).
2. Failing to maintain sufficient axial thrust. This allows the wood to force the cutting edge back towards you and the clearance angle to increase. The cutting edge wants to take an increasingly-thicker shaving, the thrust you are applying decreases as a proportion of that needed to maintain equilibrium, and a catch results.
3. You realize that the cutting edge is too steep so you reverse its rotation. The top of the shaving climbs up the cutting edge, the shaving widens, and therefore the force needed for shaving severance increases. But you are too slow to increase your thrust, the edge is pushed backwards, clearance opens, and a catch results.
4. Many turners have difficulty achieving the full 90° rotation and cheat, starting the cuts with the cutting edge too steep. This results in Gothic beads, or in the turner ceasing or even reversing the blade's axial rotation during the cut to try and correct the shape. A catch will usually result for the reason explained in paragraph **3** above.
5. The tool pivots if you fail to move the contact point between the blade and the toolrest along the toolrest during a rolling cut. Therefore the short point cannot remain in proper contact with the bead surface and cannot reach down into the cusp between the beads.

6. You can cause the cutting edge to lose support if you rotate the skew too quickly or move the blade/toolrest contact point too far. These are rare errors.
7. A blunt tool will be reluctant to penetrate, but crushes the surface making subsequent penetration more difficult. You force down too hard, the edge suddenly penetrates deeply, your thrust is insufficient, and you lose control.

EXERCISE 6.3   CUTTING FILLETS

Techniques taught	Cutting fillets
Tool required	Wide skew chisel
Workpiece	That remaining after exercise 6.2

Fillets are short discontinuities, usually straight. When one is located at the point of inflection on an "S" curve (figures 6.65 and 6.66) it can be considered as separating the curve into a bead and a cove.

As this exercise is used to produce the workpiece for exercise 6.4, you should only cut away alternate beads to produce fillets. The upper waste in figure 6.66 could be removed with a parting tool or detail gouge, but you usually use the skew you used to roll the beads to save a time-wasting tool change. You can use the overhand grip for cuts requiring very long traverses, but should use the tied-underhand grip for the short traverses in this exercise. The cuts are described in figures 6.66 to 6.74.

To cut fillets you should move the whole tool laterally, not pivot it in plan about the first contact point between the blade and the toolrest. You should cut on the short point with a side rake of 45°, and should keep the shavings fairly thin. As it is difficult to judge the shaving thickness when you start the short point into a near-vertical face, alternate the cutting direction as shown in figure 6.66.

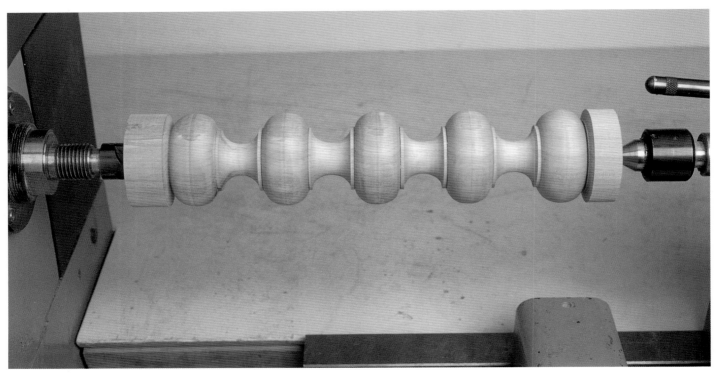

Figure 6.65   Your workpiece after exercise 6.3 and exercise 6.4.

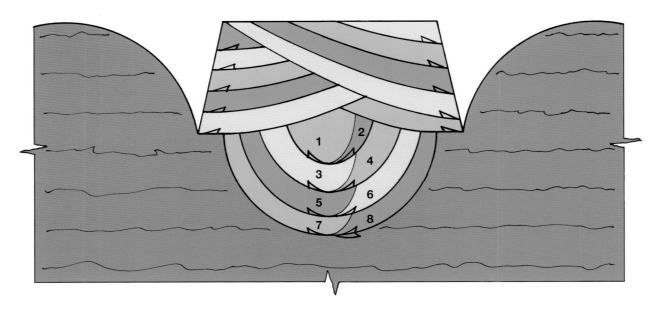

Figure 6.66   The cuts for cutting fillets and coves.
   You use a scooping action to cut pairs of horizontal fillets which lie between upstanding beads.
   The coving cuts alternate from the left and the right. You only cut towards the lathe axis to cut with the grain (see section 4.4).

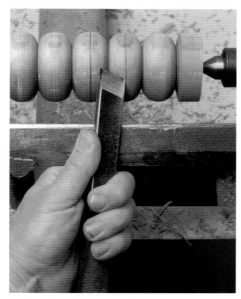

Figure 6.67 Starting to cut a fillet.
You need to thrust strongly with your left wrist and forearm throughout the cut. To keep that axial thrust within a reasonable level, you must keep the depth of cut shallow. You will find that easier when starting into a near-horizontal surface. The skew sides should be as near horizontal as possible, but take care not to damage the beads as you traverse the skew over them.

Take the entire cut on the short point. Where the traverse is very long, you commonly start by planing, and slide the skew forwards towards the end of the cut to bring the cutting down to the short point.

Figure 6.69 Starting the final fillet cut of the first series to the right.
Rather than cut the two fillets in one series of cuts to the right and one series to the left, I could have used three series. This would have avoided the need to take fine and therefore difficult cuts like this into the near-vertical, left-hand side of the remainder of the bead.

Figure 6.68 Completing the first fillet cut.
Lever the short point onto a horizontal path towards the end of the cut. You have to thrust firmly and bear the lower bevel heel adjacent to the long edge on the surface left at the start of the cut. Slow the traverse towards the end to avoid damaging the bead.

Figure 6.70 Completing the cut started in figure 6.69.
The left-hand end of the lower bevel heel is bearing on the wood.

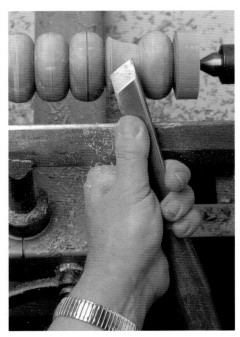

Figure 6.71 Starting the first cut to the left.
It is relatively easy to take a thin shaving when you start a cut into the gently-sloping surface left by the previous series of cuts.

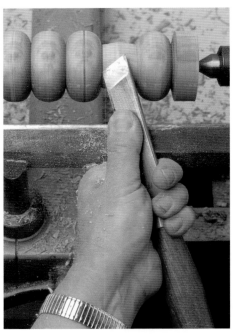

Figure 6.73 Completing the final cut to the left.
If the short point penetrates beneath the bottom of the vee left after V-cutting, a ruff of fibres will pushed out. To remove this ruff it is best to deepen the vee with the short point. If the bead surface is damaged you will have to skim the bottom section of the bead with a rolling cut.

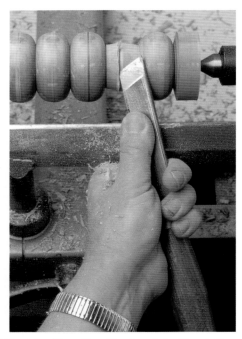

Figure 6.72   Starting the final cut to the left.

Figure 6.74 Starting a final cut to the right.

EXERCISE 6.4 CUTTING COVES

Technique taught   Cutting coves

Tool used   A medium or large detail gouge

Workpieces used   Those left after exercise 6 3

The detail gouge is a multi-purpose tool, but you use it mainly to cut coves. Figure 6.66 showed a typical series of coving cuts.

You should use your largest detail gouge which will fit within the finished cove. If you use an unduly-small gouge, you will take longer to cut the cove and will tend to leave a more-rippled surface.

A common belief is that you should cut with the tip of the cutting edge tangential to the workpiece surface. This belief is incorrect because it ignores the importance of cutting with side rake to improve the surface. Figure 6.75 shows the preferred gouge axial rotation for cutting at any gradient.

You are most likely to lose control of a detail gouge when you present it to the wood at the start of a cut. For a stable entry into the wood you need to have the blade at the correct axial rotation and in the complementary and correct presentations when viewed in plan and from the tailstock. Figure 6.76 shows the gouge axial rotation and the blade alignment in plan for cutting at any gradient.

Coving cuts tend to be three part. You first achieve a stable tool entry; then thrust the nose into the stable, preferred *cutting* position; thirdly, from this second position you cut to the bottom of the cove. Figures 6.77 to 6.82 detail this for the final coving cut of a series. The full series of cuts you use to cut a cove is then shown in figures 6.83 to 6.98.

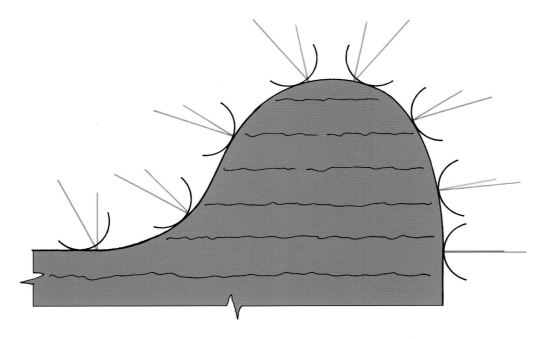

—————— **Inclination of flute**

—————— **Normal to surface**

Figure 6.75 The preferred axial rotation of a detail gouge at different profile gradients.

The green lines are normals (lines at 90° to tangents) to the surface. The red lines show the directions in which the gouge flute should point. When cutting horizontally you should angle the flute to point at 30° from the vertical in the direction of traversing to give 45° side rake. The angle between the green and red lines decreases with increasing gradient until when the gouge is cutting "vertically" (square to the lathe axis), its flute points horizontally and the blade points at the lathe axis.

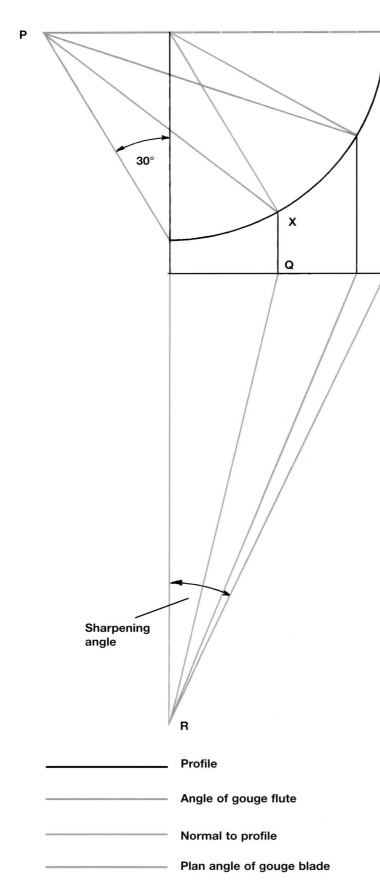

Figure 6.76 The Darlow diagram.

Figure 6.75 shows the appropriate axial rotation of a detail gouge for cutting at any gradient. There are two other variables: the blade presentation when viewed in plan; and when viewed from the tailstock. This diagram shows the gouge blade's axial rotation (and how it was derived for figure 6.75), and the blade's presentation in plan for cutting at any gradient. The diagram is not derived from mathematical formulae, but does provide solutions which are graphic, and which work. Keep it in mind as you study the photographs in this section.

The green lines are normals at 90° to the tangents to the curve. The red lines show the directions in which the gouge flute should point. To cut with side rake and reduce subsurface damage, you rotate the gouge "into the cut". The blue lines show the corresponding blade presentations in plan.

Consider cutting at point **X** where the curve's gradient is at 60° to the horizontal. The flute should point along red line **X-P**, and the blade should be angled in plan along blue line **Q-R**.

There are too many variables to allow the the tilt of the blade in elevation when looking from the tailstock to be determined simply. If you present the gouge nose too high at the start a cut, the nose will tend to skid away from the cove. If you start the gouge too low it will tend to skid into the cove. The Darlow diagram will give you a clear idea of how to present a detail gouge, but only through practice will you gain consistency and confidence.

Profile

Angle of gouge flute

Normal to profile

Plan angle of gouge blade

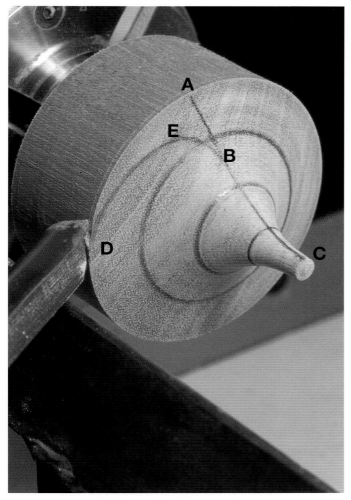

Figure 6.77 The paths of a gouge tip during the cutting of a cove.

Imagine that the half cove in this photograph was at the bottom of a deep, "U"-shaped cove. To cut the left-hand side of the "U", you would start by cutting down the vertical side to **A**. The cut would then continue along **ABC** to the bottom. If you were cutting just the semicircular cove, you could not start to cut at **A** as if the gouge had just cut down the vertical side of the "U" because the lower part of the cutting edge would catch and yank the gouge tip to the left. You can however start the cut with certainty at **D** if you present the gouge in a specific way. The ideal path for the gouge tip to follow then is **DEBC**. If you traversed the gouge tip along a lower path than **DEBC**, you would be cutting with excessive clearance and with probably less side rake and would produce an inferior surface. The cut along path **DEBC** is shown in figures 6.78 to 6.82, and is the same as cut **7** in figure 6.66.

Figure 6.78 Starting a final coving cut from the left.

For a stable and controlled start you must present the gouge tip (at **D** in figure 6.77) with the gouge flute pointing horizontally to the right, the bevel square to the lathe axis in plan, and the gouge's axis pointing exactly at the lathe axis. If you do not have these three criteria correct, especially the first and the third, a catch is likely.

Figure 6.79 Thrusting the gouge forwards and upwards.
You hardly axially rotate the gouge during this first part of the cut. Note that the bevel is no longer exactly square in plan. Its correct orientation in plan is given in figure 6.76. Do not move the gouge handle to the left in order to lever off the heel of the bevel—this will damage the rim of the cove and lead to a rippled surface.

Figure 6.80 The tip is at E, the high point on its path. At no time during this cut should the bevel heel contact the cove's surface

Figure 6.81 The tip is at B.

Figure 6.82 Completing the cut at C. The blade is square to the lathe axis in plan and the flute points about 30° clockwise from the vertical to give 45° side-rake cutting. Here as throughout, the tip is high on the wood to minimize the clearance.

Figure 6.83 Starting to cut a cove. The start of cut **1** in figure 6.66.

This and the following 15 figures to 6.98 show how to cut a semicircular cove.

Use the stance shown in figure 6.6, it will allow you to make the necessary large body movements between and during coving cuts. Take the shaking-hands grip with your right hand with the gouge flute facing up, and retain this grip throughout the series of coving cuts. Your left hand should adopt a looser version of the tied-underhand grip; a grip which positions the blade, while allowing it to slide through and rotate within. The flute should face about 45° clockwise from the vertical, but this angle should be bigger with deep, narrow coves, and smaller with wide, shallow coves.

Figure 6.84 At the end of cut 1 (and cuts **3**, **5**, and **7**), the shoulder zone of the cutting edge should be cutting horizontally with about 45° side rake. The blade is square to the lathe axis in plan and the flute should point at 30° to the vertical. You should not cut up the right-hand side of the cove.

Figure 6.85 Starting cut 2 from the right.
The gouge's starting presentation should be the same as that at the start of cut **1** (figure 6.83), only transposed right for left.

Figure 6.86 Completing cut 2.
The gouge should be positioned as it was at the completion of cut **1** (figure 6.84), only transposed right for left.

Figure 6.87 Starting cut 3. Compared with the start of cut **1**, the tool tip should be a little lower on the wood, the flute should point a little lower, and the blade should be a little less square in plan.

Figure 6.89 Starting cut 5.

Figure 6.88 Starting cut 4.

Figure 6.90 Completing cut 5.

Figure 6.91 Starting cut 6.

Figure 6.93 Cut 7 in progress.

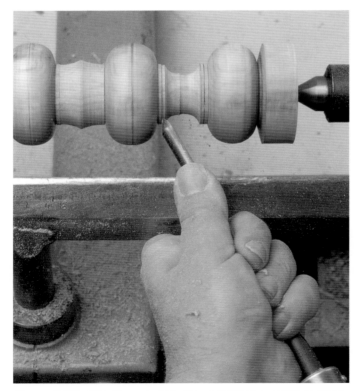

Figure 6.92 Starting cut 7. Figure 6.78 shows this in close up.

Figure 6.94 Completing cut 7.

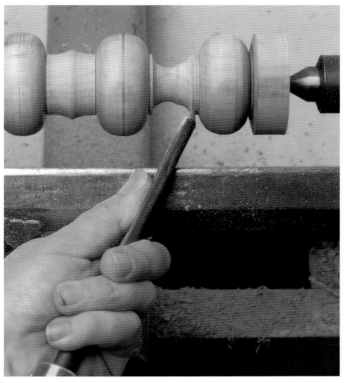

Figure 6.95 Starting cut 8.

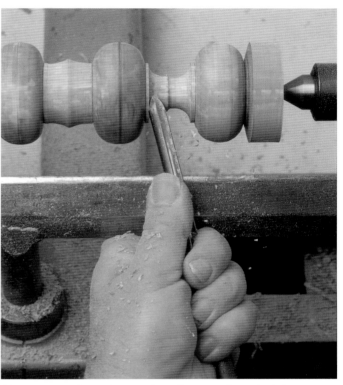

Figure 6.97 Starting a trimming cut from the left to correct the cove's shape.

Figure 6.96 Completing cut 8.

You will not always achieve your intended cove profile without having to make one or two trimming cuts as shown in figures 6.97 and 6.98.

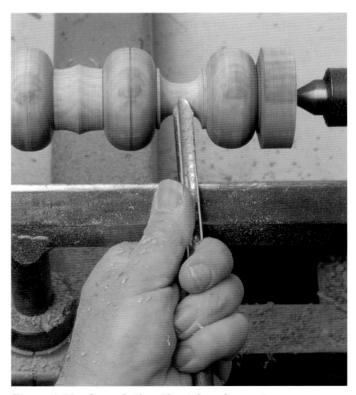

Figure 6.98 Completing the trimming cut.

EXERCISE 6.5   MAKING A TURNING TOOL HANDLE

Techniques taught   Selecting the optimum sequence of cuts
Facing a radial end-grain surface
Axial boring
Calipering to diameter
Undercutting
Finish-turning shallow curves
Sanding

Tools used   Roughing gouge
Wide skew chisel
Parting tool
Calipers
Jacobs chuck on arbor, and suitable twist drill(s)
Abrasive paper and/or cloth

Workpieces   Approximately 2 in x 2 in (50 mm x 50 mm), 13-in (325-mm) long

Figure 6.99 shows a selection of handles; figure 6.100 shows handle design details and defines the turning procedure I recommend. It's usual to make a few handles at a time, so make a pencil gauge. Modify the design to suit the ferrules you have and your own preferences. Make your handles in different tough woods and with different detailing to aid tool selection.

Although a tool handle is a simple exercise, you can order the component operations in several ways: if you have a horizontal or vertical boring machine you can bore the tang hole(s) before the turning; if boring in the lathe, the bit can be held in the tailstock or the headstock spindle; you can caliper with different tools and in different orders; and you can fit the ferrule early or late. The order shown in this exercise is efficient and uses in-lathe boring. How you order the component operations of each of your future projects is an important part of its design.

In spindle turning you rough first, then do all the cutting that you can with a skew chisel. You then complete the turning with a detail gouge before sanding. This order of roughing gouge, skew, detail gouge is efficient because each tool is used once only. However for more-complicated turnings you may have to use more than three tools, some more than once, and in a less-straightforward order.

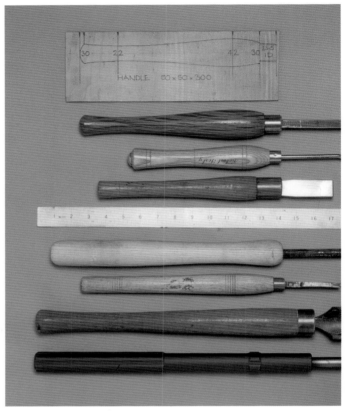

Figure 6.99   A selection of handles. *Top to bottom:* the pencil gauge for the handle immediately below; the handle made in this exercise; a small handle by Robert Sorby; a home-made handle; a Kangaroo-brand handle by Robert Sorby; a hook-tool handle by Kurt Johansson, larger in diameter and with an off-the-tool finish to help resist twisting forces; a home-made handle for a 2-in (50-mm) roughing gouge; the aluminum handle of a Glaser HiTEC bowl gouge which contains lead shot.

Take into account when you make your pencil gauge: the ferrule size (figure 6.100), the dimensions of the wood you wish to use, and your expected tool usage—if your work will usually be large, make your handles a little heavier and longer, and vice versa. Handles for hollow-turning tools are usually larger in diameter and much longer (see section 10.3).

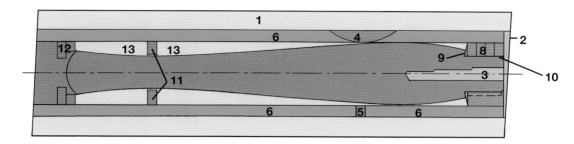

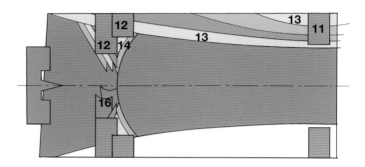

Figure 6.100 The detailing and cutting sequence for a handle. The longitudinal section is taken along a diagonal through the square cross-section. The enlarged longitudinal section shows two methods of finish-turning the left-hand end.

You can buy ferrules from turning suppliers, or you can cut them from brass or steel tube (copper is too soft). Ferrule diameters are typically between 3/4 and 1 1/2 in (20 to 35 mm). Allow about 5/16 in (8 mm) of wood between the tang and the ferrule. The length of a ferrule should be about two-thirds of its outside diameter. Take care to cut ferrule ends square and deburr them. Your tubing supplier may be willing to saw your purchase into ferrule lengths for an extra charge. You can cut and deburr ferrules in your woodturning lathe at its lowest speed if you have a suitable scroll or collet chuck.

After making the pencil gauge, cut the workpiece to length allowing at least 3/4 in (20 mm) of waste length and a minimum of 1/4 in (6 mm) of excess thickness. Punch the centers, and mount the blank in the lathe, ideally using a cone tail center. I suggest that you then turn the handle using the sequence below (the numbers of the instructions correspond with the numbers in this figure):

1. Rough the square cross-sectioned workpiece to the largest-diameter cylinder.
2. Face the right-hand end using shoulder-squaring cuts which stop just short of the tail center nose.
3. Bore the tang hole, and remount the workpiece back in the lathe.
4. Caliper the maximum diameter with a roughing gouge.
5. Alternatively caliper the maximum diameter with a parting tool.
6. Rough down to the maximum finished diameter of the handle. Slow the traverse and use 45° side rake where the periphery of the cylinder will form part of the handle's finished surface.
7. Mark out the handle from the pencil gauge.
8. Caliper the ferrule spigot.
9. Undercut at the left-hand end of the ferrule spigot so that the ferrule will seat nicely. Trim away any waste with your skew's short point.
10. Cut a tiny bevel at the ferrule spigot's right-hand end with your skew's short point. Then trial fit the ferrule. Once the fit is correct, hammer the ferrule on using another as a mandrel to drive the first ferrule home.
11. Caliper the smallish diameter where the hand will grip, and the diameter almost at the handle's left-hand end.
12. Part down to define the handle's left-hand end to a diameter of about 3/4 in (20 mm). Steps 11 and 12 are done after the ferrule is fitted because you should need to hammer on the workpiece's left-hand end to drive the

ferrule home.

13. Rough the body of the handle to near its final profile. Then plane the finished shape with a skew chisel, always cutting from larger diameter to smaller. It is better to plane with a roughing gouge presented with 45° side rake if the grain is non-axial.
14. Partially roll the handle's left-hand end with the skew chisel.
    Retract the tail center just a touch to prevent the wood immediately to the left of the end of the handle from crushing as you reduce its diameter. Use a combination of V-cuts and rolling cuts to make space and finish-turn the end of the handle. The end of the handle will show crushing damage if you don't make enough space to the left of your finishing cuts. To do this you need to leapfrog finishing and space-clearing cuts. Stop the lathe when the waste is down to about 5/16 in (8 mm) in diameter. Remove the handle from the lathe, saw or chisel through the waste, and pare off the stub. Finally, fit the blade, and polish the handle if you elected to do it out of the lathe.
15. Sand, and do any in-lathe polishing.

There is a spindle-turning technique called parting off (**16** above and figure 6.112) which you could use instead of **14** above. It is a technique which you should not attempt until you are reasonably competent because if you perform it poorly the workpiece can be thrown out. In parting off you separate the workpiece from the left hand waste while the lathe is running by V-cutting with a skew's long point or by parting through with a parting-off tool. There is little to be gained by parting off in spindle turning unless you put the next workpiece into the lathe with it still running. This second technique is better learnt under supervision.

To fit the handle, insert the tang into the tang hole. With the blade pointing vertically upwards, bang the back end of the handle down hard onto the floor. To remove a blade from a handle, hold the tip of the blade, and accelerate and slide a heavy scraper or roughing gouge flute down along the blade at the ferrule.

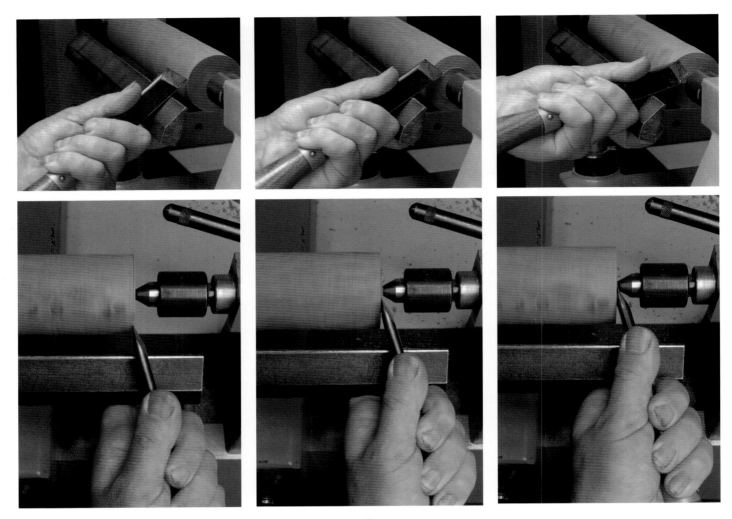

Figure 6.101 Facing the ferrule end of the handle (cut 2).

Cutting to finish-turn a flat, end-grain surface perpendicular to the lathe axis is often termed facing or facing off. Where a small-diameter section projects from the flat face, the process is often termed squaring a shoulder. You use a skew's long point, start it fairly high on the workpiece periphery, and push it along a descending arc which would finish at the lathe axis but for the presence of the tail center. If you looked from the tailstock, at the start of a cut the skew blade would be angled at about 30° above a radius from the lathe axis to the top of the toolrest. If you start the long point too high it will cut poorly, and cut radially outwards, not inwards.

During a facing cut the facing, here left-hand, bevel must follow a path exactly square to the lathe axis. To achieve this you must control and power the cut with your left hand. You may need to grip the skew further back from the rest than usual with your left hand if the facing cut is long. If you use your right hand to do more than steady the tool handle, it will tend to push the handle to the left, align the blade squarer to the lathe axis, and force the facing bevel heel against the wood surface faced earlier in the cut. As this happens the tool will start to vibrate, the noise level will increase, and a spirally-rippled and even charred surface will result.

Facing cuts must no more than 1/16-in (1 1/2-mm) thick. The thinner the better. Thick shavings tend to remain attached and will then force the long point deeper into the face.

When, as here, the face or shoulder faces right, you should tilt the cutting edge a touch clockwise from vertical. Start with 5° clearance although it will tend to spear the long point to the left. As you become more confident reduce the clearance to 1° or 2°.

After facing the workpiece's right-hand end, stop the lathe, and remove the workpiece and the toolrest from the lathe before setting up to bore the tang hole.

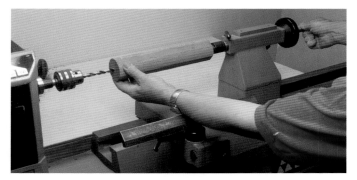

Figure 6.102 Boring the tang hole with a twist drill held in a Jacobs chuck.

Put the lathe to a low speed, almost fully retract the tailstock ram, and twist the Jacobs chuck arbor hard into the headstock swallow. When choosing the drill diameter(s), allow for the wood to be compressed when the tang is driven in. The harder the wood, the less compression you should allow. Lock the appropriate drill in the chuck. Put a piece of tape on the drill to mark the hole depth. Locate the cone-shaped hole in what was the tailstock end of the workpiece on the end of the drill. Locate the tail center in the hole left by the driving center's center pin and and lock the tailstock to the bed. Start the lathe, and stop the workpiece rotating with your left hand while winding the workpiece to the left with your right hand. Withdraw the workpiece frequently so that the bit doesn't jam.

If you are using more than one bit to produce a stepped hole, drill in order of decreasing diameter, but take care with centering.

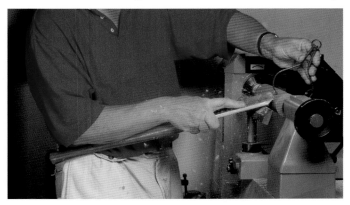

Figure 6.103 Calipering with a roughing gouge (cut **4** in figure 6.100).

After boring, remount the workpiece with the just-bored hole located over your cone tail center. A cone center is preferred because it ensures that the bored hole is centered on the lathe axis. You should then skim the cylinder truly round using roughing-gouge traversing cuts. If you are a beginner, use a parting tool and calipers to set the handle's maximum finished diameter (figure 6.107). However it is quicker to caliper the maximum diameter with a roughing gouge when you are more competent.

You should hold any tool you use with calipers beneath your right forearm so that if the tool tip catches the handle cannot be jerked upwards and hit you. You should also hold the tool well forwards for greater control. I am holding the adjusting knob of the calipers between my fore- and second fingers to prevent vibration changing the calipers' setting.

Figure 6.104 Calipering with a roughing gouge, cutting down from the left.

When you caliper with a roughing gouge you have to turn a shallow cove. It is better to do this with a skewed cutting edge.

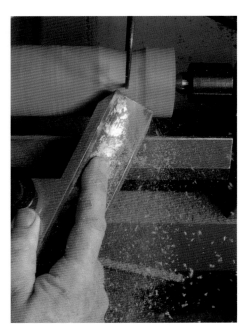

Figure 6.105 Calipering with a roughing gouge, cutting down from the right.

You can skew the cutting edge so that the blade points from right to left as you cut down from the right. I often, however, keep the edge presentation I used for the previous cut from the left.

If you caliper near the position of the maximum diameter, you need only caliper that diameter once. You then bring the whole workpiece down to that diameter by eye. When a workpiece is long or diameters are more critical, caliper more often. Planing the cylinder with a skew after roughing and before marking out would serve no useful purpose here.

Figure 6.106 Marking out the handle (cut **7**).
I use dark lines where I'm going to cut in or V-cut. I use faint lines at maximum diameters where I must not cut in.

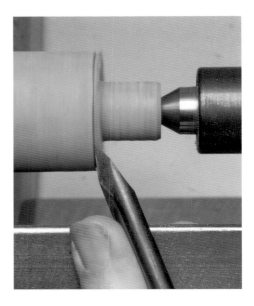

Figure 6.107 Calipering the ferrule spigot to diameter with a parting tool and vernier calipers (cut **8** in figure 6.100).

Hold the tool well forwards and beneath your forearm as in figure 6.103. The blade should be square to the lathe axis in plan. Exert a strong axial thrust to keep the clearance angle small and the tip supported. By rocking the blade from side to side on its bottom edge during the cut you widen the groove. This lessens the chance of the wood grabbing the tool tip, and allows you to safely part deeper.

If you need to skim the spigot, plane towards the left, sliding the blade forwards as you approach the shoulder to bring the cutting down to the short point.

Figure 6.108 Undercutting the shoulder to the left of the ferrule spigot with a skew's long point (cut **9** in figure 6.100). The cutting edge is tilted more clockwise and the handle is held further to the right than for a shoulder-squaring cut.

Figure 6.109 Trimming away the waste left after the undercutting with the short point.

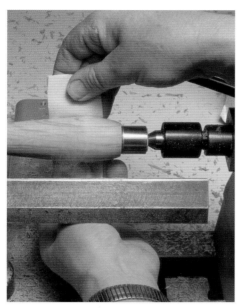

Figure 6.110 Sanding with one hand beneath the workpiece.

Sanding was introduced in section 5.4. There are two related methods for sanding spindles. This one has one hand beneath the workpiece and the other above. The lower hand pulls to prevent the triple-folded quarter sheet being carried away by the rotating wood. Keep the abrasive moving to and fro along the workpiece.

I advise you to remove the toolrest when sanding. Commercial turners usually don't, but they are aware of the risk of having a thumb dragged down between the workpiece and the toolrest, and keep their hands clear.

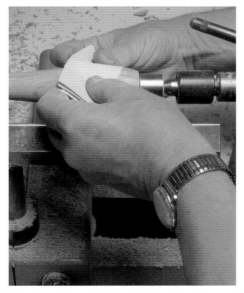

Figure 6.111 Sanding with both hands above the workpiece.

For this second method of sanding spindles you usually face the headstock. Your far hand pulls to prevent the abrasive being thrown forwards.

Figure 6.112 Parting off the handle.

You can part off this handle as it is light in weight and fully turned. The technique is quick and should leave a left-hand end with an excellent finish. As advised towards the end of the figure 6.100 legend, don't try this technique until you are a reasonably competent turner.

When you have parted down to where the left-hand end of the handle is held by a pin of about 5/16 in (8 mm) diameter, retract the tail center until the drive center is just driving. Then hold the skew or parting-off tool under your right forearm, and bring your left arm over, ready to catch the handle when it quietly comes free. (To save working cross-armed some turners part off left-handed). You then continue to part down with V-cuts with the long point or with a parting-off tool until the handle falls free.

EXERCISE 6 6   TURNING A SHORT LEG

Techniques taught

Cutting a flat face at the end of a pommel (a length of square cross-section, left unturned)
Rounding a pommel end
Roughing away from a pommel
Cutting a chamfer
Offset V-cutting
Cutting an offset bead with a vertical face
Cutting an "S"-curve profile
Sanding details

Tools used

Roughing gouge
Wide skew chisel
Medium detail gouge
Calipers
Abrasive papers and/or cloths

Workpieces

Preferably 3 in x 3 in x 10-in long (75 mm x 75 mm x 250-mm long).

The finished leg is shown in figure 6.113 and the cutting sequence in figure 6.114. This exercise introduces most of the remaining spindle-turning cuts, and gives you experience in putting cuts together to produce a turning of greater complexity. You can use these legs for an upholstered stool; either by gluing the pins into drilled holes in a rectangle of thick plywood, or by cutting off the pins and dowelling or morticing rails into the pommels.

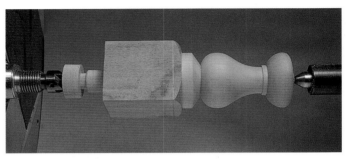

Figure 6.113   A finished leg.
Pommels or squares are usually left unturned so that rails may be easily joined into them. Take care when marking and punching the centers so that the pommel and turned sections will truly align.

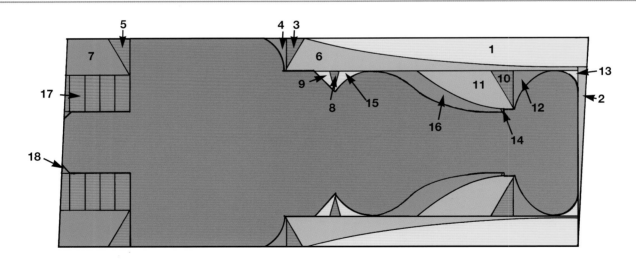

Figure 6.114   The cutting procedure.

The preferred order of spindle-turning tool use is roughing gouge, skew, detail gouge. You have to use a more complicated order for this leg because of the pommel and the pin to its left. The cuts (their numbers correspond with the numbering in this figure) are listed below:

1. After making the pencil gauge (see figure 6.125), preparing the workpieces, and mounting the first one in your lathe, rough away most of the right-hand waste.
2. Face the right-hand end of the workpiece flat, then mark out the pommel.
3. Cut the right-hand end of the pommel.
4. Round the right-hand end of the pommel.
5. Cut the left-hand end of the pommel.
6. Rough the right-hand turned section to a cylinder.
7. Rough the left-hand turned section to a cylinder.
8. V-cut.
9. Cut the chamfer with the short point.
10. Offset V-cut to the top of the fillet.
11. Remove most of the waste from above the ankle.
12. Roll the left-hand side of the foot pad.
13. Roll the right-hand side of the foot pad.
14. Offset V-cut down the left-hand side of the fillet.
15. Roll the left-hand part of the "S" curve.
16. Plane and slide cut the ankle.
17. Part down to the top of the pin.
18. Chamfer the end of the pin.
19. Sand.

Figures 6.115 to 6.134 show how to turn the leg.

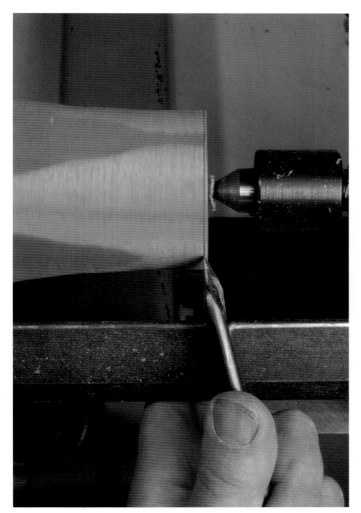

Figure 6.115   Facing the right-hand end of the workpiece (cut 2). *Facing,* a form of offset V-cutting, was described in figure 6.101.

If you have not sawn the workpieces' right-hand ends exactly square, you will need to face them flat and perpendicular to the lathe axis first to provide a proper reference from which to mark out the pommels.

It is easier to face a cylindrical end than one of square cross-section. Therefore cut away much of the right-hand waste using the roughing cuts shown in exercise 6.1 before facing the end.

If you have sawn the workpieces' right-hand ends square, you can mark both ends of all the pommels before you start the turning. You square one pencil line to mark a flat pommel end, and two lines if an end is convex (figure 6.117). On paler woods you only need to mark these lines on one side of the workpiece. On small turnings where you don't need to face an end, start turning by cutting the ends of the pommels (figure 6.116). On large turnings you might start by roughing away most of the corner waste to lessen vibration.

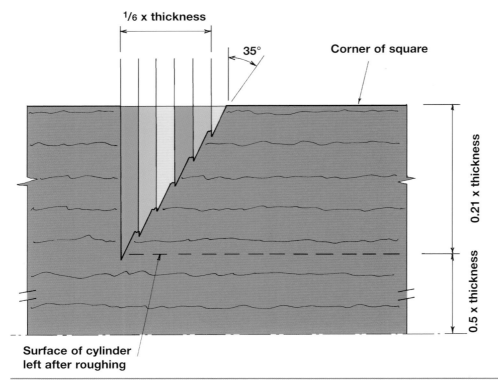

1/6 x thickness

35°

Corner of square

0.21 x thickness

0.5 x thickness

Surface of cylinder
left after roughing

Figure 6.116 **Cutting the end of a pommel.** A radial, longitudinal section through the corner of a square cross-section workpiece showing the cuts (cut **3** of figure 6.114).

You use a series of offset V-cuts. The cuts are almost identical to the facing cuts shown in figures 6.101 and 6.115, except that it is better to start each cut with the long point a little lower. Each offset V-cut penetrates a little deeper than the previous one, but you should not swing the long edge below the radius from the lathe axis to the top of the toolrest. These cuts must be thin.

The line joining the bottoms of your offset V-cuts may not be at 35° to the vertical. Its gradient will depend on the sharpening angle of your skew, and on the penetration and thickness of each cut.

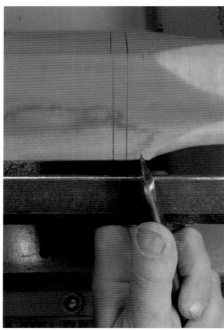

Figure 6.117 The first cut for the right-hand end of the pommel.

The right-hand face of the pommel is here defined by two lines not one because it is to be convex not flat (figures 6.120 and 6.121).

The first cut is little more than a nick. If you force these cuts the long point will be diverted from its ideal path. Each cut should feel smooth, especially when the long point starts to cut mainly wood rather than air. If you are pushing the heel of the facing bevel against the end of the pommel, the tool will vibrate, the cut will be noisy, and the end of the pommel will be rippled.

Figure 6.118 Starting the final cut to form a flat pommel end.

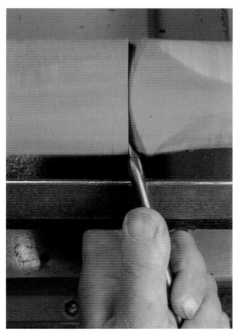

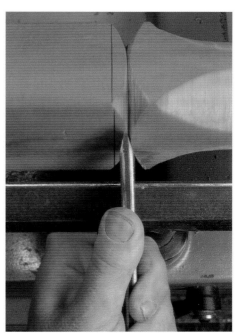

Figure 6.119 **Completing the final cut** started in the previous figure.

The forward thrust with the left hand has caused the contact point between the skew and the toolrest to move to the right while the skew's left-facing bevel remains exactly square in plan to the lathe axis. The skew's long edge has arced down through about 20° to lie along the radius connecting the lathe axis to the top of the toolrest.

After cutting the right-hand end of the pommel flat, you round it using a series of rolling cuts with the short point (figures 6.120 and 6.121). You could also use a detail gouge.

Figure 6.121 **Completing the final rolling cut** started in the previous figure.

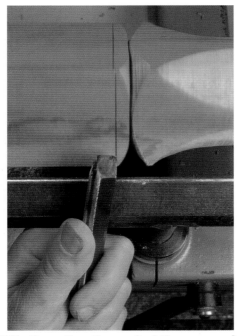

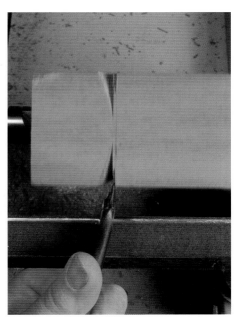

Figure 6.122 **Cutting the left-hand square face of the pommel** (cut **5**).

After cutting the right-hand face of the pommel, cut the left-hand face flat and perpendicular to the lathe axis.

Figure 6.120 **Rounding the end of the pommel.**
Starting a final rolling cut (cut **4**). This cut is taken on the short point

Figure 6.123 **Starting a roughing cut** to the right of the pommel (cut **6**).

You can rough away from a pommel or other upstanding surface with a roughing gouge. Start each traversing cut with the blade square to the lathe axis in plan and the gouge axially rotated so that the cutting edge adjacent to the pommel is horizontal. You then roll and traverse the gouge until it is in the usual traversing presentation (figure 6.124). Rough down until you have just cut the flats away and the whole surface is cylindrical. You also use this technique to rough to the left of the pommel.

Figure 6.124 **Traversing to the left** (cut **6**).

When you have rolled and traversed the gouge into this presentation, stop rolling but continue to traverse.

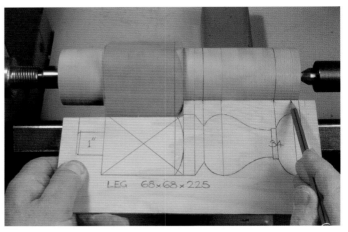

Figure 6.125 **Marking out.**

The top edge of the pencil gauge has been checked out so that it clears the rotating pommel. I have pencilled heavy lines where I shall V-cut, and light lines at other reference points.

Figure 6.126 **Cutting the chamfer** (cut **9**).

Do all the skew chisel work that you can first. I have V-cut to the bottom of the chamfer, taking care to get the depth correct, and am cutting the chamfer's surface to the left of the vee with the short point.

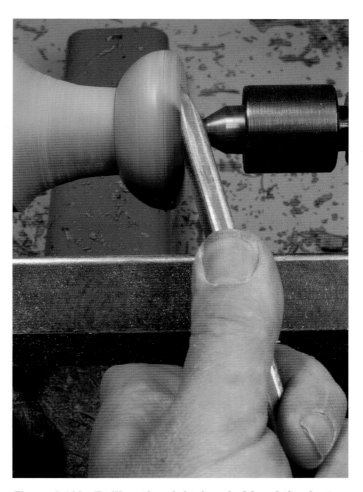

Figure 6.128 Rolling the right-hand side of the foot pad (cut **13**).

The bottom of this half bead is vertical. For the bottom of a rolling cut to be vertical, the facing (here left-hand) bevel must finish in a plane which is perpendicular to the lathe axis. To achieve this you have to move the contact point between the blade and the toolrest further along the toolrest, and roll the cutting edge about 5° past the vertical. This is an exacting cut.

Figure 6.127 Cutting away the waste above the ankle (cut **11**).

The left-hand side of the foot pad is steep. Instead of making a symmetrical V-cut, offset it to the left so that the vee's right-hand face is vertical. Use the same technique that you used to cut the left-hand end of the pommel. Then remove the waste to the left of the foot pad with scooping cuts with the skew. As you axially rotate the skew counterclockwise, you can support the tool tip by levering off the conjunction of the lower bevel, long edge, and lower face. Continue these cuts until you have cut down to produce the cylindrical surface of the fillet. Then roll the left-hand side of the foot pad.

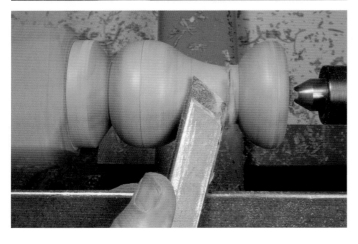

Figure 6.129 Finish-turning the ankle (cut **16**).

After offset V-cutting down the side of the fillet to the left of the foot pad, roll the left-hand side of the "S" curve. Then cut the right-hand side of the "S". You can start these cuts on or back from the short point. When you reach the point of inflexion you should however be planing with the short point exposed. As you traverse the chisel towards the upstanding face of the fillet, thrust the skew forwards to bring the cutting down onto the short point.

This "S" curve is short and shapely, more so and it would be very difficult to plane. You can cut it with a large detail gouge.

Figure 6.130 Planing the ankle (cut **16**). An end view with the fillet and foot pad removed.

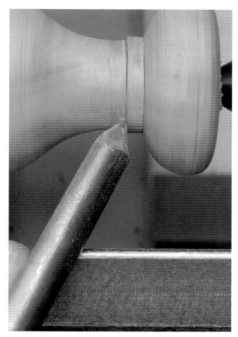

Figure 6.131 Starting to scrape back from the fillet.
If you finish-turn the ankle with a detail gouge you will leave a little waste immediately to the left of the fillet. You can remove this with the gouge. Start cutting with the gouge presented as if you were starting a final coving cut from the right. This presentation is often called *pointing*.

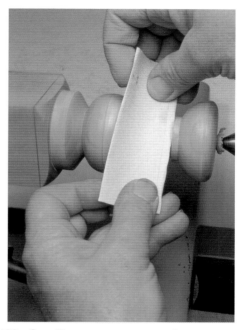

Figure 6.133 Sanding a concave surface.
To sand a concave surface you spring the triple-folded quarter sheet into a curve.

Figure 6.132 Shear scraping the ankle.
From the pointing presentation in the previous figure, pull the tool tip to the left, at the same time rotating it clockwise and thrusting it higher up the wood into a *cutting* presentation.

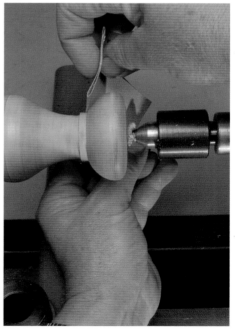

Figure 6.134 Sanding at a sharp change in direction.
To sand without destroying the crisp edges you have cut needs care. Use the folded edge to sand in corners. You can have both hands above the workpiece as in figures 6.111 and 6.133, or one above and one below as here.

EXERCISE 6.7   A HATSTAND SHAFT

Tools used   Roughing gouge, wide skew, 3/8-in
                              (10-mm) detail gouge, parting tool,
                              calipers

Workpieces   2 in x 2 in x 15 in long
                              (50 mm x 50 mm x 380 mm long)

You should clarify and express your design intents through creating the design, making the pencil or other gauges, and doing the turning. By maximizing the functional, aesthetic, and communicative aspects of a turning at its design stage, you will be more likely to create turnings which manifest, communicate, and even refine your intents. In this exercise I shall be seeking to introduce intent and demonstrate how you apply it. I shall show how you can influence the impression that your turning is likely to create in others by seemingly minor adjustments.

This exercise is the spindle component of a woman's hatstand. This spindle or shaft has been designed holistically with the hatstand's top and base, not in isolation. The whole hatstand needs to be stable and look good both with and without a hat on it (figures 6.135 and 6.136). The dimensions are given in figure 6.137. Its turning is described in figures 6.138 to 6.141.

Some project instructions specify diameters at small, regular intervals of length along a spindle. This is valid for patternmaking, but not for hand woodworking. In this exercise some diameters should be calipered, some should be gauged by eye. You should minimize your need to caliper by training your eyes to be active, to compare diameters, to judge depths, diameters and profiles. You also need to understand and appreciate the nuances of your design so that you can previsualize the profile you are about to turn because you know how it relates to the rest of the design. And as you turn your design, you should be experiencing the impressions that you intend others will experience.

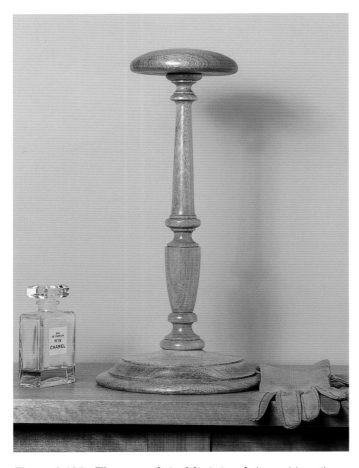

Figure 6.135 The completed hatstand. It combines the shaft from this exercise with the mushroom top from exercise 8.1 and the base from exercise 8.2.

Figure 6.136 The hatstand with a hat. The hat is from the extensive and costly Alice Darlow collection.

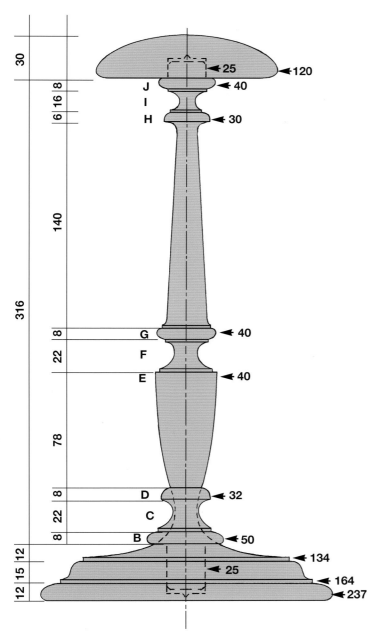

Figure 6.137 The hatstand's design.

This design is late-eighteenth-century English in style, a delightful, almost feminine style which should be popular with most women. The shaft design is appropriately based on a typical bedpost of the period. The base is generous to give real and visual stability, while the mushroom is nicely rounded.

The hatstand design was sketched, and the sketch then gradually refined until it looked right to me. I designed within wood's commercially-available widths and thicknesses. I did not calculate any ratios of the lengths or diameters of the different features of the design, but my guess is that the ratios are complex. Having designed many similar items over the years, the designing went quite quickly. I have through twenty years of study and designing built up a mental library of shapes, details, and relationships. In short the "secret" of successful designing is to work at it. Certainly some are more naturally gifted and may achieve design success more readily, but it is within the reach of all turners.

To make the turning easier, I made the maximum diameters at **E**,**G**, and **J** all 40 mm. The lowest scotia (cove) **C** follows the flow of the lower part of the shaft into the base. The lower a scotia is on the shaft, the greater is its minimum diameter. The minimum diameters in the three scotias are above the centers of their lengths to give visual lift. Similarly the torus (bead) at **B** is offset downwards and those at **G** and **J** are offset upwards, again to reinforce the impressions of support and uplift respectively. At **D** and **H** a cavetto is next to an ovolo. This has more tension than the torus, fillet, cavetto combination used at **G**, and adds to the variety of detailing in the hatstand.

In general the differences between maximum and minimum diameters are large. Fillets are used to add visual definition and crispness. Abrupt changes in direction are at 90° or close to it. Curves are strong and vary in curvature along their lengths. Regions which are detailed are separated by regions of gradual change to give variety.

My aim was to create a lively, delightful design. I have not copied an 18th century design. That my design is in a style which was prevalent in a particular country at a particular time was a means to an end rather than the end in itself. I could have used several other styles which could have been similarly effective. But the modernist or international style of the 20th century with its more limited turning vocabulary is less suited to the impression I wanted this hatstand to create.

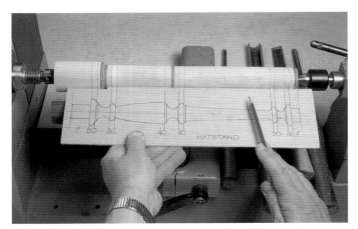

Figure 6.138 Marking out the roughed blank. The gauge has a stepped front edge to allow the 40-mm- and 50-mm-diameter zones to be marked out accurately.

The square blank has been roughed to a stepped cylinder with diameters of 50 mm and 40 mm. I calipered the diameters using a parting tool at the locations indicated by the red rings. These locations are adjacent to but not at points where these surfaces are retained in the finished shaft.

The turning procedure.

You can use your tools in a variety of sequences because the maximum diameters of the shaft's beads and half beads (toruses) are not all the same. I would caliper the 40-mm and 50-mm and 1-in diameters, but eye the 32-mm and the 30-mm diameters. You could carry down the marking out of beads **D** and **H** from the 40-mm surface, or mark them out from your pencil gauge after you have locally reduced the diameters at **D** and **H** to 32 mm and 30 mm respectively. There is not much between the two options, but I shall use the former.

If you cannot get the 50-mm diameter for bead **B** out of your blank, you can reduce the size of part or all of the design, or turn bead **B** as a loose ring in either axially- or radially-grained wood.

Figure 6.139 Slide cutting half bead H down to 30-mm diameter.

I have taken offset V-cuts down to just below the maximum finished diameters of half beads **D** and **H**. To bring **H** down to 30-mm diameter, I slide cut from left to right until I judge that the radius at **H** is 5 mm below the 20-mm radius to its right.

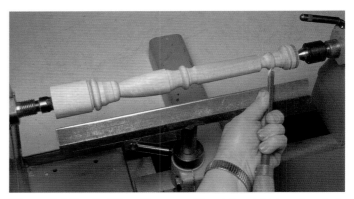

Figure 6.140 Cutting the cavetto at the right-hand end of the tapering section between **G** and **H**.

Figure 6.141 Planing the tapering section between G and H. By this stage the spindle has become slender and will bounce under the tool. To damp this vibration, use your left hand as a steady. By keeping your left thumb in contact with both the toolrest and the skew's long edge you improve the efficiency of your steadying and have more control over the skew.

After planing this section, cut the central hollow **F**, then the hollows at **I** and **C**. Finally cut the shaft's top and bottom pins, and sand.

Chapter Seven

CUPCHUCK TURNING

Knobs, finials, egg cups, scoops, some bowls, and most lidded boxes are cupchuck turned: firstly because they are axially grained like spindles; and secondly because to produce them you need unrestricted access to fully turn, sand, hollow, or bore one end of the workpiece. Workpieces for cupchuck turning are almost always turned inboard with their left-hand ends held rigidly in alignment with the lathe axis by chucks. You shape cupchuck turnings using spindle turning techniques, axial hollowing, and drilling.

7.1 CHUCKING

"Chucking" in the workholding sense was in use by 1869, and I assume derives from its older meaning "throwing". Cupchuck turning is so-called because the workpiece was traditionally held in a cupchuck (figure 7.1) screwed onto the right-hand nose of the headstock spindle. The title has stuck despite the increasing substitution of other chuck types (figures 7.2 to 7.8). All except the screwchuck demand that you preturn a chucking spigot which is left as waste in the chuck after you part off the finished turning.

The holding power of a chuck is related to the contact area between the wood and the chuck. Therefore you usually select the chuck or jaws which accept the largest-feasible-diameter chucking spigot. The hold is also sounder if the wood is compressed radially inwards by the chuck as this overcomes wood's tendency to split along its grain. Hold and chucking concentricity are also improved by preturning a shoulder on the workpiece to bear against the chuck's right-hand vertical surface(s). Only when turning at workpiece projections exceeding 6 to 8 in (150 to 200 mm) should flexing become a problem.

Choosing a Chuck

When you buy a chuck consider:

1. The cost of the chuck.
2. How accurately the chucking spigot has to be turned – cupchucks and collet chucks require them to be turned precisely, scroll chucks have a wide range of adjustment. Collet chucks in part compensate by having collets of different capacities.
3. The availability of accessory jaws, and the ease of converting the chuck from one purpose to another.
4. The diameter of the chuck relative to the workpiece diameter, and the ease and safety of tool access close to the face of the chuck.
5. The chucking spigot diameter(s) and length(s).
6. The chuck's holding power.
7. Whether the chuck permits a workpiece to be readily and accurately rechucked.
8. Whether the chuck has any projections or recesses which can catch a tool or your flesh.
9. The weight of the chuck and the load-bearing capacity of your headstock.
10. The speed and ease of using the chuck.
11. Whether the chuck has a dedicated thread and will only fit one specification of spindle nose, or whether it takes inserts which allow it to be fitted on differently-threaded spindle noses both inboard and outboard.

Besides using proprietary chucks, you will sometimes make wooden chucks, either to save buying a proprietary chuck or because a home-made one is more suitable for that application. The most-common home-made chuck is the press-fit (or jam-fit) chuck used in exercise 7.2. You can make wooden cupchucks (figure 7.1) for occasional use by turning a hole with a diametrical taper of about 1-in-20 in a disk cut from an interlocked-grained hard wood plank screwed onto a faceplate.

A form of chucking which is becoming more used, but is not covered in this book, is vacuum chucking. Atmospheric pressure will force a workpiece against or into a chuck when a cavity adjacent to the workpiece's headstock-facing end or face is evacuated. Although rarely used in cupchuck turning, vacuum chucking may be used to supplement the frictional holding power of a press-fit chuck.

TIP   Mounting a chuck

When you mount a chuck or faceplate, always screw it firmly against the spindle flange. If you don't, when you switch the lathe on the spindle flange will snap against the back of the chuck or faceplate. You will then need to apply massive leverage to remove the accessory.

Figure 7.1 **Cupchucks** with mouth-of-bell diameters from
1 1/2 in (37 mm) to 3 5/8 in (92 mm).

A cupchuck is a straight-tapered bell narrowing towards its
headstock end. To chuck a workpiece, you hammer its chucking
spigot *(top right)* into the bell. The chucking spigot has to be
turned to the same taper as the bell's to hold well (figures 7.11
and 7.12). The 1/4-in (6-mm) distance between the two pencil
lines on the the chucking spigot shown top right illustrates how
far a chucking spigot is typically driven in by hammering (figure
7.13).

The central, vertical turning is an extractor used to drive a
chucking spigot from a bell after the finished turning has been
parted off. Its lower cylindrical section is a sliding fit in the
threaded hole of the cupchuck. The upper section acts as stop
to prevent damage to the cupchuck.

Cupchucks are relatively cheap to buy, hold very well, and
have no dangerous projections. Because they have relatively-
small outside diameters, they enable good tool access to part
off or turn much of an item's left-hand end. Chucking the
workpiece and extracting the waste spigot left in the chuck is a
little more time consuming than with most other chucks, but you
quickly learn to hammer the workpiece into the chuck just hard
enough. The chuck's only disadvantage is that it does not allow
accurate rechucking.

Figure 7.2 **The headstock spindle swallow** as a
cupchuck.

To turn the chucking spigot, caliper the diameters at the
ends of the drive center's taper and replicate them the same
distance apart on the chucking spigot with a parting tool. It is
best to turn the central length of the chucking spigot's taper
slightly waisted so that the taper fits snuggly within the swallow
after a tap. To eject the waste, use the largest-diameter knock-
out bar which will pass through the headstock spindle.

Figure 7.3 **Jacobs chucks** are only suitable for short,
small-diameter workpieces. Be alert for the chuck's arbor to
start to slide out of the spindle swallow. You may find it best to
preturn a cylindrical chucking spigot on the workpiece rather
than whittle a three-sided one.

Figure 7.4 Screwchucks hold poorly in end grain and are therefore restricted to short, smallish-diameter workpieces. Here the left-hand plywood waste disk prevents tool contact with the steel chuck face. The right-hand waste disk was preturned to the diameter of the knob flange, acts as a reference diameter, and allows limited tool access to the left-hand side of the knob flange.

In the foreground are two Glaser screwchucks.

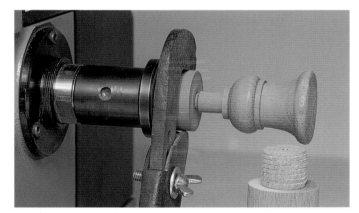

Figure 7.5 The Woodfast Screw Cupchuck invented by Bruce Leadbeatter.

Modelled on a thread-cutting die, it allows accurate rechucking, is compact in diameter, and holds very well through cutting a thread on the workpiece chucking spigot. Screwing in the chucking spigot can be demanding. Leave enough projecting waste to grip when you part off the finished turning so that the chucking spigot can be screwed out.

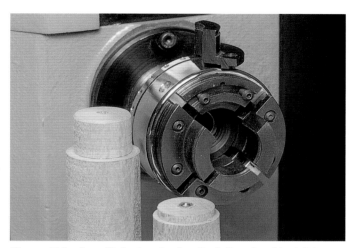

Figure 7.6 A collet chuck, the Craft Supplies Maxi-Grip 2000

Unlike most earlier collet chucks, the Maxi-Grip can grip by contracting onto a spigot or by expanding into a recess. It can hold both axially- and radially-grained workpieces. Jaws of different capacities and for different purposes are available, but their range of radial adjustment is limited. When used for cupchucking, a long cylindrical chucking spigot gives the greatest hold. A short, dovetailed one can be used where the workpiece length is barely sufficient, or where you wish to conserve wood.

Figure 7.7 A lever-operated scroll chuck, the Nova chuck made by Latalex of New Zealand, with 45-mm Spigot (cupchucking) half jaws fitted.

Woodturners' four-jaw scroll chucks have a wide range of adjustment and hold very well. They grip through both expansion and contraction, and have a large range of interchangeable accessory front half jaws which screw onto the rear half jaws which engage with the scroll. The cupchucking half jaws are internally serrated to hold better, and can grip round or square spigots.

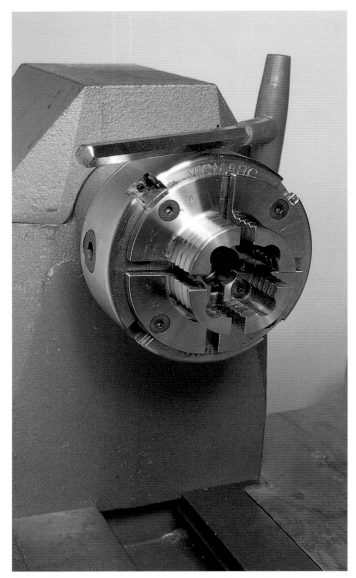

Figure 7.8 A key-operated scroll chuck, the Vicmarc VM 120 with 45-mm Shark (cupchucking) half jaws fitted.

You often feel the need for a third hand when using lever-operated scroll chucks. Key-operated chucks overcome this problem, are heavier and more expensive, but offer the ultimate in chucking convenience and versatility.

Scroll chucks are relatively large in diameter and this can restrict tool access to a workpiece's left-hand end. Their irregular peripheries make them more risky to use than other chuck types, so guarding is advisable—even a short length of car tyre inner tube stretched around greatly reduces the risk.

EXERCISE 7.1   TURNING A PEG

Techniques taught	Chucking with a cupchuck Turning chucking spigots Facing an end square Rolling full beads
Tools required	Cupchuck or other chuck Roughing gouge 1-in (25-mm) skew chisel 1/4-in (6-mm) parting tool 1/2-in (13-mm) detail gouge Outside or vernier calipers Abrasive papers
Workpieces	About 1/4 to 3/8 in (5 to 10 mm) thicker than the peg's maximum diameter, and, depending on your chucking method, about 2 in (50 mm) longer than the peg's length

The techniques and procedure used to turn the peg in figure 7.9 are similar to those needed to turn most items which have their right-hand ends fully turned and sanded. The most-common examples are knobs, finials, handles, and short legs and feet.

You could turn the figure 7.9 pegs between centers. Their mushroom ends could then be hand finished outside the lathe, but would show a central dark patch after polishing where the fibres had been disturbed in a different way from the surrounding "turned" fibres. You could avoid that problem by rechucking each peg by its 1-in (25-mm) spigot to finish-turn and sand the top of each mushroom in the lathe. However in this exercise you should turn all the chucking spigots, then chuck each workpiece once in a cupchuck or other suitable chuck to complete its turning.

Figure 7.9 Coat pegs 3 in (75 mm) long turned from casuarina.

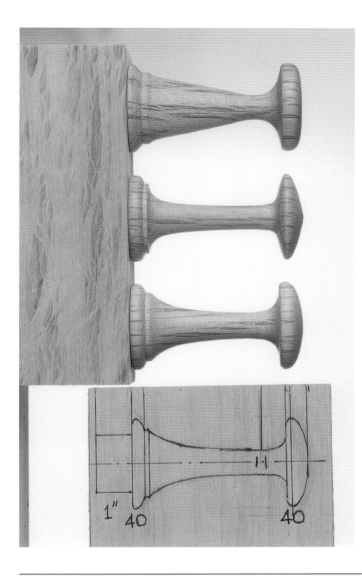

Figure 7.10 **Design clarity.** A finished peg alongside its pencil gauge, and two interpretations which still conform to the setting-out points and diameters specified on the gauge.

Besides teaching you techniques, this exercise emphasizes the concepts of design clarity and intent. The intended peg is pictured on the gauge. Some points on the peg can be definitely established by setting out from the gauge and calipering, but the majority of its surface has to be turned freehand. You could keep checking against templates, but this is slow and difficult. Monitoring against a reference sample mounted immediately behind and above is more efficient. But unless you have a clear understanding of why you have chosen a particular design, your chances of repeating it are slim.

This peg design has clarity, definition, and function. The mushroom is defined without being mean or gobby. The necking immediately to the left of the mushroom defines the mushroom, but does not look likely to snap. The neck then increases in diameter to the left to take the increasing bending moment of a heavy coat. .All curves flow nicely into one another. The fillet distinguishes the flange from the neck, but is not so dominant as to divorce them. The flange has a small half bead on its left to give a discrete shadow line and disguise any lack of planeness in the mounting board. As the flange is skewed it gives the perception that it is actively supporting the cantilevering neck and mushroom. Unless through the design process you have become conscious of the functional, emotional, aesthetic, and communicative intents of your design, the turning process is less likely to be either rewarding or successful.

There is one unsatisfactory aspect in the design. The tangents to the curves immediately above and below the fillet are not parallel. I could have kicked the fillet up and/or varied the curve gradients adjacent to the fillets, but on-paper trials did not yield an improved result, at least to me. And this illustrates an important aspect of design: unless a design is dictated to you, you are the judge. Unless there are failings in the functional area, ultimately your judgement on a design is as valid as anyone else's, even if not necessarily as sound.

Figure 7.11 **The cupchuck bell and chucking spigot** used for this exercise 7.1. All dimensions are in millimeters. You will need to select your most-suitable chuck or chuck/jaw combination. The diameter(s) of the chucking spigot held within the chuck jaws or bell should be as large as possible so that workpiece flexing is minimized. You may be able to use a larger chuck or jaws if you leave small flats on the spigot. Establish the correct diameter(s) and calipering position(s) for your chucking spigot using this figure as a guide. Make a pencil gauge for the peg similar to that shown in figure 7.10.

Calculate the required length of the peg blanks. To the total finished length of the peg you will need to add the length of the chucking spigot appropriate to your chuck, an allowance for parting off, the length of the penetration of the drive center pin into the blank, and 1/8 in (3 mm) for the facing cuts numbered **4** in figure 7.14 which are made to the right of the mushroom.

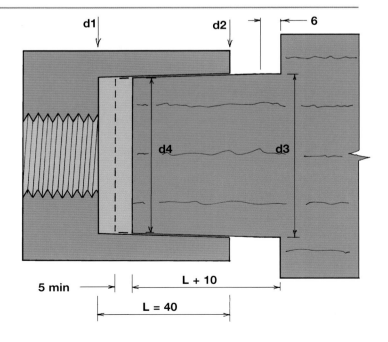

Figure 7.12 Turning the chucking spigot. Rolling away the roughing gouge after parting to diameter **d3** defined in figure 7.11.

It is better to preturn the chucking spigots on all the blanks first. Mount each blank between centers and rough almost to a cylinder—this is so that if the blank is not later cupchucked truly axially, you should still be able to achieve the peg's full diameter. You can caliper and turn the chucking spigots at the tailstock end by several methods:

For a cylindrical chucking spigot. Use a succession of adjacent parting tool cuts with calipering. Alternatively, you can caliper just at one or both ends of the spigot and remove the remaining waste using a roughing gouge, detail gouge, or skew. The parting tool should leave a serviceable finish on the shoulder, but you can skim it clean and vertical with a skew's long point so that it can be better butted against the face of the chuck to improve the hold and workpiece alignment.

For a tapered chucking spigot. You can caliper once, and monitor the taper by comparing it to your pencil gauge or to a correct sample as in this figure. Alternatively you can caliper at both ends of the taper. It is a good idea to trial fit each spigot until you are confident of getting them correct. If the chucking spigot bottoms in the your cupchuck bell, it is too small in diameter. If its taper does not match that of the bell, the hold will be poor. If the tapered chucking spigot is too narrow, saw it a little shorter—it may now fit even without returning.

You do not need to turn a clean, vertical shoulder to the left of the chucking spigot for a cupchuck. Once you have mastered calipering with a parting tool followed by removing the waste with a roughing gouge, try doing both operations with a roughing gouge. You form a rough shoulder by digging the left-hand corner of the roughing gouge into the wood, and then roll the gouge away clockwise to the right to remove the waste.

Figure 7.13 Hammering in the workpiece.
One crisp blow is usually sufficient. Try to drive the chucking spigot in axially. The bottom end of the cupchuck is protected from the concrete by a piece of waste wood. The chucking spigot extractor described in figure 7.1 is in the foreground.

Figure 7.14 The sequence of cuts for turning the peg.
It is desirable to conform to spindle turning's preferred order of tool usage (roughing gouge, skew, detail gouge). However the need to preserve workpiece stiffness to the left of the area being turned takes precedence. You therefore work from right to left, and would not, for example, turn the neck to the left of the mushroom before turning the mushroom.

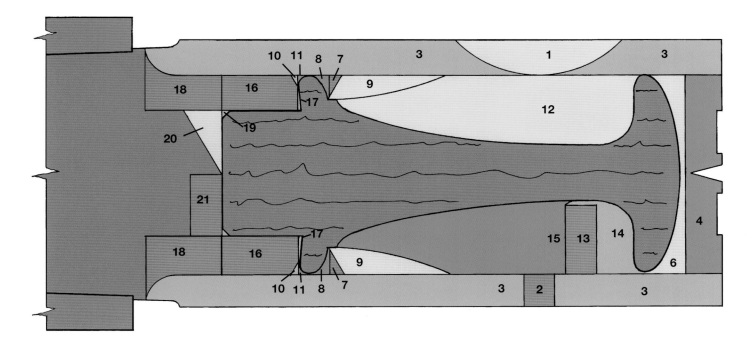

The order of the cuts I recommend to turn the peg is indicated by the numbering in the drawing. The cuts are described below and are correspondingly numbered.

1. Calipering to the peg's outside diameter using a roughing gouge.

Or

2. Calipering to the peg's outside diameter with a parting tool. You don't need to allow any waste diameter if you don't caliper exactly at the rim of the mushroom or flange.

Then

3. Traversing to a cylinder with a roughing gouge, increasing the side rake and decreasing the shaving thickness as you approach the final diameter. Do not be too heavy with these cuts or you may force the workpiece out of axial alignment.

4. Facing cuts (figure 7.15) to remove the drive center's imprint. About 1/16-in (1-mm) thickness of waste is left so that the whole front of the mushroom can be later formed by one final rolling cut and thus have a uniform surface.

5. Marking out from the pencil gauge pictured in figure 7.10.

6. Rolling the front of the mushroom with a detail gouge (figures 7.16 to 7.18) or a skew (figure 7.19).

7. Offset V-cutting almost down to the top of the fillet, leaving a little waste to the right of the bottom of the bead.

8. Rolling cut(s) with a skew to form the offset half bead.

9. Slide cuts with the skew's short point to form the fillet.

10. Offset V-cutting.

11. Fine rolling cut(s) with the skew.

Then

12. Coving cuts with a detail gouge. Concentrate on turning the back of the mushroom first before reducing the stiffness of the shank.

Or instead of 12

13. Parting down with calipers, allowing a little thickness to trim away the disturbed wood.

14. Cutting the back of the mushroom with a detail gouge

15. Forming the shank with a detail gouge. Forming it with a skew is also a possibility.

After 12 or 15 you would sand. Then

16. Parting down with calipers and a parting tool to form the pin.

17. Undercutting with a skew's long point.

18. Parting down into the waste to make room for parting off

19. Cutting a lead-in bevel with either the skew or the parting tool.

Then

20. Parting off with the skew's long point.

Or

21. Parting off with a parting tool or a parting-off tool.

Then

22. Extract the waste chucking spigot. After parting off the finished turning, stop the lathe. Remove the cupchuck from the lathe. Hold the cupchuck with its bell pointing down, insert the narrow section of the extractor (figure 7.1) down through the chuck's threaded hole, and hammer the top of the extractor to expel the waste.

Figure 7.15   Facing the end. (Cuts numbered **4** in figure 7.14).

    The workpiece has been turned to the diameter of the mushroom and flange. The right-hand end of the workpiece still contains the imprint of the drive center. Remove this using shoulder-squaring (often called facing) cuts. Push the long point along an arc descending to the lathe axis. As with other similar cuts already described in exercises 6.5 and 6.6, you need to arc the left hand and tool forwards as a single unit to maintain the skew's left-hand bevel in the correct presentation, square to the lathe axis in plan and in an almost vertical plane.

    After facing off the driving center imprint, mark out the peg from the pencil gauge allowing about 1/16 in (1 mm) of waste to the right of the mushroom. The mushroom top's finished surface can then be rolled in one finishing cut (figures 7.16 to 7.18, or 7.19).

Figure 7.16 Starting to roll the mushroom. (Cuts numbered **6** in figure 7.14). At the start of the final rolling cut with a detail gouge present the blade square to the lathe axis in plan with its flute facing 30° clockwise from the vertical.

You can roll the right-hand face of the mushroom with a skew or a detail gouge. Practice both. It is less risky to use the gouge where the mushroom is flattened rather than being near-hemispherical.

You should use a series of rolling cuts to form the mushroom top. The first just takes off the corner. Each succeeding cut involves more rotation and more horizontal and vertical movement of the gouge nose. Ideally the depth of cut should be approximately constant throughout a cut, and should tend to decrease through the series.

Figure 7.17 Continuing to roll. To keep a zero clearance presentation as the cut proceeds, you will need to thrust the gouge forwards, roll it clockwise, and move its handle to the right.

Figure 7.18 Completing the final rolling cut.
When you complete the cut, the gouge axis should point at
the lathe axis, the flute should point horizontally to the right, and
the bevel must be square to the lathe axis in plan. This presentation is identical to that used at the start of a final coving cut
from the left (see exercise 6.4).

Figure 7.19
Rolling the mushroom with a skew. This rolling cut is the final cut of the series, and is similar to that used to form the right-hand half-bead of the stub leg in exercise 6.6. The left-hand bevel should lie in a plane perpendicular to the lathe axis at the end of the cut. You therefore have to rotate the blade about 4 1/2° past the vertical, and move its contact point with the toolrest well to the right.

To complete the peg you then work basically from right to left, using the sequence of cuts described in figure 7.14.

EXERCISE 7.2   A LIDDED BOX

Techniques taught   Making waste allowances
                          Parting through
                          Hollowing
                          Fitting spigots to sockets
                          Reverse chucking

Tools required   Roughing gouge
                          1-in (25-mm) skew chisel
                          Medium detail gouge
                          Parting tool
                          Parting-off tool (optional)
                          Scraper(s) (see figure 7.26)
                          Inside and outside calipers
                          Abrasive papers

Workpieces   Square in cross-section,
                          approximately
                          5 in (125 mm) longer than the
                          height of the box, and 1/4 to
                          3/8 in (6 to 10 mm) greater in
                          thickness than the diameter

Wood for Boxes

Wood for boxes needs to be selected with care. Loose and soft woods tend to crush when being hollowed, so prefer a harder, crisp-turning wood. The wood must also be fully-seasoned if you wish the box lid and base to fit well long-term. Even then stability is not assured. Seasoned wood is usually damper inside than near the surface, and is often internally stressed. Therefore during and after the hollowing and external shaping, the wood remaining as the base and lid will season further and warp. And the internal stresses in equilibrium in the original blank will relax into new equilibriums causing further warping. These processes take hours or days depending on the circumstances. Therefore when making lidded boxes of the highest quality, and especially of larger diameters, it is best to preturn the lid and base with thick walls, dechuck them without parting off, allow them to further season and stabilize, and then rechuck them for finish-turning. As cupchucks are ill suited to rechucking, prefer a different chuck type. Intermediate seasoning is omitted in the steps for this exercise, and the chuck used is, but does not have to be, a scroll type.

Figure 7.20   The finished box, its pencil gauge, and internal templates.

You should practice turning a specific box, not just any one. The gauge and templates will help you to achieve the desired shapes consistently. Using the templates will confirm that a hollow always looks wider across its bottom than it really is.

This box is similar to a natsume, a Japanese tea box. The design at the junction of the top and base in this exercise differs slightly from that used in natsumes, but is the simplest and the most commonly used. The lid's rim is usually made thicker than the base's spigot because during the turning and in later use the rim is put into circumferential tension whereas the spigot is put into circumferential compression.

Preparing the Blank

You need to allow the three types of extra length shown in figure 7.21 in a lidded box blank:

Chucking spigots   A chucking spigot should be turned at each end of the blank. These spigots should be sized to suit your chuck jaws. Here they are 1 in (25 mm) long by 1 3/4-in (45-mm) diameter. (When it is important to minimize these allowances, you may be able to use chucking spigots about 1/8 in (3 mm) long, gripped in compression within dovetail jaw ends as shown in figure 7.6). At the inside end of each spigot leave a vertical shoulder. Force this shoulder against the chuck jaws as you tighten the chuck. This will improve the chuck's hold and help you chuck the workpiece axially.

Parting-off allowances   The shaded areas adjacent to the chucking spigots allow for limited tool access to turn the left-hand ends of the top and base and for parting off. The minimum lengths of these parting-off allowances will vary with the diameter and shape of the lid and base, your chucking method, and how much of the two left-hand ends you intend to finish-turn before parting off. Here the parting-off allowances are about 3/4 in (19 mm) long.

A parting-through allowance The two unshaded lengths are the heights of the base and lid. Between them is the parting-through allowance which you cut through to separate the original blank into base and lid workpieces. It also allows length for you to face the right-hand ends of the lid and base workpieces after you chuck them. By having the lid and base facing each other within the blank, and by separating the blank into two workpieces for hollowing, the grain mismatch across the meeting between the lid and base is usually barely noticeable.

The parting-through and parting-off allowances can be minimized if you use a narrow parting-off tool. Minimizing these allowances saves wood, and minimizes the cantilevering length of each workpiece and therefore any workpiece flexing during the hollowing cuts. Minimizing the parting-through allowance minimizes grain mismatch.

The Turning Sequence

The whole surface of a natsume and of this box are fully turned. To enable this, the procedure for each box is:

1. After preparing the blanks, mount each between centers. Rough each almost to a cylinder, mark out, turn chucking spigots at each end, and separate into a lid and a base workpiece.
2. Chuck the lid workpiece, true its periphery and right-hand face, hollow it, sand the hollow, finish-turn as much of the lid's outside as possible, and part off. You turn the lid first because it is shorter than the base and is therefore less likely to be levered off the base spigot when later reverse chucked (figure 7.38).
3. Chuck the base workpiece, true its periphery and right-hand face, hollow it, and sand the hollowed inside.
4. Turn the base's spigot so that the lid fits quite tightly.
5. Reverse chuck the lid by pushing it onto the base spigot, and finish-turn the area where the lid was parted off earlier.
6. Finish-turn most of the outside of the base leaving a substantial spigot between the base and chuck, and sand the outside of the lid and base.
7. Remove the lid and if required slightly reduce the diameter of the base spigot by turning and/or light sanding. Further finish-turn and sand the left-hand end of the base. Part off the base.
8. Reverse chuck the base by forcing its spigot into an annular recess in a disk of scrap wood (a press-fit chuck). Finish-turn and sand the area where the base was earlier parted off.

Figure 7.21 Parting the blank into lid and base workpieces with a Sorby 2-mm parting tool. The parting-off and parting-through allowances are colored grey.

Sorby's 2-mm parting (-off) tool cuts a smooth-sided groove. Hold it in both hands except when using it with calipers or to part off. You simply thrust this tool forwards and down at minimum clearance. Do not axially oscillate it as you might a parting tool. Do not reduce the spigot diameter to much below 1/2 in (13 mm) or the spigot will snap – it can be twisted asunder or sawn through after you have stopped the lathe. Instead of a parting-off tool, you can use a parting tool, or make a single V-cut and then saw through.

Figure 7.22 Marking the lid's internal diameter.

After you chuck the lid workpiece, skim its outside just to a cylinder with a roughing gouge presented with 45° side rake. Then face the workpiece's right-hand end perpendicular to the lathe axis with a skew's long point as shown in figure 7.15.

Mark the perimeter of the hollow from the gauge with a pencil. You can also use wing dividers set to the hollow's radius. You still position the toolrest square to the lathe axis in plan, but raise it so that the dividers point slightly down. Carefully put the dividers' right-hand point into the exact centre of the face of the wood and gently slide the left-hand point forwards to scribe.

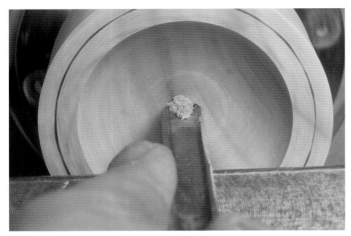

Figure 7.23 Hollowing the lid with a detail gouge. The start of a hollowing cut.

You hollow cupchuck turnings before you finish-turn their outsides because when hollowing you are more likely to force a workpiece out of alignment.

Use a 1/2-in (13-mm) or slightly larger detail gouge. Adjust the height of the top of the toolrest so that when the gouge blade is horizontal the bottom of its upwards-facing flute is at lathe-axis height. Position the toolrest square to the lathe axis and far enough back from the face of the lid so that you can use the tied-underhand grip. Shine a desk light or similar into the hollow to help you see.

The first action in hollowing is to thrust the gouge forwards with the bottom of its flute facing upwards and coincident with the lathe axis. Penetrate about 1/8 in (3 mm) for heavy cuts; less for finishing cuts. If the gouge tip does not remain truly coincident with the lathe axis throughout the forward thrust, a central spike will be left. To remove the spike, position the nose of the gouge or a scraper just below it, and lever downwards on the tool handle.

To prevent injury to your elbow during hollowing remove the tail center and move the tailstock to the right-hand end of the bed, or remove the tailstock from the lathe.

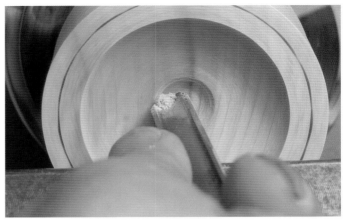

Figure 7.24 Cutting across the bottom. The figure 7.23 hollowing cut continues with levering the gouge nose horizontally to the left at axis height while axially rotating the blade counterclockwise towards a maximum of 45°.

In all hollowing cuts work as far as possible with the grain. Therefore cut by pulling or pushing the tool in the direction of increasing hollow diameter.

By rotating the nose into a shear-scraping presentation you lessen subsurface damage and gain control. Transfer the cutting to the shoulder zone of the cutting edge as you start to pull the gouge towards you—you will probably need to start to clear the handle to your right to achieve this. Do not rush the tool movements; give the tool time to cut. Hollowing should feel surprisingly sweet.

Figure 7.25 Shear scraping with the shoulder of the cutting edge towards the end of the figure 7.23 hollowing cut.

As you pull the gouge towards you, clear the handle well to the right to keep the cutting on the shoulder zone. Take care not to bell open the mouth of the hollow.

Figure 7.26 Scraper shapes for cleaning up the lid and base hollows.

A gouge is likely to leave unevenness and subsurface damage. You should therefore gouge the hollow slightly under-size, confirming its accuracy with a template. Then use a sympathetically-shaped and freshly-sharpened scraper to improve the surface.

The scraper on the left is used in the lid. It has three scraping zones: a sightly-domed end, a right-hand corner of tight radius, and a side-cutting zone along its left-hand edge. You could use either the center or the right-hand scraper within the base.

If you do not have separate lid and a base scrapers for this exercise, I suggest the smaller of the two base scrapers. You would however have to tighten its right-hand corner, or retain some of the surface that you produced with the gouge.

Figure 7.27 Trimming with a flat scraper.

Before starting to scrape, raise the top of the toolrest to about lathe axis height. The scraper will then be safely pointing slightly down when it cuts at axis level it.

Cutting end grain will quickly blunt the burred edge, so resharpen for the final cut.

You should skim the walls while pulling the scraper towards you to work with the grain. You could cut while either pulling or pushing the scraper where the walls are cylindrical.

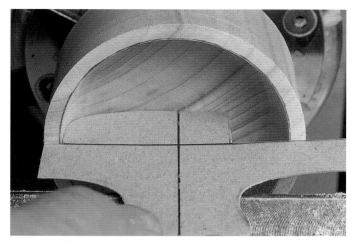

Figure 7.28 Checking the hollow's shape with a template.

Figure 7.29 Using inside spring calipers to check that that part of the hollow which is to mate with the base spigot is truly cylindrical. The lathe must not be running.

Figure 7.30 A hook tool on end grain should leave almost no subsurface damage . Use it or a ring tool presented with zero clearance and at least 45° side rake after removing the bulk of the waste with a detail gouge. As you start to cut more parallel to the lathe axis the likelihood of a catch increases with hook and ring tools.

Figure 7.32 Sanding inside the lid with a third of a quarter of a standard sheet folded once. I take great care as I approach the rim not to bell open the near edge. Sand lightly—heavy sanding will tend to destroy the inside rim's circularity.

Sand a hollow in its the bottom-front quarter. If you allow your finger(s) to stray across the lathe axis they will experience a painful whip.

Figure 7.31 A hollowing tool (a Woodcut Mighty Midget) will also give a better surface than a gouge.

Figure 7.33 Parting off the lid, here with a 1/4-in (6-mm) parting-off tool.

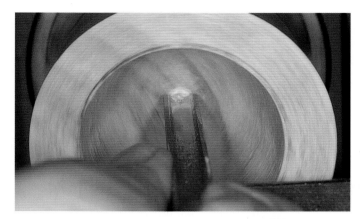

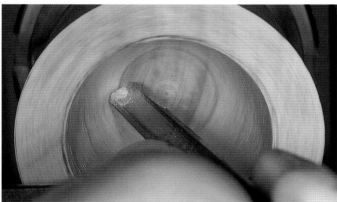

Figure 7.34 Hollowing the base with a 1/2-in (13-mm) detail gouge using the same technique as that used in the lid.

Figure 7.35 Trimming the base hollow by taking fine cuts with a flat scraper "on the pull".

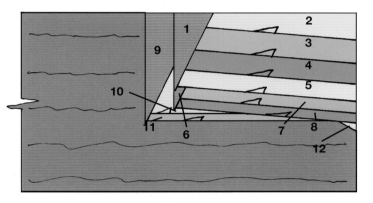

Figure 7.36 Cutting the spigot, the preferred procedure.

Make an offset V-cut (**1**) to the right of the intended vertical face of the shoulder. This cut must not be so deep that it will leave a groove on the cylindrical surface of the finished spigot. You then take a series of slightly-uphill cuts on the short point (**2** to **5**, then **7** and **8**). During these cuts you are likely to need to slightly deepen cut **1** (cut **6**). Try the fit of the lid as you approach the finished diameter, preferably with the lathe stopped.

When the correct fit is achieved close to the right-hand end of the spigot, make the finishing V-cut **9**. It should penetrate to just below the finished diameter of the spigot. Take a couple of horizontal cuts with the short point to form the finished surface (**10** and **11**). Then cut a tiny bevel (**12**).

When an exceedingly fine cut is needed to finish the spigot's cylindrical surface, you can choose to sand lightly instead. Heavier sanding however tends to create a spigot which is elliptical rather than circular in cross-section.

The fit of the lid should be reasonably tight at this stage to allow the lid to be finish-turned while being held on the spigot. If you want a lift-off lid, you slightly reduce the diameter of the spigot after the lid has been finish-turned, sanded, and removed. However even a lift-off lid should not have any noticeable looseness.

Figure 7.38 Finish-turning the lid where it was earlier parted off (cut **1** in figure 7.39). Use a detail gouge with its flute pointing horizontally to the right—it is far less risky than a skew.

If the fit is initially too tight when you press the lid on, skim the spigot with the short point, and/or sand lightly. If the lid's fit is too loose, pack out with thin paper. If you are not confident that the lid will hold, temporarily tape it to the base.

Figure 7.37 Trimming the base spigot.

By cutting slightly upwards with the short point you turn a spigot with a taper which increases in diameter from right to left. You should retain this taper as you reduce the spigot's average diameter until the lid just fits at the spigot's right-hand end. You then cut away the taper to leave a cylindrical spigot onto which the lid fits fairly tightly. If the grain direction is not axial you may have to shear scrape the spigot with the tip of a spindle gouge to prevent tear-out.

The figure 7.36 procedure is not the fastest. If you caliper the lid's inside diameter with vernier calipers, you can then cut down with a parting tool while calipering the outside of the spigot with the verniers' main jaws. Before calipering, open the jaws about 1/16 in (1.5 mm) to allow you to skim off the subsurface damage left by the parting tool with your skew's short point after forming the finished shoulder with an offset V-cut.

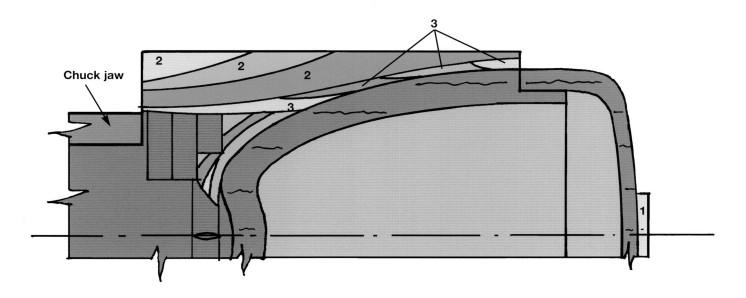

Figure 7.39 The sequence of cuts to turn the body.
After cuts **2** and **3**, sand the lid and the finish-turned part of outside of the base, remove the lid, and do any trimming of the base spigot.

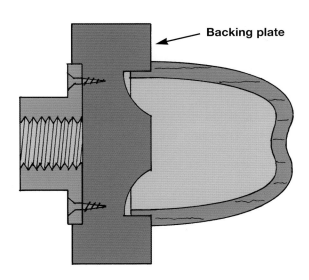

Figure 7.40 Reverse chucking in a press-fit chuck.
You can use any disk of scrap wood (the grain direction doesn't matter), plywood, or suitable board. You may hold the disk in a chuck, on a screwchuck, or on a faceplate. If on a faceplate, beware the screws as you cut the annular recess. Skim the disk's periphery true, and its right-hand circular face flat using techniques appropriate to the grain direction. (Use the techniques described in exercise 8.1 if the disk's grain is radial). Mark the outside diameter of the base spigot with a pencil or dividers, and cut a groove or recess just inside it as shown in figures 7.41 to 7.45. If doing a number of boxes, leave the all the base reverse chucking until the end. You can then use the same chuck for all, starting with the smallest-diameter spigot first.

Figure 7.41 Cutting the annular recess. Have the toolrest half the width of the gouge below lathe axis height. At the start of the cut the flute is pointing horizontally, and the angle in plan between the bevel and the face of the disk is 30° to 40°. This cut is the same for radial or axial grain.

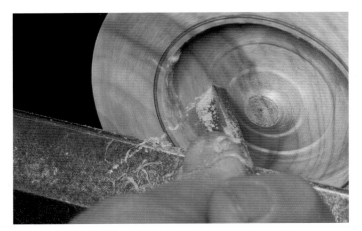

Figure 7.42 Cutting the annular recess, part-way through the cut started in figure 7.41.

As soon as the tip has penetrated, roll the gouge clockwise until the flute faces about 30° above horizontal. Push the gouge handle forwards and to your right during the cut so that the tip cuts an arc in plan.

Figure 7.43 Cutting the recess. As the gouge tip approaches the end of the cut started in figure 7.41, axially rotate the gouge counterclockwise until the flute faces about 10° above the horizontal. If the wood is axially grained, you can cut the outer, cylindrical wall of the recess without having to alter the gouge's presentation. You just have to pull the gouge bodily towards you: the cut is a shear scrape taking place on the lower shoulder zone of the nose.

Figure 7.44 Widening a recess in a radially-grained disk with a pointing cut. The bevel is parallel to the lathe axis in plan, the flute faces horizontally to the right, and the base of the flute is horizontal and at lathe axis height.

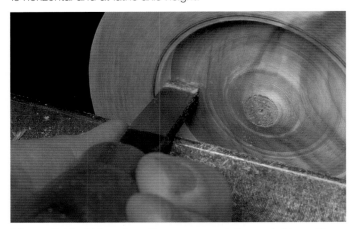

Figure 7.45 Trimming the recess. A tip- and side-cutting scraper can be used to increase the diameter and depth of a recess irrespective of the grain direction. Ideally you should first raise the top of the toolrest to about lathe axis height so that the scraper will point slightly down.

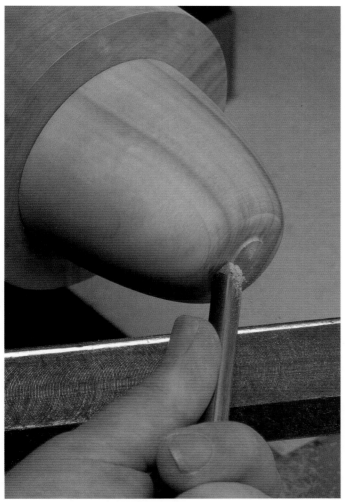

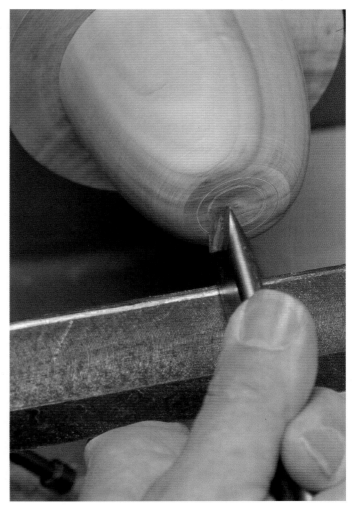

Figure 7.46 Finish-turning the bottom of the reverse-chucked base.

A detail gouge with a convex bevel is the ideal tool, but a conventionally-sharpened gouge will do well unless the bottom is very concave.

A perfectionist would want to sand the whole of the box's outside in the same rotational direction. This would need the base to be reverse chucked outboard or sanded inboard with the lathe in reverse.

Figure 7.47 Cutting two fine V-cuts 1/8 in (3 mm) apart.

You must present the skew's long point exactly at lathe axis height or it will tend to skid sideways. Between the V-cuts I later sign my name and write the wood species with a hot-wire pyrograph (figure 9.40).

Chapter Eight

FACEPLATE TURNING

Faceplate turnings are produced from disks cut from planks. I call their grain direction "radial" although it is continuously changing relative to your tool tip as a disk rotates. This necessitates using different but related techniques to those you have learnt so far.

You usually cut detailed faceplate turnings entirely with detail gouges. The bowl-turning tools and techniques described in chapter 9 can also be used when the design is plain. Many turners use flat scrapers and/or shear scrapers when faceplate turning. I rarely do because a gouge leaves less subsurface damage.

There are three basic detail-gouge cuts. *Rim-skimming* is used on the periphery, the cylindrical surface of a disk. *Face-scraping* and *face-peeling* are used to cut along the face of a disk. As you will see, particularly in exercise 8.2, cutting curves is usually just transferring from one of the three basic presentations to another.

Faceplate turnings are usually mounted inboard on a screwchuck or faceplate. Outboard mounting is better when there are concave sections because you often need to present the gouge with the handle well down.

Subjects for faceplate turning include bread boards, table and stool tops, plates, curtain rings, circular mouldings and frames, and bases. Disk-like bases commonly have stems dowelled into them—in lamps and candlesticks for example. Exercises 8.1 and 8.2 are the mushroom top and base of the hatstand in figure 8.1, the stem of which you may have turned in exercise 6.7. Exercise 8.3 is a fishing reel, and involves turning deep, narrow scotias (coves).

EXERCISE 8.1   A MUSHROOM TOP

Techniques taught	Truing a blank Rim-skimming Face-scraping Face-peeling Preparing a profiled backing plate
Tools required	1-in (25-mm) drill Jacobs chuck on an arbor Medium-sized detail gouge Small screwchuck
Workpieces	Disks 5-in (125-mm) diameter cut from planks approximately 1 1/2 in (37 mm) thick. Saw one disk for the backing plate plus the number you decide for the mushrooms.

Through turning the mushroom top of the hatstand in figure 8.1 you will be able to master the three basic faceplate-turning cuts. You will also gain an insight into the sometimes demanding chucking procedures dictated by particular design features.

You can shorten the time to turn the mushrooms by bandsawing the blanks from a plank which has been machined flat and to the finished thickness. You could also predrill the 1-in (25-mm) holes (figure 8.2) in a drilling machine, and chuck each disk by gripping its hole wall with an expanding-jaw or other chuck. You may not have the machinery to plane, thickness, and drill. I shall therefore describe how to produce the mushroom from a sawn blank totally in the lathe.

If you can bandsaw the disks, allow about 1/8 in (3 mm) of waste all around for truing the disk and finish-turning. If you do not have a bandsaw (or a jigsaw), you could cross cut the plank into square blanks about 1/4 in (6 mm) larger across than the mushroom's diameter. However starting faceplate turnings from squares is risky even for experienced turners. At the least, saw off the corners to produce octagons.

Figure 8.1   The hatstand detailed in figure 6.137. Exercises 8.1 and 8.2 show you how to turn its mushroom top and base.

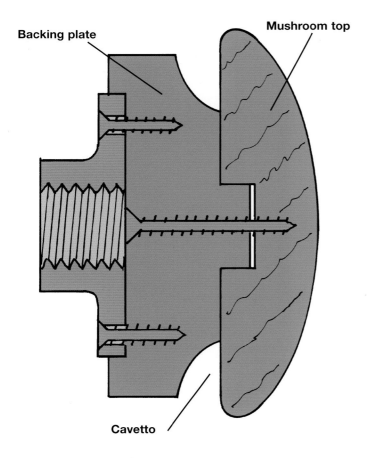

Backing plate

Mushroom top

Cavetto

Figure 8.2 Chucking the mushroom blank. You only need a faceplate for this method.

The screw through the backing plate and the screw of a screwchuck both act in the same way. They pull the left-hand face of the workpiece against the right-hand face of the backing plate or screwchuck. If you take a heavy cut the workpiece will tend to slow while the chuck doesn't. Friction will be generated between the two surfaces in contact. The potential frictional force is proportional to the pull of the screw and the roughnesses of the two surfaces, and is usually sufficient to ensure that the workpiece doesn't slip. You could find that without a screw the latent friction between the cylindrical surfaces of the 1-in (25-mm) spigot and the hole in the mushroom will prevent the mushroom spinning relative to the backing plate, but it will work for only a couple of mushrooms. Hence I use what is a home-made screwchuck. The central screw should be at least 10 gauge.

The turning procedure described in figures 8.2 to 8.18 does not leave any fixing holes to mar the finished mushroom. Its steps are:

1. Mount the mushroom workpiece on a faceplate by screws into its top.
2. True the periphery of the mushroom. If the right-hand face of the disk is reasonably true, you may be able to mark the finished diameter on the face and rim-skim the periphery to the finished maximum diameter of the mushroom—if not you can mark the mushroom's diameter later.

3. Face-skim the right-hand face (the base) of the mushroom flat.
4. Drill the shallow 1-in (25-mm) hole in the base to the correct depth, sand the right-hand face, and remove the disk from the faceplate.
5. Repeat steps 1 to 4 for all the mushroom workpieces.
6. Mount the backing plate workpiece on a faceplate, and true its periphery and right-hand face.
7. If you have a small faceplate, turn a shallow recess in the right-hand face of the backing plate into which the faceplate will fit snuggly. Remove the backing plate, screw the small faceplate into the recess, and mount the assemblage on the lathe. The recessed backing plate cannot then move about on the faceplate, and therefore always remains concentric. If you only have a large faceplate, just true the backing plate's periphery and flatten its right-hand face in the lathe; remove the faceplate from the lathe and the backing plate from the faceplate; then screw the large faceplate concentrically onto the just-flattened face of the backing plate.
8. Turn a short locating spigot on the backing plate that is just greater than 1-in (25-mm) in diameter. Try the hole in a mushroom for fit. The fit should be tight. Turn a cavetto in the rim of the backing plate so that you will have good tool access to turn the mushroom.
9. Drill a central pilot hole through the backing plate in the lathe. The pilot hole should be sized to allow you to screw a 10 gauge or coarser screw through it.
10. Remove the faceplate and backing plate assemblage from the lathe and screw in the screw.
11. Mount the home-made screwchuck in the lathe and screw on a mushroom workpiece.
12. If the mushroom workpiece diameter is oversize, mark the diameter of the mushroom on the workpiece's right-hand face and bring the workpiece to diameter using rim-skimming cuts.
13. Mark the thickness and the position of maximum diameter.
14. Skim the mushroom to its finished thickness, then finish-turn and sand it.

Like the mushroom at the end of the peg in figure 7.10, this mushroom top is exacting to turn because of the extensive sections which have to be eyed. Draw the mushroom's profile on the pencil gauge (figure 8.14) for reference. You could also use a template to monitor your shaping of the mushroom, but should not need to.

Figure 8.3   Using rim-skimming cuts with a detail gouge to true the periphery of a mushroom workpiece.

The mushroom workpiece is first held by screws into its top face. The screws should penetrate less than 3/8 in (10 mm) and be as far from the disk's center as possible to prevent screw holes being left in the top of the finished mushroom.

You use the shoulder zone of the cutting edge for rim-skimming. To achieve zero clearance and at least 45° side rake, have the handle low and axially rotate the gouge so that the flute points partially in the direction of tool traverse. Work inwards from the disk's outside faces to avoid splitting fibres out from them. Keep the gouge tip's overhang below 1 in (25 mm) or you will risk losing control.

If the right-hand face of the disk is initially fairly true, you could mark the finished diameter of the mushroom first. You can then use the rim-skimming cuts to produce a cylindrical surface of the mushroom's finished diameter.

When you have trued the disk you may wish to increase the lathe speed.

Figure 8.4   Facing the base of the mushroom very slightly concave using face-scraping cuts. The flute is facing about 20° above horizontal. By presenting the gouge rotated to face the disk, the tool is rotationally stable with the toolrest parallel to the lathe axis. The cut is a flat scrape if you pull the tool tip towards you along a radius. If you drop the handle as you pull it, the tip will follow an arc and shear scrape, leaving less subsurface damage. Both cuts are taken on the shoulder zone of the cutting edger.

The advantage of face-scraping is that you don't need to move the the toolrest to lie approximately parallel to the face you are about to cut. Face-scraping usually leaves an acceptable finish on side-grain surfaces, but the surface deteriorates as you start to cut end grain. The cut puts high and varying forces onto the tool tip, and at long overhangs and with slender blades, chatter from blade flexing is a problem.

Figure 8.5 Flushing the base of the mushroom using face-skimming cuts.

Face-skimming leaves a better surface than face-scraping, but does require you to position the toolrest parallel and close to the face, and well below the lathe axis.

As in face-scraping, you can vary the side rake and thus the balance between subsurface damage and rippling by how you present the cutting edge. The lower the gouge handle, the greater the side rake.

Figure 8.6 Drilling the shallow hole in the base of the mushroom with the drill held in a Jacobs chuck. The masking tape on the drill shows how deep to drill. You should reduce the lathe speed for this.

The point of the drill should leave a sufficient pilot hole for the fixing screw used later to pull the mushroom against the backing plate. If not, you can easily enlarge the pilot hole in or out of the lathe.

After drilling, sand the base of the mushroom. You cannot sand it in the lathe later.

Figure 8.7 Scribing the outside of the recess in the backing plate shown in figure 8.2.

Screw the backing plate workpiece onto a faceplate, and true its periphery by rim-skimming cuts and its right-hand face by face-scraping or -skimming cuts. Set the dividers to the radius of the faceplate. Adjust the toolrest so that the dividers point slightly down with both legs on the toolrest. Locate the right-hand point in the exact centre of the wood, then gently push the left-hand point forwards to scribe the circle.

Figure 8.8 Recessing the backing plate by shear scraping with a detail gouge. The gouge flute is facing about 45° above horizontal.

When you start the gouge into wood, the first bit of cutting edge to contact the wood should align with the velocity of the wood at the point of contact on the wood for there not to be a risk of a catch. When you start these cuts into the center of the disk you can have the flute facing about 45° above horizontal throughout.

Figure 8.9 Trimming the recess with a detail gouge
with its flute facing horizontally to the right and its bevel parallel
to the lathe axis in plan. The gouge blade is horizontal and at
lathe axis height. The cutting edge at the gouge tip is therefore
vertical and aligned with the velocity of the wood at contact.
This pointing presentation prevents a catch and leaves a better
surface than a scraper.

Figure 8.10 Using a side-and-end-cutting scraper to
trim the recess in the backing plate. It is easier to trim minute
amounts away with a scraper than with a gouge. The scraper
should point slightly down.

Figure 8.11 Cutting the 1-in (25-mm) diameter spigot
on the backing plate.

The backing plate has been reversed and mounted on the
small faceplate. Take care that the length of cutting edge which
will first contact the wood will align with the velocity of the wood
at the point of first contact. Also align the section of bevel which
will provide support parallel to the lathe axis.

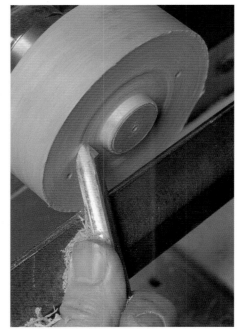

Figure 8.12 Cutting the face of the backing plate
slightly concave using a face-skimming cut.

Figure 8.14 Marking the thickness and maximum diameter on the periphery of the mushroom workpiece. The shallow screw holes from the first mounting are visible on the face of the disk.

If you did not bring the mushroom down to its finished diameter during its first mounting on the lathe, you should do so before this marking out. You may have to do a preliminary face-scrape or face-skim if the disk face is very uneven so that you can mark the mushroom's finished diameter from the gauge.

Figure 8.13 Cutting a cavetto (a half-cove profile) in the the backing plate. The cavetto will allow access to cut the ovolo (a half-bead profile) on the left-hand side of the mushroom (figure 8.2).

Although the gouge's orientation changes little during the cut, the cutting action changes from a type of rim-skim to a face-skim. If the toolrest was aligned parallel to the lathe axis, you would have to axially rotate the gouge counterclockwise during the cut to convert it from a rim-skim to a face-scrape.

After cutting the cavetto, mount a drill in a Jacobs chuck in the tailstock and drill a pilot (not a clearance) hole for the screw through the backing plate.

After completing the backing plate, remove the faceplate from the lathe. Screw in the central screw. Its length should be such that about 3/8 in (10 mm) projects from the right-hand face of the backing plate. The faceplate-and-backing-plate assemblage is then screwed back onto the right-hand spindle nose. You can then screw the mushroom workpieces onto the centering home-made screwchuck for finish turning.

Figure 8.15 Face-skimming the mushroom workpiece to its finished thickness.

Figure 8.16   Turning the small ovolo.
Start the detail gouge in a face-scraping presentation, but have the handle low to give a shear scrape rather than a flat scrape. The cut finishes as a rim-skim. During the cut the handle is dropped further and moved to the right while the gouge is axially rotated counterclockwise. Take this cut slowly so that you have time to manipulate the gouge correctly.

Figure 8.17 **Finish-turning the top of the mushroom** with the toolrest parallel to the lathe axis. The cut starts as a face-scrape and gradually converts to a rim-skim.

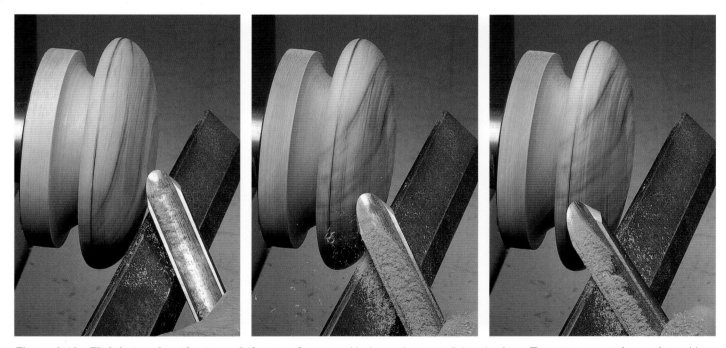

Figure 8.18 **Finish-turning the top of the mushroom** with the toolrest parallel to the face. The cut converts from a face-skim to a type of rim-skim.

After completing the finish-turning, sand. You usually create more subsurface damage on faceplate and bowl turnings than on spindle turnings, and therefore should start sanding with a coarser-grit paper or cloth.

EXERCISE 8.2   A HATSTAND BASE

Techniques taught   Turning moldings on
                         radially-grained workpieces

Tools required   1-in (25-mm) drill
                         Jacobs chuck on an arbor
                         Medium detail gouge
                         Small screwchuck

Workpieces   Disks 8-in (200-mm) diameter x 2-in
                         (50-mm) thick

This base is similar in design to many used for lamps and
candlesticks. Its turning is described in figures 8.19 to 8.28.

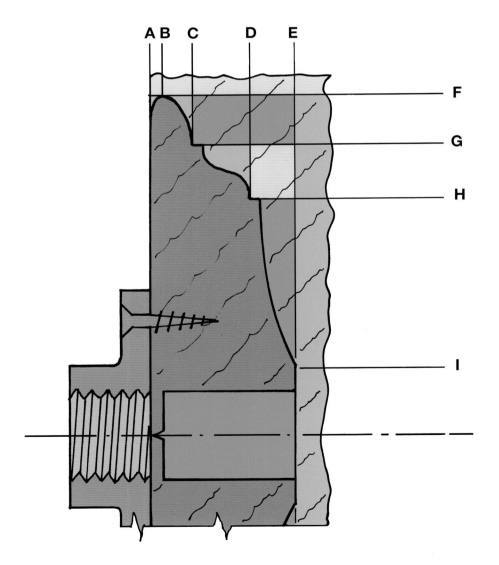

Figure 8.19 The base design and
cutting procedure.

As in exercise 8.1, you can choose
from several chucking methods, and
order the various operations in different
ways. Here I suggest you be a little
cruder than in exercise 8.1. Screw the
disk onto a faceplate with short screws
at a wide radius or onto a screwchuck.
True the periphery with rim-skimming
cuts. Turn the right-hand face (the
underside of the base) slightly hollow
using face-skimming cuts, sand it, and
pencil on a circle just greater in
diameter than the outside diameter of
the faceplate you will next mount it on.
Remove the workpiece and faceplate or
screwchuck from your lathe.

You need to mount the workpiece
on a faceplate next, not a screwchuck,
because you need to bore a 1-in
(25-mm) diameter hole to glue the stem
into later. Screw the faceplate centrally
onto the underside of the base, using
the pencilled circle as a guide

Figure 8.20 Mark the finished thickness of the base onto the rotating, trued periphery from your pencil gauge. Then bring the disk to thickness using face-skimming cuts.

Figure 8.21 Mark the diameters F, G, H, and **I** defined in figure 8.19. Then drill the 1-in (25-mm) axial hole. Take care not to drill so deeply that the drill hits the faceplate.

Figure 8.22 The workpiece marked out ready to start detailed turning.

Use rim-skimming cuts to bring the disk to the maximum finished diameter. Mark the thickness of the torus (line **C** in figure 8.19) and the high point on it (line **B**). The shaded surfaces show the ring of wood which you next cut away to define the circular line **C-G**.

Figure 8.23 Cutting away the ring outside C and G. During each cut traverse the gouge tip to the left while you rotate it counterclockwise from a rim-skimming presentation to one of face-scraping.

At the completion of each cut the gouge should be able to cut a square corner. Rotate the gouge too far and it will catch. If you don't rotate it sufficiently and have moved the contact point between the gouge and the toolrest too far to the left, you will not be able to cut the corner square.

Figure 8.24   Later in cutting away the ring outside C and G.

To finish correctly I have to start the cut with the contact point between the gouge and the toolrest further to the right than in figure 8.23. This contact point remains almost fixed throughout each late cut except in situations where the ring is very wide.

Figure 8.25   Cutting the right-hand half of the torus.

You cut the right-hand side of the torus using a series of cuts similar to that used for rolling a bead except reversed in direction. Each new cut of the series involves more traversing, radial movement outwards, and clockwise axial rotation of the gouge tip than the previous cut. With the last cut in the series, start the gouge in the same face-scraping presentation it finished in at the end of the cuts in figures 8.23 and 8.24. During this last cut you take the cutting action from a face-scrape through to a rim-skim. Take the cut slowly. Look at the profile at the top of the workpiece rather than at the gouge tip. You have to lower the gouge handle and move it to the left as you axially rotate the gouge clockwise.

You cut the left-hand side of the torus in a similar, but transposed, way (see also figure 8.16).

Figure 8.26 Cutting away the next ring of waste outside D and H.
If you leave the toolrest's position unchanged, parallel to the lathe axis, you will have to work at a long and therefore risky tool overhang. To avoid this, position the toolrest approximately parallel to the surface you are about to cut. The cut starts as a rim-skim and ends in a face-scraping-with-side-rake presentation.

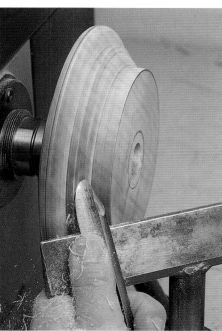

Figure 8.27 Cutting the ogee with an angled toolrest.
Start this cut as a face-scrape, convert it into a rim-skim, then revert it back to a face-scrape.

Figure 8.28 Cutting the shallow cavetto using a face-skim.

EXERCISE 8.3 A FISHING REEL

Techniques taught   Turning deep, narrow scotias

Tools required   Roughing gouge, skew, medium-sized detail gouge, parting tool, parting-off tool, calipers
1-in (25-mm) and 3/8-in (10-mm) drills
Small drills for the holes for the round-head screw and to tie on the line
Jacobs chuck on an arbor
Small inboard screwchuck
Small outboard screwchuck or faceplate

Workpieces   Disks 5-in (125-mm) diameter and 2-in (50-mm) thick for the reel body
Squares 2 x 2 x 6 1/2 in (50 x 50 x 160 mm) long for the main spindle
Squares 1 x 1 x 3 in (25 x 25 x 75 mm) long for the winding handle
Cubes 2 x 2 x 2 in (50 x 50 x 50 mm) for the keeper disk
Waste disk for reverse chucking the reel, minimum size 7-in (175-mm) diameter, 1-in (25-mm) thick

The reel is shown in figures 8.29 and 8.30. It's importance is as an exercise in cutting scotias into radially-grained disks, and it is a useful item if you fish off jetties or boats. I show the reel body being turned outboard—you will find it far more difficult to turn its front face inboard over the bed.

To chuck the reel body workpiece, you could:

1. Drill the 1-in (25-mm) through hole first in a drilling machine, then center and mount the drilled blank on a backing disk with a spigot, similar to that shown in figure 8.13. You could also expand the small-diameter spigot jaws of a scroll or collet chuck into the hole, or use a pin chuck.
2. Mount the blank on an outboard screw chuck and drill the through hole later.
3. Screw the disk onto a small outboard faceplate. This is the method shown in figure 8.31, but the workpiece disk has first been glued onto a waste disk to avoid unsightly screw holes being left in the back face of the reel body.

After preparing the pencil gauges and chucking the reel-body workpiece, the first turning operation is to flush the front face of the disk. Use face-skimming cuts with a detail gouge as shown earlier in figure 8.5. Then bring the reel rim down to its finished maximum diameter with rim-skimming cuts (figure 8.3). Pencil the edges of the scotia onto the disk rim, and cut the scotia as described in figures figures 8.31 to 8.34. You then mark out and cut a recesss and the scotia into the face of the disk (figures 8.35 to 8.37), before drilling it (figure 8.38).

Figure 8.29 The finished reel. For casting you hold the rear handle on the main spindle and point it in the direction of casting. You reel in your catch in the conventional way.

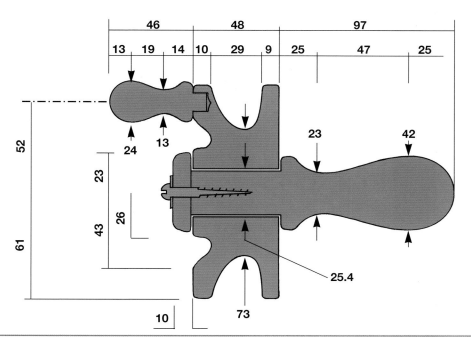

Figure 8.30 A longitudinal section through the reel. The dimensions are not critical. The reel body's through hole should be an easy sliding fit on the spigot of the main spindle. Wax the spigot to make the reel spin more smoothly.

Figure 8.31 Cutting a scotia in the rim of a disk. Starting a cut with a pointing presentation.

Cutting a scotia into the rim of a disk is a similar process to that of cutting a cove in a spindle except that you enlarge the scotia by cutting radially outwards to work with the grain. You can use face-scraping (figures 8.31 and 8.32), face-skimming (8.33 and 8.34), or any presentation between. To deepen the scotia before widening it you cannot however avoid cutting radially inwards, against the grain. If you are going to widen the scotia by face-scraping, you first deepen the scotia by making a pointing cut with the gouge flute facing horizontally and the blade pointing at the lathe axis in elevation. The angle in plan between the gouge bevel and the lathe axis does not have to be 90°, and is usually less as here.

Figure 8.32 Cutting the side of the scotia by face-scraping.

Once you have suitably deepened the scotia, start to scrape radially outwards. You can continue the face-scrape to the edge of the scotia. If you wish to reduce the subsurface damage, you can modify your tool presentation towards that of a face-skim as you bring the nose out.

Figure 8.33 Deepening the scotia by rim-skimming.

The more open the scotia, the lower the risk if you enlarge it using a gouge presentation near that of face-skimming. And the closer your presention for cutting the sides of the scotia will be to face-skimming, the nearer your starting presentation for deepening the scotia at the start of the cut can be to rim-skimming. As in figure 8.31, you can decrease the risk of a catch by presenting your gouge with your right hand well to the left of square if you are about to cut the right-hand side of the scotia, and vice versa.

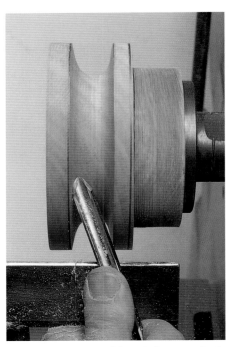

Figure 8.34 Cutting the side of the scotia by face-skimming.

You can widen the scotia by levering the gouge nose away from the lathe axis in any presentation between face-scraping and face-skimming. The nearer that presentation is to face-skimming, the less the subsurface damage and the greater the risk of a catch. The shallower the scotia, and the narrower the gouge while still being stiff, the lower the risk of a catch.

Figure 8.35 Turning a "V"-shaped recess into the front of the disk.

Figure 8.38 shows how to hold the reel to axially bore it. Unless the central area of the left-hand face of the reel is in hard contact with the press-fit chuck, the wood will splinter when the drill tip emerges through that face. You can minimize that splintering by turning a "V"-shaped recess where the drill will emerge. The recess should be a touch larger in diameter than the drill. After marking the radius of the through hole and the extents of the scotia, use pointing cuts at lathe-axis level to turn the recess.

Figure 8.36 Starting a cut to enlarge the scotia in the face of the reel body.

You can cut this scotia in almost exactly the same way that you would a cove in a spindle because the disk's grain is "parallel" to the toolrest. However the wood is only moving vertically downwards at lathe axis level. Therefore if the initial contact between your gouge's cutting edge and the wood will not be at axis height, you need to modify the way you present your gouge to counter the sideways force.

Figure 8.37 Completing the cut started in the previous figure.

After completing the outboard turning, sand the accessible parts of the reel body in the lathe. The next operation is to reverse chuck the reel body to finish turning the reel's back face and bore the through hole.

Figure 8.38 Drilling the through hole with a 1-in (25-mm) sawtooth drill held in a Jacobs chuck.

There is little risk of a workpiece coming out if it fits tightly into a press-fit chuck. However experience has convinced me of the value of insurance. I often screw down small rectangular pieces of plywood to give greater security.

Before drilling the through hole, finish turn the right-hand face of the reel using radial-skimming cuts (figure 8.5). Then sand.

To complete the reel:

1. Turn the main spindle between centers with the spigot which passes through the reel body at the tailstock end. The imprint of the tail center then gives you a central recess in which to start the drill when you hand drill the pilot hole for the threaded part of the screw.
2. Spindle turn or better cupchuck turn the small winding handle.
3. Chuck a 2-in (50-mm) cube of wood with its grain radial on an inboard screwchuck. Faceplate turn the keeper disk which holds the reel onto the rear handle. Bore the clearance hole for the screw with the drill held in a Jacobs chuck mounted in the tailstock. Then part off the keeper disk, ideally with a parting-off tool.
4. Bore the pilot hole into the end of the main handle's spigot to hold the fixing screw, the hole to hold the winding handle, and the hole to secure the end of the fishing line.
5. Glue the winding handle into the reel body.
6. Varnish with polyurethane or marine varnish.
7. Fully assemble the reel, finishing by screwing through the keeper disk into the pilot hole in the main spindle.
8. Proceed to your favorite fishing spot.

Chapter Nine

BOWL TURNING

This chapter introduces bowl turning and includes one exercise. Its illustrations show a bowl being turned outboard. The advantages of not having the bed in the way were discussed in section 3.1. If you have to turn bowls inboard, you will have to imagine the illustrations transposed. You may also need to use your gouges in nearer-horizontal presentations than those shown.

9.1   BOWL DESIGN

Design Guidelines for Bowls and Hollowed Forms:

1. Clarify your intents. How do you want someone to react to your bowl? Your design, the wood you select, any non-turning techniques you apply, and any finishing, should be sympathetic to and reinforce your intents.
2. What overall feeling do you want your bowl to convey? A thin-walled, "V"-shaped bowl rising from a tall, narrow base will not cause the same reaction as a thick-walled, shallow, "U"-shaped one squatting on a wide base.
3. The walls and base should be of an equal and constant thickness unless you decide otherwise. The intention of this guideline (it is not a rule) is to get you to actively think about wall thicknesses, both the average and any departures from the average.
4. A turning's finished design should not be dictated by features required for its chucking. A finished bowl should not retain recesses, shoulders, etc. which were only there for chucking purposes.
5. Use strongly-defined flowing curves. Make sudden changes in direction at 90°. Avoid simple ratios of bowl height to maximum diameter, base diameter to maximum diameter, and total height to the height to the maximum diameter.
6. Give attention to the design of the rim and the base. How wide should the base be to achieve your aesthetic and any functional intents?
7. Concentrate on the overall shape, rather than adding distracting V-cuts, beads, etc.
8. If a major intent is to display the wood's grain pattern, colors, or other features, is there a design which will be especially suitable? Figure 9.1 shows an example.
9. If you want a bowl to be functional, does this commend particular design features? A fruit bowl is better wide and shallow, with a wide base for stability. In a deep bowl only the top fruit is displayed, that below rots unseen. A sharp rim could damage fruit. Fruit would tend to roll off a wide, horizontal rim.
10. Does the standard sanded surface best convey and complement your intentions? Would your normal or a more extreme off-the-tool surface suit better? If you apply a finish should it be clear, tinted, or opaque, and with what gloss level?

Other Intents

Your intents need not be limited to the aesthetic and functional. Your bowls can communicate (figure 9.2). A bowl's design can cause people to recall a person, location, event, etc.; you can communicate political or social messages through painting, carving, or lettering.

You can further your intents by combining other creative processes with turning. Carving, laminating, tooled-surface effects, staining, painting, and even charring are used. You can add or incorporate plastic or metal components, feathers, rope, etc.

Figure 9.1   Special design features. The inside is finely sanded. The outside has an off-the-tool finish. Sanding the outside would round the junctions between the turned surface and the outer surface of the sapwood, revealed undamaged after blasting off the bark with a high-pressure water jet. The bowl is thick and massive, a treatment which suits this burl jarrah.

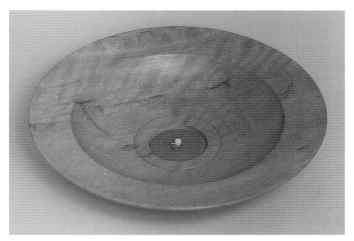

Figure 9.2 A Plug Bowl communicates the question "What is my plug for?" We haven't found the answer yet.

9.2 WOOD PREPARATION

It is unlikely that you will be able to buy seasoned timber for larger bowls because the probability of degrade is too high to make seasoning large cross-sections commercially worthwhile. If such timber was commercially available it would be prohibitively expensive. Even buying unseasoned timber often seems expensive because unless you have the techniques and equipment to turn nests of bowls, 90% or more of a bowl blank ends up as shavings. An important part of bowl turning is therefore obtaining suitable wood at an affordable cost.

For your first bowls you may have to buy disks from a specialist supplier. Although most disks are sold surface sealed, they are not necessarily properly seasoned. You can also laminate them from seasoned planks, but if you decide to concentrate on bowl turning it is certain that you will become involved in wood harvesting and seasoning. Being in a turners' club is an advantage because you will find members who are willing to sell or swap wood or join with you to harvest it.

Wood harvesting, processing, and seasoning are detailed in *The Practice of Woodturning* and elsewhere. Wood starts to degrade as soon as it ceases to "live". It starts to crack in from the ends, from the pith, and from under the bark; it starts to stain and rot through fungal action; and it continues to be attacked by insects. The sooner you deal with wood after it ceases to live, the less wood you will have to ultimately reject. You should cut wood intended for bowls into disks and turn them with the minimum of delay. If you need to store the wet disks, ensure that they cannot dry out by keeping them wet or sealed—unfortunately this does not eliminate the problems of staining and rot.

9.3 OUTLINE TURNING PROCEDURES

Figure 9.3 explains the three main paths to a finished bowl.

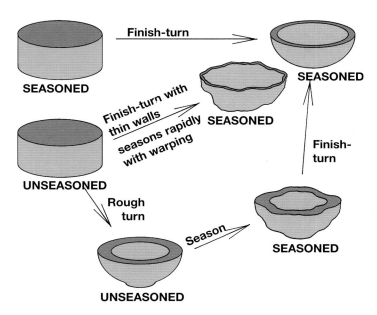

Figure 9.3 The three paths for turning wooden bowls.

Top path, starting from a seasoned blank Even a seasoned blank will be wetter inside than near its surface. It is also likely to have internal stresses: remnant stresses from the growing tree (such as those in branch wood), and stresses induced by seasoning. But the seasoned blank will be in a state of equilibrium. When you turn it into a bowl, the moisture contents and internal stresses have to relax into a new equilibrium, and the bowl therefore warps or cracks. This happens during the turning and during a period afterwards. You should therefore turn a bowl quickly to minimize any deformation-related chucking and sanding problems.

Diagonal path If your workpiece is unseasoned and you require the finished bowl to be free of cracks but do not demand that it remains round, you can turn it directly to a very thin wall thickness throughout. As the wood seasons and shrinks, the thin walls are flexible enough to warp freely. Thick walls would be stiff and would resist warping. Some areas would therefore become highly stressed and crack.

Bottom path If you want your finished bowl to remain round, you first rough turn the unseasoned blank to a thick-walled bowl. Once this bowl is seasoned, you then re-turn it to produce the finished bowl. This finished bowl should remain stable and is unlikely to crack.

Avoiding Degrade

How thin should you turn a bowl and how much will it warp if you take the diagonal path in figure 9.3? How thin should you turn the rough bowl and how likely is it to season without unacceptable degrade if you take the bottom path. The answers depend on:

1. *The size* The larger the blank, the more likely you are to have problems.
2. *The shrinkage* The greater a species' typical shrinkages during seasoning, the greater the warping and the likelihood of cracking.
3. *The wood's grain and growth* Straight-grained wood from large, mature, forest-grown trunks is the most stable. High local stresses, warping, and cracking are likely when the grain is contorted. Large medullary rays and tightly-curved growth rings increase the probability of degrade.
4. *Internal stresses* Wood from areas of contorted grain or from areas which were highly stressed in the tree will want to warp more when its equilibrium is disturbed by being hollowed.
5. *The bowl's design* Wood cracks when it it is stressed above its breaking stress. Below that stress it warps. The thinner the wall the more flexible it is, and the more stress can be dissipated by warping.
6. *How you cut the blank* A blank is more likely to degrade when it contains sapwood, the pith, or contorted grain.
7. *Your seasoning expertise and equipment* Most turners have to rely on air drying. You can take steps to lessen the degrade during air drying, but for substantial reductions in degrade you have to season in a kiln. A major factor in kilns' lessening of degrade is that they keep the wood hot. Hot wood is somewhat plastic and therefore does not become as highly stressed during seasoning.

Although the factors which cause degrade are understood, little research has been done on bowl seasoning. Until that happens, my qualitative advice is:

1. Avoid species which have high shrinkage coefficients and which are notorious for degrade.
2. Do not have the pith in the blank.
3. Reject or cut away wood which is already cracked.
4. Be aware of sapwood's greater tendency to degrade. I am not saying exclude sapwood. The color contrast between sapwood and heartwood is often aesthetically desirable, and including the sapwood often greatly increases the possible size of the bowl.
5. Avoid areas of contorted grain. However the appeal of such wood often makes the increased risk of degrade worthwhile. Very highly-contorted burl wood seasons to produce even, fine cracking rather than major cracks.

6. Rough turn the wall thickness of a bowl to be seasoned to about 1/8 th of the bowl's maximum diameter. The thickness of a rough-turned bowl must accomodate the warping which occurs during seasoning and allow the desired finished bowl to be turned afterwards.

A less-common "seasoning" process is *stabilization*. In stabilization the *combined water* bound within the wood's cells (there is also *free water* between the cells) is replaced or modified so that the wood remains stable irrespective of changes in the ambient atmosphere.

9.4 CHUCKING

You have to chuck a bowl at least twice during its turning to tool its whole surface. Design guideline 4 in section 9.1 holds that "A turning's finished design should not be dictated by features required for its chucking". Chucking is therefore a major area of interest in bowl turning.

Chucking is usually two or three stage (figure 9.4). There may also be a preliminary stage. The range of bowl-chucking equipment continues to expand (figure 9.5 shows only three types of scroll-chuck accessory-jaws). But this chapter through exercise 9.1 concentrates on lower-tech chucking methods because:

1. You are unlikely to have the equipment for some of the higher-tech methods.
2. It is useful to know the lower-tech methods to cope with situations in which a higher-tech approach may not be feasible, for example for an especially-large bowl.
3. Higher-tech equipment may save time but it doesn't make anything new possible. You can chuck anything on a simple faceplate if you have some waste wood and fasteners.

And a faceplate is the lowest-tech and most-flexible item of chucking equipment as exercise 9.1 demonstrates.

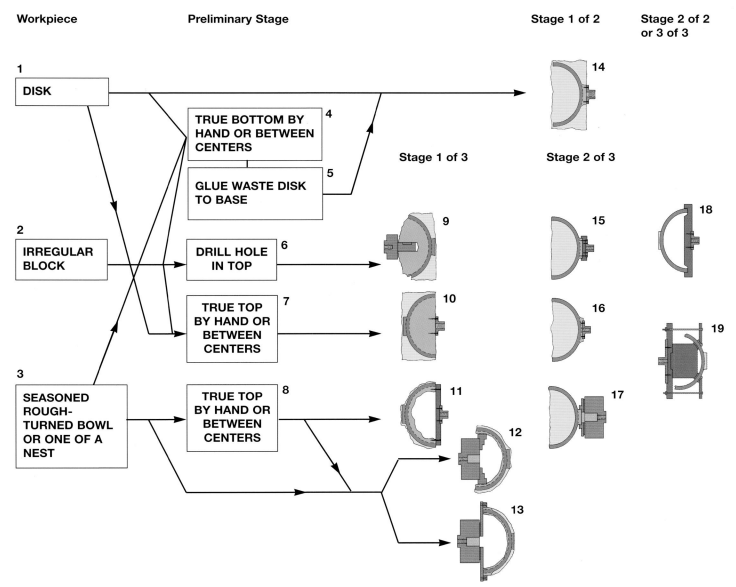

Figure 9.4 A flow chart of chucking options showing the two- and three-stage chucking procedures commonly used in bowl turning. The finished bowl has a convex base. The numbering of the notes below corresponds with the numbering on the chart.

Notes on the Options

2 You often start from an irregular blank for natural– (or waney)–edged bowls.

3 A seasoned, rough-turned bowl blank is likely to have a flattish, thickened base area. A blank produced using a nesting device will have a uniform thickness and a convex base. When you are preparing blanks for seasoning allow sufficient thickness to allow for the warping during seasoning and for any shoulder, recess, etc. which you need for later chucking.

4, **7**, **8** You can use a hand plane for truing.

5 You can glue on a waste disk where the wood is too crumbly to hold screws or where you have insufficient thickness to turn a temporary chucking feature such as a shoulder.

9, 12, 13 Workpieces chucked in this way are often turned inboard so that the tailstock can be used to provide extra security.

9 to 13 The chucking feature you turn on the base should be compatible with the chucking method you use in **15, 16,** or **17**.

12 To use this option you have to rough the inside of the bowl blank close to the rim with a constant diameter and a shoulder. You must not expand the chuck jaws too enthusiastically when you grip the blank. It is better to grip a small bowl by contracting the jaws.

19 This annular-ring chuck type is used inboard so that the tailstock can be used to align the workpiece axially in the chuck and provide support during the early part of the turning.

Figure 9.5 Proprietary bowl chucking equipment. *Top left,* Cole jaws mounted on a Nova chuck grip bowl rims with radially-adjustable rubber studs; *bottom,* the dovetail jaws of a Vicmarc VM 120 can be contracted to grip a base spigot, or expanded to grip inside a base recess; *right,* the scroll-chuck-mounted chuck plate system invented by Mike Darlow in 1984, and used primarily to grip bowl rims.

9.5 AN INTRODUCTION TO BOWL-TURNING TECHNIQUES

There is no consensus on the best way to turn a "standard" bowl. Some believe that they can produce faster by relying on power sanding. Others finish-turn the surface by shear scraping. A minority will rely on high-rake-angle and high-side-rake cutting. There are differences in approach. Some may suit particular woods or bowl shapes or not be noticeably inefficient, but the conservatism of many turners ensures that they continue to use and promote inferior techniques.

The Purist Approach

In this chapter's exercise I recommend that you take a purist approach and aim for the best-possible off-the-tool finish. It is an approach which is applicable to all woods and bowl shapes. It will remain relevant if you choose to adopt a less-purist approach later.

Bowl-turning techniques are intimately related to the techniques used to turn other items. For a fine off-the-tool finish you want the best compromise between subsurface damage and a rippled macro-cut surface. You need a high side rake and a thin shaving to minimize subsurface damage. To minimize rippling you need a shaving with a wide horizontal component, which you achieve by using a cutting edge with a curvature close to that of the surface you are cutting. *Cutting* will almost always leave the best surface, but can be more demanding. The relative effectiveness of different approaches such as scraping or shear scraping depends on how the wood reacts. If you are unsure of the approach to use, ask the wood by comparing the alternatives.

EXERCISE 9.1   A BOWL WITH A PLAIN RIM AND A DIMPLED BOTTOM

Techniques taught	Mounting the blank Turning the outside Hollowing Monitoring wall thickness Three-stage chucking Measuring to turn the base Sanding
Equipment required	Bowl gouge(s) Faceplate Calipers
Workpieces	Disks about 10-in (250-mm) diameter and 5-in (125-mm) deep Waste disk for reverse chucking, 11-in (275-mm) diameter, at least 1 in (25 mm) thick

The Design

Your bowl's design need not be identical to that in figures 9.6 and 9.7, but I suggest that it be similar. Its size can also be substantially smaller without affecting the value of the exercise. Its finished base has no abrupt changes in direction, chucking recesses, or shoulders, and is therefore testing to turn and requires reverse chucking.

I recommend that once you have your blank, you finalize the bowl's cross-section on cardboard. You can then cut inside and outside templates directly from the cardboard.

Rather than use a simple flat or round rim, I am using a design I first developed for burl bowls to separate the tooled outside from the sanded inside (figure 9.1). I have designed a constant wall thickness—I see no benefit in varying it here although rims and bases are sometimes designed with extra thickness.

Designing the chucking procedure is an intrinsic part of the design. The exercise demonstrates three-stage chucking using a faceplate. Once you have mastered this low-tech chucking, you will be better able to assess the alternatives.

The Turning Procedure

The first operation is to mount the workpiece on a faceplate by screwing into the waste within what will be the top of the bowl. Four 1-in (25-mm) screws should suffice. You may need to flatten the top of the disk with a hand plane or chisel so that it will not rock on the faceplate. Using figure 9.4 chucking options **10, 15,** and **18,** the steps are:

1. True the workpiece at a low lathe speed. Once the workpiece is trued you should consider raising the lathe speed.
2. Rough the outside of the bowl.
3. Turn any temporary chucking feature, here a spigot. Then refine the outside's shape and surface, and check that it conforms to the template.
4. Sand the outside—it is better to do this early in case the bowl warps as you hollow it.
5. Chuck the bowl by its base so that it still rotates concentrically about the lathe axis.
6. Rough the rim and the inside.
7. Finish-turn the rim and the inside to conform to the inside template.
8. Sand the rim and the inside.
9. Remove the bowl from the faceplate or chuck, and reverse chuck it.
10. Turn off the bottom waste to conform to the template. Sand, make any required V-cuts to guide your signing of the bowl, remove it from the chuck, and write the wood's name and your signature on the base.

These steps in turning the bowl are shown in figures 9.6 to 9.40.

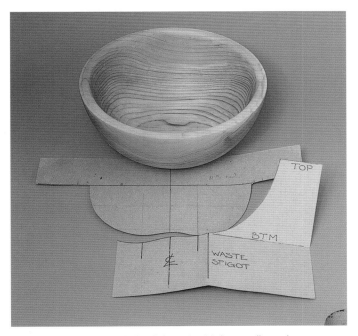

Figure 9.6   The finished bowl with its cardboard templates. Cardboard is an ideal material because you can flex and fold it (figure 9.18).

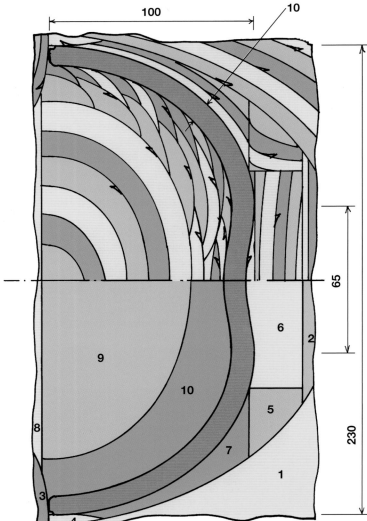

100

10

65

230

6

2

9

10

5

8

7

1

3

4

Figure 9.7 The bowl's design and the cutting procedure. The order of cutting is shown by the numbering

To be able to monitor the outside profile with the template, you have to turn the outside of the rim to its designed diameter, mark the radial projection of the intersection of the waste chucking spigot with the bowl's outside wall after truing the outside, and then establish the intersection accurately. To use the template you first have to bend the template at the spigot/wall intersection (figure 9.18).

You should finish-turn the inside in bands, working from the rim towards the bottom. This ensures that the band which you are finish-turning is stiffened by the adjacent thick wall.

Figure 9.8 Roughing the outside of the workpiece with a bowl gouge.

It is quicker and safer to start from a bandsawn disk. There are no troublesome projections, and because the blank is likely to be well balanced you will be able to run the lathe faster. If you do not have a bandsaw, you can use a hand or chain saw to cut a radially-grained square blank as here. However a far better compromise is a hexagonal or octagonal blank.

You start by roughing away the wood at the edge of the base of the blank. A ground-back bowl gouge is the preferred tool.

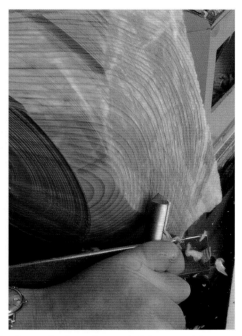

Figure 9.9 Completing the outside roughing cut started in figure 9.8. During the cut raise the handle and axially rotate the gouge clockwise.

You could alternatively use face- and rim-skimming cuts with a detail gouge, but a bowl gouge allows you to take a heavier cut and not be in the path of escaping shavings, etc.

Figure 9.10 Truing the bottom of the disk with a bowl gouge.

You can traverse the gouge towards or away from the lathe axis. The nearer the cut is to a finishing cut, the more side rake I use and the more I cut on the end of a flange rather than at the bottom of the flute.

Figure 9.11 Face-skimming cuts along the top face.

If you continue roughing towards the headstock as in the two previous figures, you will start to split away the unsupported fibres running across the top face of the workpiece. You should turn the top of the bowl down to its finished diameter before this starts to happen.

Because I unwisely started from a square block, I have aligned the toolrest square to the lathe axis and am using face-skimming cuts with a detail gouge.

Figure 9.12 Finish turning the top of the outside wall using rim-skimming cuts.

Once the workpiece periphery at its headstock end is fairly round, you can position the toolrest parallel to the bowl's nearside and use a spindle gouge (figure 9.13) or a bowl gouge (figure 9.14). The latter will leave a less rippled surface.

Try raising the lathe speed once the bowl is fairly true.

Figure 9.13   50°-side-rake cutting. A close up of the previous figure.

Figure 9.14   A bowl gouge at 70° side rake gives a slightly better surface than the rim-skimming shown in the two previous figures because of the wider band of cutting-edge support.

Figure 9.15   Face-skimming cuts with a detail gouge. The waste spigot prevents a bowl gouge being presented with side rake.

I have turned the base of the waste spigot to be a tight fit into the press-fit chuck (figure 9.18). You need to take care to correctly locate the junction of the waste spigot with the outside of the bowl wall to provide a reference for the outside template.

Figure 9.16   Cutting with the flute facing down.

This presentation avoids the slight risk of the corner at the top of the flange catching. It also prevents you seeing the cutting.

The shape of your bowl gouge tip affects the ways you might present it. If you have sharpened it square across, axially rotating it will not affect the side rake. This bowl gouge is ground back at 15°. To achieve a desirable 60° side rake, present it as here or as in the next figure.

Figure 9.17 Cutting with the flute facing up.

As with all *cutting* you need to present the cutting edge with the optimum clearance. If the clearance is too small the bevel will bounce. If the clearance is too large the tool will stutter. Once you are sensitive to these initially faint signals, you will be able to make the minute changes in presentation during a cut which will ensure maximum control and surface quality. Increase the side rake, slow the speed of traverse, and thin the shaving to improve the surface.

Figure 9.18 Checking the wall profile. The bowl will next be held in the faceplate-mounted, press-fit chuck to the left.

You can accurately monitor the outside wall profile by turning the outside of the rim to the designed diameter and folding the template at the diameter of the waste spigot.

The waste spigot fits tightly into the recess of the press-fit chuck on the left. Although it should not be strictly necessary, I advise that you screw through the faceplate and the bottom of the chuck recess into the waste spigot. This will ensure that you do not lever the bowl out of the chuck when hollowing near the bowl rim.

Figure 9.19 Skimming the top flat. Near the edge you should work towards the lathe axis to avoid splitting fibres away.

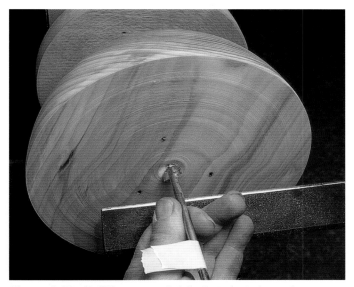

Figure 9.20 Drilling an axial hole to just above the bottom of the bowl with a spear-point drill. This operation is optional. The majority of turners would omit it and take major cuts right to the lathe axis.

A conventionally-sharpened drill will not work because the workpiece is spinning clockwise. It is easy to reverse the sharpening of a spear-point drill or spade bit.

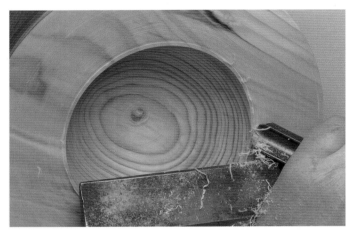

Figure 9.21 Starting a hollowing cut with the gouge handle well to the right before cutting a tight quarter circle to enter the hollow. Experienced turners do not need such a large margin of safety.

As you start a hollowing cut, your gouge tip may catch and veer off, usually towards the outside. You can prevent this by starting the cut as shown, or by:

1. Having the first length of cutting edge which touches the wood's surface in line with the velocity of the wood at the point of contact. If that contact is to be at axis height, you will need to lift the handle and/or axially-rotate the gouge (figure 9.22)
2. Positioning the left-hand end of the toolrest inside the hollow and approximately parallel to the lathe axis. This allows you to cut with an internal peripheral skim.

Once you have safely started the cut, cut along an arc which is slightly convex in elevation (figures 9.22 to 9.25). This allows you to cut down to the center late in the cut.

It is always best to minimize tool overhang. You may be able to angle a straight toolrest into the hollow if you can get the toolrest low enough without fouling the bowl. A better solution is to use a toolrest curved in plan. (The top section should still be narrow and bevelled).

Figure 9 22 Starting a hollowing cut with the cutting edge at the base of the flute vertical and at axis height. The bevel in plan is pointing along the inside wall.

Figure 9.23 Thrusting upwards and forwards. The gouge has been axially rotated clockwise so that the flute is pointing at about 40° from the vertical. If you have a square-across bowl finishing gouge, use it with the flute at 20° to 30° to the vertical for finishing cuts.

Figure 9.24 The tool tip is at its highest as you thrust it around the bend into the bottom. The blade is continuing to be axially rotated counterclockwise.

Figure 9.25 Thrusting down towards the center. The flute is facing almost horizontally towards you.

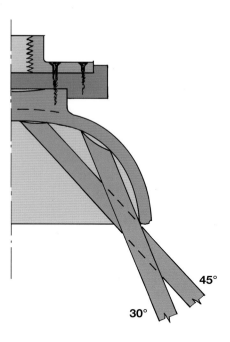

Figure 9.26 The influence of the sharpening angle. How it affects how far a gouge can turn into the bottom of a bowl.

As you turn into the bottom of deep, square bowls with a gouge with a relatively small sharpening angle (here 30°) you will find that the gouge blade's movement is blocked by the rim. You can continue to turn "round the bend" with a larger-than-optimum clearance angle if you make the cut thin, but this requires extra care and is still risky. Alternatively you can change to a different tool; a gouge with a larger sharpening angle (45°) as here and in figure 9.27, or a hook or ring tool (figure 9.28), a flat scraper (figure 9.29), or a shear scraper (figure 9.30). The differences in the subsurface damage left by the four tools will vary with the wood, but the hook or ring tool will almost always leave the least. Make trial cuts to investigate the best tool(s) to use with a particular piece of wood.

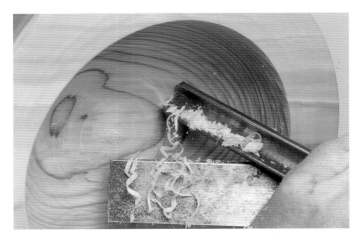

Figure 9.27   Turning round the bend with a bowl gouge with a 45° sharpening angle.

Many turners use bowl gouges with coarse sharpening angles for all their bowl turning. This allows them to use the same gouge to turn most or all of each bowl's surface. The penalties are that such gouges leave more subsurface damage than large-rake-angle *cutting,* and their users have to push harder because their gouges are "blunter".

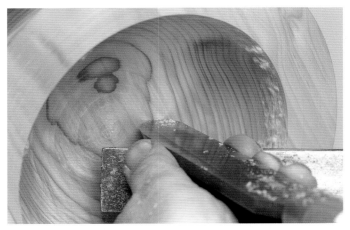

Figure 9.29   Flat scraping minimizes macro surface unevenness, but leaves the greatest subsurface damage. Present flat scrapers pointing slightly down and at short overhangs.

Figure 9.28   A HSS ring tool is my preferred tool for turning bowl bottoms.

Figure 9.30   Shear scraping is especially useful for taking out ripples.

Figure 9.31 Calipering wall thicknesses.

You can achieve your designed internal shape by turning it to agree with a template, or by turning the bowl wall to the designed thicknesses. In practice it is best to caliper the wall between the rim and the start of the bottom, and use a template to monitor the bottom. You can use normal spring or fixed outside calipers, proprietary calipers specially made for measuring the walls of bowl and hollow turnings, or home-made calipers bent from wire (figure 10.24). The home-made caliper shown can be used with the lathe running. It is sawn from 3/4-in (19-mm) plywood. The plastic strip which slides in a saw cut is cut from a milk container.

I have marked circles with a pencil where I want to monitor wall thicknesses. I first set the caliper gap to the wall thickness at the rear pencil line keeping the line through the caliper jaws square to the surface. When I bring the caliper to the front where the wall is at the finished thickness, the gap is the thickness which still has to be turned away at the rear pencil line. Similarly I can also estimate the excess thickness at the front pencil line.

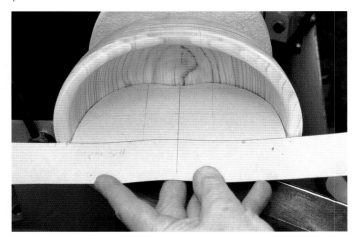

Figure 9.32 Checking the bowl's inside shape.

Figure 9.33 Drying the wood's surface with a heat gun.

When you sand unseasoned wood the coated abrasive cloggs rapidly. You can largely overcome this by drying the wood's surface with a heat gun, and completing the sanding before the internal moisture has time to rise to the surface. This technique is not equally suitable for all woods. Some, and especially those with a high resin content, will develop fine surface cracks if overheated by a heat gun or by too much sanding.

Figure 9.34 Hand sanding.

Always hand sand with the abrasive trailing. If you allow the abrasive to cross to the other side of the lathe axis the wood's velocity will be in reverse, and your fingers can experience a painful whip.

Progress through the grits as with other sanding. You usually need to start with 100 grit or coarser. You may need to sand difficult areas with the lathe stopped before resuming sanding with the lathe on.

Figure 9.35 Power sanding.

It takes longer to sand radially-grained bowls than axially-grained spindles. The absense of fine detail also suits power sanding. You can use an electric drill, preferably with a side handle, and/or an angle sander. The best form of sanding disk has a thick foam backing and is faced with Velcro. These pads come in a range of sizes, and compatible felt-backed abrasive disks in all diameters and grit sizes are readily available. An alternative system uses freely-rotatable sanding pads which are driven by the rotation of the wood.

Power sanding can rapidly cut grooves into the wood. Keep the disk moving over the surface and do not use a pad diameter which is too large or too small for the curvature of the surface.

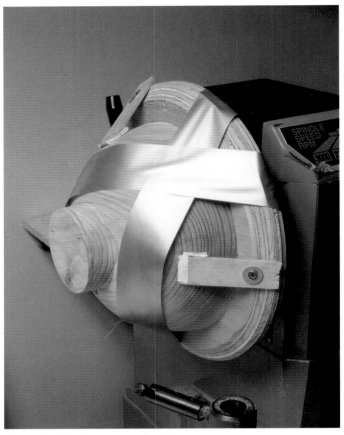

Figure 9.36 Reverse chucking.

The simplest reverse-chucking equipment for bowls with a plain rim is the press-fit chuck. Alternative proprietary systems are available (figure 9.5). To ensure that the bowl cannot come out you could use adhesive tape or plywood cleats. Use packing under the ends of the cleats to prevent damaging the bowl surface. If you cut the chucking recess a touch too large, pack the gap with tape, cloth, or paper.

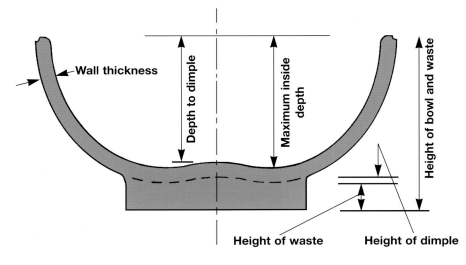

Wall thickness

Depth to dimple

Maximum inside depth

Height of bowl and waste

Height of waste

Height of dimple

Figure 9.37 The measurements you need to take to accurately turn off the waste spigot if you have not prepared templates. Figure 9.38 shows how to take them.

Waste height = Height of bowl and waste —
Maximum inside depth —
Wall thickness

Dimple height = Maximum inside depth —
Depth to dimple

Figure 9.38 Taking the measurements shown in figure 9.37.

You can take the three depth measurements with a rule and a straight edge. Use calipers to measure the wall thickness. To find the diameter across the circle of maximum inside depth, feel with your thumb and forefinger and then measure across them after pulling your hand out of the bowl.

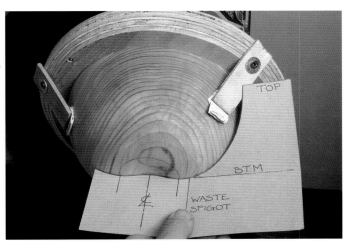

Figure 9.39 Checking the base shape before sanding.

Figure 9.40 Signing and naming the wood with a hot-wire pyrograph.

Chapter Ten

HOLLOW TURNING

David Ellsworth's article on hollow turning in the May/June 1979 *Fine Woodworking* was a revelation. He showed how to excavate a large cavity through a small hole to create a highly-incurved vessel called a *hollow turning* (figure 10.1). Although not a new process, there was a freshness to David Ellsworth's approach which was inspirational.

Hollow turning is now an important turning specialty. Its potential for aesthetic and technical exploration has ensured a growing popularity. The apparent technical difficulties also seem to be an attraction. They are mainly caused by having to hollow through a relatively-small hole, and include:

1. Controlling the downward forces exerted by the wood onto the tool tip at long tool overhangs.
2. Controlling the twisting forces (moments) on tools.
3. Removing the shavings through the small entrance hole.
4. Cutting where straight tools cannot reach.
5. Knowing where your tool tip is even though you cannot see it. This enables you to perform the desired cut, and be prepared to counter the forces which the wood will apply to the tool tip during the cut.
6. Monitoring the wall thickness.
7. Chucking large, cantilevering workpieces.

Since 1979 the horizons of hollow turning have continued to expand. Each technical advance has revealed new aesthetic possibilities, and these in turn have inspired the development of a new generation of technical advances.

Figure 10.1 Some simple shapes for hollow turnings. The sphere is the basic hollow-turning shape, but is often stretched or squashed. Additional features and detailing may be added. The flattened cone shape on the left has a diameter of 6 3/4 in (172 mm) and a height of 3 5/8 in (93 mm). All the turnings have a wall thickness of about 1/8 in (3 mm).

The flattened cone shape, *left,* and the tapered cylinder shape, *right,* were both shown in David Ellsworth's 1979 article. Exercise 10.2 shows you how to turn the flattened cone form. Exercise 10.1 shows you how to turn the inverted egg shape, *second from left.* *Second from right;* Englishman, Melvyn Firmager was among the first to develop tools and techniques for producing necked vessels.

The woods are, *left to right:* jarrah burl, camphor laurel, London plane, and Australian red cedar.

10.1   TECHNICAL PROGRESS

In his 1979 article David Ellsworth described hollowing with straight scrapers and scrapers cranked at 40° (figure 10.2). He used cranked scrapers to reach areas which straight scrapers could not. He narrowed his scrapers' tips to lessen the downward forces which the wood would apply. His tools had heavy shafts to lessen chatter and long handles to aid control.

As hollow turnings got bigger, the tip overhangs got longer, and handles had to be lengthened to help counter the increasing moments. Jim Thompson of South Carolina was a leader in this and developed tools up to 6 feet (1.8 meters) long. So long and heavy did handles become that it became sensible to use a rest to support the back end of the handle and thus hold the tool horizontally. This extra rest is called a *backrest*. It is a wide, horizontal rest aligned at 90° to the lathe axis in plan. Jim also developed a lathe with features which made it especially suitable for hollow turning.

In 1988 Denis Stewart of Oregon introduced the Stewart System for cupchuck, bowl, and hollow turning (figures 10.3 and 10.14). Among its features: an armbrace handle increased a user's ability to resist the downward and rotational forces applied to the tool tip; a side handle assisted in controlling rotational forces; a question-mark-shaped hooker tool allowed cutting in difficult spots while avoiding the need for the turner to resist rotational moments; and a flexible wall-thickness gauge enabled you to monitor the wall thickness while actively hollowing.

Also in 1988 Australian Harry Arnall introduced a gate rest and scrapers (figure 10.4). The downward and rotational forces applied by the wood were absorbed by the gate rest. Hollowing thus became a process of hand machining. Harry Arnall also introduced special calipers which speeded wall thickness measuring.

Although most hollow-turning tools scrape, you can shear scrape with straight tools around the bottom of a hollow. For inboard hollowing you would typically achieve this by axially rotating the tool 30° to 45° counterclockwise before presenting it to the wood. You can also shear scrape by axially rotating the cutter rather than the whole tool. The Crocodile is one of several offset tools which allows this, and thus enables you to scrape with side rake along the walls of the hollow (figure 10.5).

Scraping and shear scraping are not the only cutting methods used in hollowing. Straight and offset hook tools allow *cutting* (figure 10.6), but the side rake is usually near zero except near the bottom of the hollow. Ring tools can be used in the same way as hook tools, but are only available with straight shafts.

The Mighty Midget in figure 10.7 represents a new generation of *cutting* tools which are specially designed for hollowing. It is developed from the hook tool. Its guard cover allows you to restrict the shaving thickness, and provides an upper fulcrum about which you can axially

rotate the tool to bring it to cut. Melvyn Firmager's angle tools also have an upper fulcrum which acts in the same way (figure 10.8). Melvyn Firmager has also introduced three unique bowl-gouge grindings for hollow-turning.

An *outrigger* is a device for maintaining rotational stability (figure 10.9). Lyle Jamieson of Michigan in the March 1997 *American Woodturner* described a rear outrigger which houses in a slot in a backrest to resist both downward and rotational forces (figure 10.10).

Early hollow turnings were basically squashed or stretched spheres. Offset and hook-shaped tools allowed access to spots which straight tools could not reach. But even short, integral necks dramatically increase access problems. Jerry Glaser's articulated tip (figure 10.11) helped. Then in the June 1997 *American Woodturner* Hugh McKay of Oregon described his articulated hollowing system which allows you to create turnings with long and narrow integral necks (figures 10.12 and 10.13).

New hollow-turning hardware continues to be introduced. The next stage will surely be the combining of the best features from the different systems. Those who wish to turn very thin walls will have to further develop shear scraping, or better *cutting* with side rake to lessen subsurface damage.

Hollowing hardware is not the only area where there has been progress. In hollow turning you are working blind. You therefore need to use a methodical procedure to lessen the risk of the wood applying unexpected and large forces to your tool tip. The basic procedure was described in David Ellsworth's seminal article. Others have developed related procedures, notably John Jordan and Melvyn Firmager.

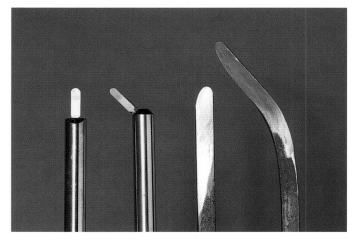

Figure 10.2   David Ellsworth hollow-turning tools. The current tools, *left*, have glued-in HSS tips. *Right*, the original tools were made from carbon tool steel.

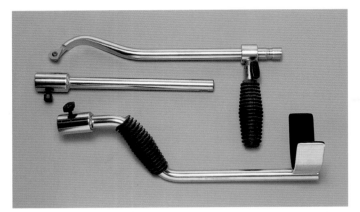

Figure 10.3   The Stewart System. The hooker, extension shank, and armbrace handle.

Figure 10.4   The Arnall gate system. The vertical clearance within the gate is a touch greater than the thickness of the scrapers' blades. Therefore the scrapers' rectangular cross-section blades can neither tilt nor rotate. The three scrapers have larger tips than most other hollow-turning tools because the greater potential downward forces onto the tips are easily resisted by the gate.

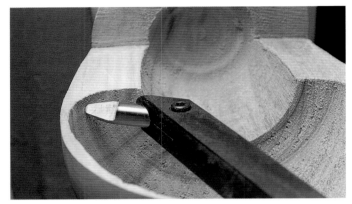

Figure 10.5   The tip of a Crocodile tool by Bierton Craft Turnery in England. I have axially rotated the HSS cutter so that it will shear scrape.

Figure 10.6   Straight and offset hook tools in carbon tool steel by Kurt Johansson from Sweden.

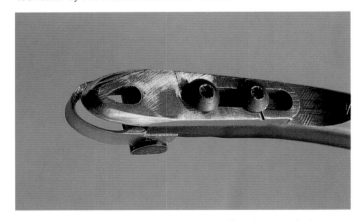

Figure 10.7   The Mighty Midget hollowing tool developed in New Zealand by Ken Port from a concept by Paul Beckett. Heavier and hook-shaped versions are available. All need an entrance hole of at least 7/8-in (22-mm) diameter. There is a later and similar hollowing system also produced in New Zealand called the Exocet.

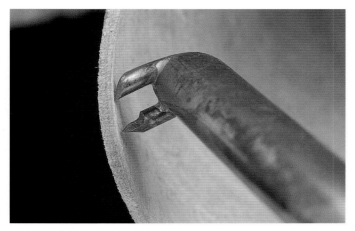

Figure 10.8 The tip of a Melvyn Firmager angle tool, a tool which reduces the risk of a catch. This version is for inboard use. Outboard versions are also available.

Here the top point is bearing against the inside wall surface, but the bottom point is just clear and therefore cannot catch. By axially rotating this tool clockwise and levering about the top point, the bottom point can be brought to cut, and the depth of cut varied.

You move or return the tool tip to the start of a cut with the bottom point out of the wood. You then axially rotate the tool clockwise to start the cutting. Once the cut is finished, axially rotate the tool counterclockwise to free the bottom point, and move or return the tip to the start of the next cut.

Whether you are using a *cutting* or a scraping tool, you can axially rotate it to start it cutting or increase the aggressiveness of its cut. If turning inboard that axial rotation must always be clockwise, that is so as to increase the rake angle. If you rotate a tool in the opposite direction to start to cut I can confirm that a catastrophic catch is likely.

Figure 10.9 An experimental hollowing tool by Bruce Leadbeatter of Sydney.

This tool combines three features: a HSS cup-shaped cutter made by Latalex in New Zealand for a ring gouge which it once marketed; an adjustable, flexible, wall-thickness gauge made from curtain spring; and an integral outrigger which prevents axial tool rotation.

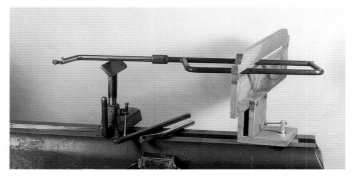

Figure 10.10 The Lyle Jamieson combined backrest and gate allows you to hand machine a hollow because the tool is prevented from tilting or axially rotating..

Any 3/4-in (19-mm) boring bar can be locked into the coupling of the vaguely "P"-shaped handle. The backrest is square to the lathe axis in plan and projects about 10 in (255 mm) forwards and 26 in (660 mm) backwards from the lathe axis.

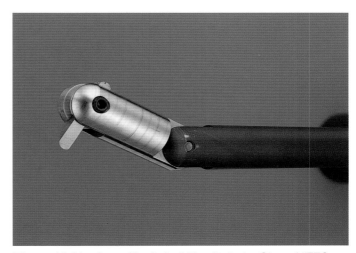

Figure 10.11 An articulated tip, that of a Glaser HiTEC hollow-turning tool.

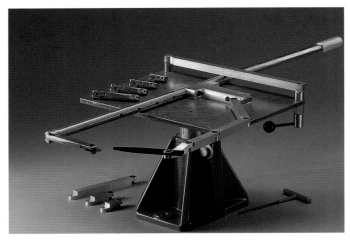

Figure 10.12   Hugh McKay's HM-1 articulated hollowing system with a 36-in long, 3/4-in diameter boring bar. The system has a gate and an outrigger. The important advance is the articulated cutting arm. You axially align this arm to feed it down a long, narrow neck; then swing and click it to 45° or 90° for hollowing a chamber (see figure 10.13). Different lengths of cutting arm are shown at the back of the gate support platform, and enable the turner to hollow a chamber in stages.

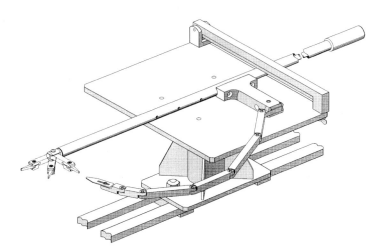

Figure 10.13   A diagram of the Hugh McKay system.
The articulated caliper assembly enables you to monitor the wall thickness with the lathe running.

10.2   THE CHOICES

There is a wide choice of equipment and approach in hollow turning. Each works. Some are better suited to particular sizes or shapes of hollow turning. Some are expensive, some less so. Some take time to set up, and are more fiddly to use. Some are more suited to a particular workpiece grain direction. Some attempt to deskill the process, or at least lessen the risk of losing control.

I cannot recommend one particular type or brand of tool. Overall I marginally prefer the *cutting* tools to those which scrape, particularly when the grain is axial. The cutting tools are faster, leave a better finish, and for a given shaving cross-section there is less force onto the tool tip. However scraping tools are simpler to use, don't clogg, and are more versatile.

I prefer to hand hold the tools for the more straightforward hollow turnings such as those in figure 10.1 because I experience more involvement in the process. A gate rest may prevent you losing control of the tool if there is a catch, but the forces between the wood and the tool tip are the same. You are therefore more likely to lever the workpiece off its faceplate when using a gate rest.

The methods and equipment you choose and the designs you apply them to will result from particular technical, cost, aesthetic, and quasi-moral judgements which you have to make. These judgements may not always be conscious. They will concern:

1. How technically difficult you want to make the turning, especially when the aesthetic return or selling price may not be commensurate.
2. How much you are willing to spend on equipment. You will need to spend extra to increase the potential size and technical difficulty of your hollow turnings. By spending more you can also convert the hollowing from a hand process to one of hand machining.
3. The practice of producing apparently very technically-difficult hollow turnings by inletting neck pieces or bottom plugs in such a way that the joint is barely visible.
4. How far you want to go towards achieving a high quality of finish and an even and thin wall thickness in the hollow. Should you take great care with internal surfaces which can neither be seen nor felt? "No" is a valid decision. However if your intent is to minimize weight so that your turning's lightness will amaze, a small and constant wall thickness is necessary, even if sanding is not. When an internal surface is visible and/or feelable, its surface finish should be compatible with your design intents. If this means sanding, you will have to make special sanding equipment such as small sanding pads on flexible arms.
5. Whether you should reverse chuck hollow turnings so that their exteriors are fully turned.

6. Particular shapes or features may be associated with particular hollow turners. Plagiarism is a hot issue in hollow turning, but is not discussed here.

The choices are yours to make. However I think that you should first master turning hollow turnings of modest size and difficulty with hand-held tools. Exercises 10.1 and 10.2 reflect this recommendation.

10.3 EQUIPMENT

Lathe Modifications

A standard-sized lathe of good specification will do well for hollow turnings up to medium size. If your lathe has a fixed headstock and you will be hollow turning inboard, you should increase the distance between the bed and any wall behind to 3 feet (900 mm). Have the bench top behind your lathe and its support removable so that you can operate from between the bed and the wall. Sitting or standing astride the bed is another option. A swivelling headstock allows you to avoid the backache from leaning over the lathe bed, and still have a lathe bed to fit a backrest to if required.

Outboard hollow turning is freer and more comfortable than any inboard form, but some hollow-turning tools are only available in versions for inboard use.

You often need two hands to safely enter or withdraw a tool. You may need to stop the lathe while still holding the tool with both hands. Melvyn Firmager is one of several who strongly and rightly advise a foot switch.

Handles

Handles for hand-held hollow-turning tools are usually long (figure 10.14). A total tool length of 2 1/2 to 3 feet (750 to 900 mm) is typical. Where the active part of the cutting tip is offset from the main axis of the tool, I suggest you follow David Ellsworth's advice and leave the surface of the wood off-the-tool, unpolished, and of larger-than-usual diameter so that you are better able to resist torsion. Such handles are also better for straight tools. Some hand-held tools are supplied with steel handles which may be telescopic, or can be filled with lead shot. The shot probably acts through adding weight and inertia rather than damping vibration through any movement of its own.

Most hand-held hollow-turning tools have shafts of round bar. If your tool catches and is not restrained in a gate rest, a circular shaft is less likely to damage the rim of the entrance hole than one with a square or rectangular cross-section.

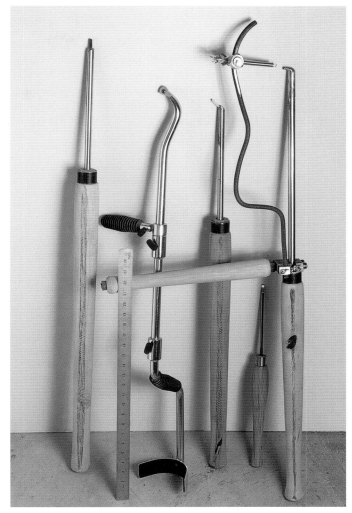

Figure 10.14 Handles for hollow turning. *Left to right:* a 30-in (770-mm) handle on a David Ellsworth straight tool; a Stewart System hooker tool on an extension shank and armbrace handle, total length 38 in (970 mm); a David Ellsworth offset tool with a 26-in (660-mm) handle; a parting-off tool with a typical, spindle-turning handle 12 in (300 mm) long; and a Melvyn Firmager angle tool with a 23-in (590-mm) handle, fitted with a wall thickness gauge of my own design (see also figure 10.25) and a side handle. A side handle gives welcome added control in some situations, but is not needed for most offset tool use.

I have spokeshaved flats along the tops of my wooden handles. These blue-colored flats tell me the axial orientations of my tool tips when the tips are hidden inside hollow turnings.

10.4   THE PROCESS

Many hollow turnings are finish-turned from unseasoned wood because of the problems of seasoning large cross-sections quickly and without degrade. Alternatively you could follow the process commonly used in bowl turning, and rough-turn, season, and then finish-turn.

You usually have to go through the following stages to produce a hollow turning:

1. Design the turning's outside shape and wall thickness. Although many hollow turnings are started with minimal if any prior design work, you should at least do a full-size sketch. You can then use the sketch in the same way that you use a pencil gauge. You can also use the sketch to check that the entrance opening is large enough to allow your tools to reach into all parts of the intended hollow.
2. Prepare the blank for turning. This may include mounting the blank between centers to true its periphery and flush the end by which it will be chucked.
3. Mount the blank on a faceplate or in a chuck.
4. Rough, then finish-turn the outside. You can use the tailstock to give additional support. Leave sufficient diameter in the region adjacent to the chuck or faceplate so that that wood will not flex during the hollowing. I sometimes leave external waste in the area around the entrance hole so that it is less liable to fracture if a tool bangs against it. I trim this excess thickness away after the rough hollowing is completed.

    If the turning is likely to warp, you should sand the outside before starting to hollow.
5. Drill an axial hole to almost the full finished depth of the hollow.
6. Remove the bulk of the waste using one or more straight tools. You might also use offset and hook-shaped tools for some shapes.
7. Remove further waste in layers, leaving the walls thick enough not to flex during the final wall trimming. You can use straight, hook-shaped, and offset tools, the last two types being greatly used for more demanding shapes. For small hollow turnings you might combine stages **6** and **7**. Trim the inside walls to the finished thickness working back towards the headstock.
8. Do any sanding inside the hollow.
9. Turn off the extra thickness left around the entrance hole if not done earlier, and sand the area.
10. Finish-turn and sand the outside adjacent to the faceplate or chuck.
11. Part off or saw off the workpiece from the waste. Hand finish the bottom of the turning, or better, reverse chuck it and finish the bottom in the lathe.

The orientation of any dominant grain direction should influence the hollowing procedure you use because you should work as far as possible with the grain. You should also obey the cupchucking dictum and work as far as possible towards the headstock.

Catches during hollowing are caused by the wood exerting large and especially unexpectedly-large forces on the tool tip. These can particularly occur when a side of the cutter instead of the narrow tip contacts the wood, or when the cutter attempts to cut grain which has a higher-than-expected severance stress—for example end grain instead of side grain. To minimize the possibility of the unexpected you need to have a good idea where your tool has been, is now, and is to go. It is important to develop tool usage patterns which promote this.

Removing the shavings from the hollow is tedious. You can deflect them out with the lathe running if the access hole is relatively large, or scrape them out with the lathe stopped. You can use a vacuum cleaner, but you may have to make a suitable nozzle .You can blast the shavings out with compressed air, but this sprays dust and chips widely. Or you can remove the faceplate and workpiece from the lathe and tip the shavings out.

EXERCISE 10.1   AN AXIALLY-GRAINED HOLLOW TURNING

Techniques taught	Hollowing through a narrow entrance opening Reverse chucking with a funnel chuck
Tools used	One straight and one offset hollow-turning tool Spindle-turning tools A drill to bore the axial hole down to the bottom of the hollow A small faceplate
Workpieces	Axially-grained, 9 1/2-in (240-mm) long, 5 1/4-in (135-mm) diameter Waste disk for reverse chucking, about 5-in (125-mm) diameter, 2-in (50-mm) thick

Hollow turning is surprisingly easy if you work within the potential of your equipment, and to an ordered procedure. It demands care and concentration rather than great expertise in tool manipulation.

The design of this exercise is shown in figure 10.15. The turning procedure is outlined in figures 10.16 to 10.27.

Figure 10.15 The hollow-turning exercise. It is 8 in (200 mm) high and 5 in (125 mm) at its maximum diameter. It has an entrance hole diameter of 1 in (25 mm), and a wall thickness of about 1/8 in (3 mm). You might increase the size of the entrance hole and the wall thickness for your first attempts. If your tools are smaller than those shown, reduce the size of the exercise accordingly.

Figure 10.17 Chucking the workpiece with six, 1-in (25-mm), 10-gauge screws through a small faceplate. This is a secure holding method for both axially- and radially-grained workpieces.

You may need to drill extra holes through your faceplate so that you can use more screws. You will increase the hold if you minimize the diameter of the screw pilot holes you predrill. It is quicker and less straining to drive the screws with a power screwdriver or a brace with a screwdriver bit. You can hold small turnings in jaw chucks.

Before screwing through the faceplate, I had roughed the blank between centers and turned its right-hand end slightly concave. After mounting the workpiece in the lathe, turn and sand the outside. You can leave extra thickness around the entrance hole.

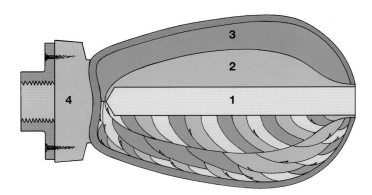

Figure 10.16 The hollowing procedure for exercise 10.1, an axially-grained hollow turning.

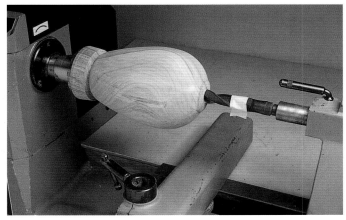

Figure 10.18 Boring to almost the bottom of the hollow using a long-series twist drill.

The tape on the drill shaft is positioned to align with the end of the workpiece when the drill tip is almost at the bottom of the hollow. Take care to withdraw the drill about every 1/2 in (15 mm) so that it doesn't jam in the hole.

You can use other drill types (see figure 10.19), but for deep holes it is wise to at least bore a pilot hole with a drill mounted in the tailstock. This will eliminate the risk of drilling off-line and leaving an axial cone of wood which is awkward to cut away.

Figure 10.19   Boring with a Sorby spear-point drill. I have preturned a conical recess to start the drill using pointing cuts with a detail gouge. There isn't a mark or tape on the drill's shaft because the hole's depth is equal to the drill's exposed length.

You can use other types of drill to bore the axial hole. For long holes you could use an auger with the screw point ground off, a short twist drill welded onto an extension rod, or a modified spade bit on an extension shaft.

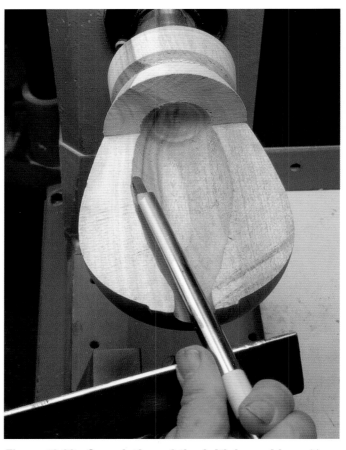

Figure 10.20   Completion of the initial roughing with a straight tool. The tape on the tool shaft aligns with the front of the opening when the tool tip is cutting at the designed full depth of the hollow.

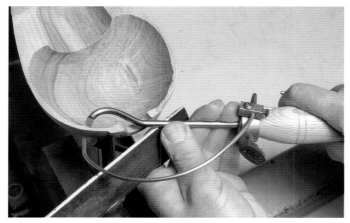

Figure 10.21   Trimming just inside the entrance hole with a Robert Sorby 850H shallow hollowing tool. My larger offset tools could not reach here. Another solution would have been to steepen the top of the turning. The wall thickness gauge of the 850H pivots. You press the end of the gauge wire against the tool handle when gauging. You pivot the gauge wire anticlockwise in plan to aid entering and withdrawing the tool. You vary the gauging gap by bending the gauge wire.

Figure 10.22 The start of a roughing cut with an offset tool (here from David Ellsworth). The cut's completion is shown in the next figure.

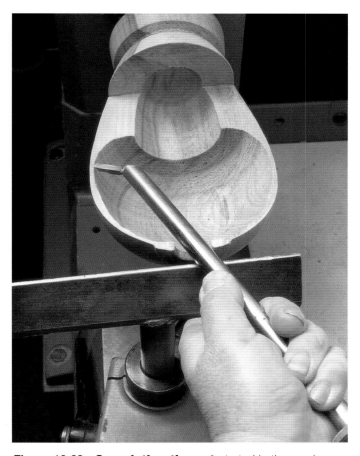

Figure 10 23 Completing the cut started in the previous figure.

Because you have to hollow blind, it is sensible to remove waste using several series of cuts, each series consisting of a number of similar cuts. If the cuts are relatively short, they can be controlled by clenching your left hand's tied-underhand grip during the cut, and slackening it on the return.

To start this cut, feel for the corner at the junction between the cavity left from the earlier initial roughing and that from the current series of widening cuts. Then lever to the right with your right arm while pulling the tool towards you. At the completion of the cut, run the tip of the cutter in light contact with the surface just cut back to start the following cut.

I have marked on the tool's shaft the full depth of the hole. You can also monitor your tool tip's position using a flexible wall thickness gauge, although once you have experience there is generally no need until you start trimming the walls.

Hollowing larger vessels is slow and hard going. At long overhangs there is more noisy chatter which reduces cutting efficiency, and when cutting near to the lathe axis the wood is more reluctant to sever because of its low speed.

Cutting along the bottom of the hollow is exacting. Whether you are cutting or scraping, it is best to present the edge with side rake. Also the severity of any catch will be minimized if the clearance angle is low, about 2°. Some cutting tips are ground with too much clearance.

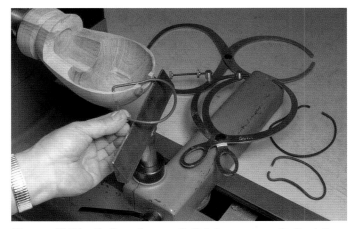

Figure 10.24 Calipering wall thicknesses with the lathe stopped. Two calipers from Robert Sorby and three home-made from fencing wire of 0.16-in (4.1-mm) diameter.

The range of calipers designed for measuring the wall thicknesses of bowls and hollow turnings is increasing. However one or two calipers will not cover all situations. The homemade, "U"-shaped calipers are quite rigid. For especially difficult locations you might need to use a pivoting or a springy caliper. For the latter you can use the 0.087-in (2.2-mm) diameter wire from dry cleaners' coathangers.

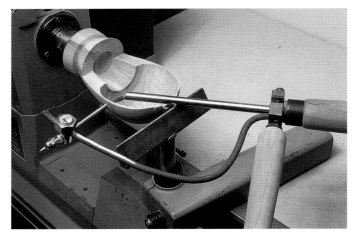

Figure 10.25 Skimming the wall to its final thickness.
This arrangement can be used with the lathe running. A David Ellsworth offset tool fitted with a home-made side handle and wall thickness gauge. The arm of the gauge is rigid, being bent from 0.4-in (10.1-mm) diameter steel. The flexible tip of the gauge is a coiled tension spring which is screwed onto a screw. This allows the gauging gap to be varied. The flexible tip assembly can be moved along the rigid curved arm and locked in any required position. This is necessary because for calipering to be accurate, the line joining a gauge's two tips needs to pass squarely through the wall. The wall thickness gauges shown in figures 10.12, 10.13, and 10.14 also have adjustments which allow gauging to be made square to the wall.

Direct measurement is not the sole means of monitoring wall thickness. You can monitor a workpiece's wall thickness visually with the lathe stopped where there are large-enough holes or cracks in the wall. The sound emitted during turning and the sound emitted by tapping with the lathe stopped can give an approximate indication of wall thickness. And if you run a small, high-intensity light along the inside of the walls, the light transmitted through will give you an approximate idea of the wall thickness.

Once the hollowing is completed, rough turn the outside of the hollow turning nearest to the headstock. Then finish-turn and part off or saw off the turning from the waste.

Figure 10.26 About to reverse chuck the hollow turning in a funnel chuck. To hold the workpiece into the funnel I shall use moderate tail-center pressure because this hollow turning is long. You could use thin foam or double-sided tape to increase the grip and soften the contact between the inside surface of the funnel and the outside of the hollow turning.

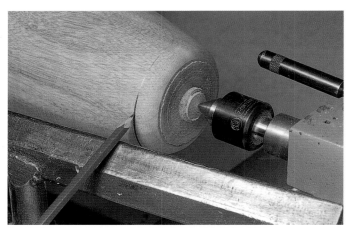

Figure 10.27 Using a pencil to check how the turning's axis is offset from the lathe axis.
It can be tricky to locate a turning truly axially in a funnel chuck. Locate the tail center into the waste stub as centrally as possible by eye, and advance the tail center just far enough so that the turning will remain in the lathe. Switch on or spin the lathe by hand and touch a pencil point onto the wood. Switch off and slacken the tail center a touch. Tap the area containing the pencil line with your hand to force the turning into true alignment. Advance the tail center, switch on the lathe to check the new alignment, and adjust again if necessary.

Once the turning is truly aligned, skim off the waste with a gouge leaving a spigot of about 5/16-in (8-mm) diameter. Sand the turned area, stop the lathe, trim off the remaining waste spigot by hand, and sand.

EXERCISE 10.2   A RADIALLY-GRAINED HOLLOW TURNING

Techniques taught   Hollowing a radially-grained
                          workpiece

Tools required   One straight and one offset hollow-
                          turning tool
                          Spindle-turning tools
                          A drill to bore the axial hole down to
                          the bottom of the hollow
                          A small faceplate

Workpieces   Axially-grained, 5-in (130-mm)
                          long, 7-in (180-mm) diameter.
                          Waste disk for reverse chucking,
                          about 5-in (125-mm) diameter,
                          2-in (50-mm) thick

This exercise is pictured in figure 10.28. Its turning process is outlined in figure 10.29, and is similar to that for exercise 10.1, but modified because the grain is radial not axial. You should reverse chuck the turning in a funnel chuck.

Figure 10.28   A good shape for your a first exercise in radially-grained hollow turning. It is 3 5/8 in (93 mm) high, and 6 3/4 in (172 mm) in maximum diameter. It has a wall thickness of 1/8 in (3 mm), and an entrance hole diameter of 1 in (25 mm).

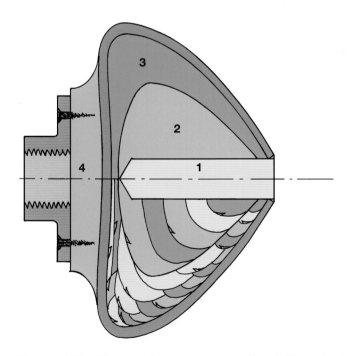

Figure 10.29   The turning process outlined. Throughout your turning you should work as far as possible with the grain.

WHERE NEXT?

You have absorbed the information in this book and worked diligently through the exercises. You have kept your options open by not specializing at the start of your turning and by developing a full range of turning skills. Where next? Most turners' turning evolves. They follow their fancies or are nudged by outside influences, and why not? But with your greater knowledge and range of skills you could make an informed decision to concentrate on one or more areas of turning, for example:

1. Items for home, relatives, and friends
2. Turnings for galleries and collectors
3. Restoration and replacement turnings
4. Antique-reproduction and traditionally-styled turnings
5. Architectural turnings: columns, balusters, finials, patera, etc.
6. Woodware
7. Giftware, souvenirs
8. Objects virtu
9. A particular class of item. For example David Springett in chapter 1 concentrates on lace bobbins
10. Patternmaking
11. Pole lathe turning, ornamental turning, oval turning or other specialties requiring non-standard equipment
12. Combining turning with other techniques such as cabinetmaking or carving
13. Demonstrating, teaching, promotion, supplying turners, developing equipment, administration, writing
14. Collecting

Your turning may become an occasional pastime or an obsession; your turning ambitions modest or great. You can treat turning vicariously—some enthusiastic and long-term members of woodturners' associations don't have a lathe and have little interest in getting one. You may even become a collector—unfortunately for gallery turners a rare breed.

Many turners make a little money by selling at markets, through group exhibitions, shops, or their own outlet. Only a tiny proportion of readers might consider turning professionally. Some will make it, most won't.

However you treat woodturning in the future, I hope that this book has fulfilled my intention and helped you to master the fundmentals of woodturning.

Figure 11.1 The Your Dial mirror depends for its success on viewers being familiar with the use of the word "dial" for a human face. Yes, my specialty is humorous turning, an area not universally appreciated. Some believe it undermines the dignity of turning.

APPENDIX 1

NATIONAL WOODTURNERS' ASSOCIATIONS

The number of woodturners' local clubs and national associations is growing strongly throughout the world. The list of national associations below is far from complete. I would be grateful for details of other national associations or changes to the details of those already listed. Please send them to me in Australia, and I will include them in future editions.

Australia has many local clubs, but no national association.

The Association of Woodturners of Great Britain
1800 members, 26 affiliated groups.
Secretary in 1997   Peter Einig, Keepers Cottage, Lee, Ellesmere, Shropshire, SY12 9AE, England.
Newsletter   *Revolutions*, published four times each year.
Major regular events   seminar every two years.

Irish Woodturners Guild
Secretary in 1997   Kevin Lee, Croneyhorn, Carnew, County Wicklow, Ireland.

National Association of Woodturners New Zealand (Inc)
1250 members, 39 affiliated clubs.
Secretary in 1997   Don Tietjens, 24 Maxwells Line, Palmerston North, New Zealand.
Magazine   *Faceplate*, published four times each year.
Major regular events   Turn Again seminar held every three years, Art of Turned Wood judged exhibition held every two years.

American Association of Woodturners
6600 members, 90 local chapters.
Administrator   Mary Redig, 3200 Lexington Avenue, Shoreview, MN 55126, USA.
Journal   *American Woodturner*, quarterly.

Iceland
Contact   Villi Sigurjonsson, Digranesvegi 18a, IS 200 Kopavogur, Iceland.

The Society of Ornamental Turners
Founded 1948, 320 members.
Secretary 1997   Mr N.S. Edwards, 188 Bromham Road, Bedford, Bedfordshire, England MK40 SBP.
Bulletin   twice each year.
Meetings   four times each year in London.

INDEX